GOD'S
POWER
to
CHANGE

GOD'S
POWER
to CHANGE

JOHN LOREN & PAULA
SANDFORD

Charisma
HOUSE
A STRANG COMPANY

Most STRANG COMMUNICATIONS BOOK GROUP products are available at special quantity discounts for bulk purchase for sales promotions, premiums, fund-raising, and educational needs. For details, write Strang Communications Book Group, 600 Rinehart Road, Lake Mary, Florida 32746, or telephone (407) 333-0600.

GOD'S POWER TO CHANGE by John Loren and Paula Sandford
Published by Charisma House
A Strang Company
600 Rinehart Road
Lake Mary, Florida 32746
www.strangbookgroup.com

Unless otherwise noted, all Scripture quotations are from the New American Standard Bible. Copyright © 1960, 1962, 1963, 1968, 1971, 1972, 1973, 1975, 1977 by the Lockman Foundation. Used by permission. (www.Lockman.org)

Scripture quotations marked KJV are from the King James Version of the Bible.

Scripture quotations marked NIV are from the Holy Bible, New International Version. Copyright © 1973, 1978, 1984, International Bible Society. Used by permission.

Scripture quotations marked NKJV are from the New King James Version of the Bible. Copyright © 1979, 1980, 1982 by Thomas Nelson, Inc., publishers. Used by permission.

Scripture quotations marked TLB are from The Living Bible. Copyright © 1971. Used by permission of Tyndale House Publishers, Inc., Wheaton, IL 60189. All rights reserved.

Cover design by Justin Evans
Executive Design Director: Bill Johnson

Library of Congress Cataloging-in-Publication Data

Sandford, John Loren.
  God's power to change / John Loren and Paula Sandford.
      p. cm.
  Includes bibliographical references.
  ISBN 978-1-59979-068-8 (trade paper)
  1. Holy Spirit. 2. Healing--Religious aspects--Christianity. 3. Change
(Psychology)--Religious aspects--Christianity. I. Sandford, Paula. II. Title.

  BT123.S26 2007
  231.7--dc22

                        2007007407

Portions of this book were previously published as *Healing the Wounded Spirit*
by John and Paula Sandford, copyright © 1985 by Victory House, Inc., ISBN
0-932081-14-2.

10 11 12 13 14 15 — 9 8 7 6 5 4 3 2
Printed in the United States of America

CONTENTS

INTRODUCTION

I n the first book of this Transformation Series—*Transforming the Inner Man*—we established how today's truncated theology of the process of sanctification and transformation has impaired the church's view of the process of salvation. In that book, we taught how to recognize habits that died positionally when we received Jesus but that have sprung back to life to defile many. (See Hebrews 12:15.) In this sequel—*God's Power to Change*—we intend to equip the body of Christ (as in Ephesians 4:11–12) to minister to each other's deep wounds and habits with truly saving grace.

Once we have accepted God's free gift of salvation and have come to Him in confession of sin, asking Him to become the Lord and Master of our lives, we are instructed to cease walking in the darkness of our sin, and to become children of light:

> For you were formerly darkness, but now you are light in the Lord; walk as children of light (for the fruit of the light consists in all good-ness and righteousness and truth), trying to learn what is pleasing to the Lord.
>
> —Ephesians 5:8–10

Many Christians are trying their best to walk as children of light, but they too often fall into what we call "PO"—*performance orientation*—striving, disillusionment, and, ultimately, self-condemnation. They are blindsided and driven from deep within by that of which they have been unaware.

They have rightly celebrated salvation as a free gift (Eph. 2:4–5, 8; Rom. 6:23), but they may not have understood that they are to grow up (1 Pet. 2:2; Eph. 3:14–19) or that they are to work out that salvation in fear and trembling (Phil. 2:12). They have celebrated with Paul that "by one offering He has perfected for all time those who are [being] sanctified" (Heb. 10:14). But they may fail to understand sanctification as a process, without acknowledging along with Paul, "Not that I have already...become perfect, but I press on in order that I may lay hold of that for which also I was laid hold of by Christ Jesus" (Phil. 3:12).

Many Christians tend to "press on" in terms of managing their behavior rather than renewing their minds (Rom. 12:2) and receiving a new heart and spirit within (Ps. 51, Ezek. 36:26), which would naturally result in changed behavior. They have not, in reality, done away with childish things (1 Cor. 13:11), but they have controlled them while allowing them to remain as a part of the treasure in the storehouse of the heart (Luke 6:43–45).

When feelings that have been accumulating for years in the heart come out of the mouth as eruptive expressions, then these people strive all the more to control the expression or rebuke the devil rather than follow Jesus's command (Luke 6:46–49) to "dig deep" into the foundation of their lives. (The foundation is what was trained and practiced into the fiber of the person's character and personality in the first six years of experiencing and reacting to life and forming attitudes, judgments, and expectations by which to interpret each succeeding experience.) Their "eye" is bad; therefore, their body is full of darkness (Matt. 6:22–23).

CLEANING THE INSIDE OF THE CUP

Matthew 5:29 prescribes a drastic solution for this way of seeing that causes one to stumble: "Tear it out, and throw it from you." Jesus is able to transcend time and space to deal with the deep cracks in our foundations and to establish every hidden part of us securely on the rock that He is. But we must give Him access through prayer.

Many Christians have tried to forget the sins of the past by ignoring them rather than by allowing the Holy Spirit to search the innermost parts of their hearts (Ps. 139:23–24). They have attempted to put aside the flesh with its practices (anger, wrath, malice, slander, and so forth—Col. 3:8–10; Eph. 4:22ff), as if those were present external expressions only. But Jesus called the Pharisees (and us) to clean the *inside* of the cup (Luke 11:39–41). Jesus knew that our speech may be smooth as butter while at the same time our hearts are at war (Ps. 55:21). God has always desired "truth in the innermost being" (Ps. 51:6).

Paul spoke these words to born-again Christians:

> And do not participate in the unfruitful deeds of darkness, but instead even expose them; for it is disgraceful even to speak of the things which are done by them in secret. But all things become visible when they are exposed by the light. . . . For this reason it says, "Awake, sleeper, and arise from the dead, and Christ will shine on you."
>
> —EPHESIANS 5:11–14

We, the body of Christ, the Church, are that sleeper. Our flesh has been crucified with Him. We have attempted to "die daily" (1 Cor. 15:31) by willful efforts to conform to Christian standards. But we have not yet experienced the fullness of that process of inner sanctification and laying down of our lives by which we can come into the fullness of resurrection power now.

This book, which deals with healing wounds and sins of the spirit, is another step in the direction of that deep revealing and inner transformation. It can help make possible experiential living in the fullness of our inheritance in the Lord—an experience that has been positionally ours from the moment we accepted Jesus Christ as Lord.

We offer to you what the Lord has given to us, for . . .

> No one after lighting a lamp covers it over with a container, or puts it under a bed; but he puts it on a lampstand, in order that those who come in may see the light. For nothing is hidden that shall not become evident, nor anything secret that shall not be known and come to light.
>
> —LUKE 8:16–17

It is our sincere desire that as you read this foundational book, you will be introduced to the realities of the wounds and sins of the personal spirit in each of us. May you see clearly the principles we have discovered for awakening, repairing, and restoring your personal spirit into full healing.

CHAPTER 1

THE FORGOTTEN FUNCTIONS OF OUR SPIRIT

The spirit of man is the lamp of the LORD, searching all the innermost parts of his being.

—PROVERBS 20:27

T he purpose of this book is to reveal the process for healing the wounds and sins of the personal spirit in each of us. In this context, *healing* means not only forgiveness through the blood of Christ, not only death on the cross to practices built in childhood in the hidden inner recesses of our character, and not only resurrection to new life. It also means comfort and balm, which repairs and restores.

Sometimes we preach and teach forgiveness and crucifixion so ardently that we lose sight of the other aspects for which Jesus came:

Surely our griefs He Himself bore,
And *our sorrows He carried*;
Yet we ourselves esteemed Him stricken,
Smitten of God, and afflicted.
But He was pierced through for our transgressions,
He was crushed for our iniquities;
The chastening for our well-being fell upon Him,
And by His scourging we are healed.
All of us like sheep have gone astray,
Each of us has turned to his own way;

But the LORD has caused the iniquity of us all
To fall on Him.

—ISAIAH 53:4–6, EMPHASIS ADDED

You may be thinking, "Isn't resurrection healing in itself?"

Our answer is yes, but it doesn't cover all the ground. Perhaps a simple analogy will help. If, as a boy, I leave my hoe in the garden and leap the back fence to play basketball (which, in fact, I did more than once), I have committed a sin of disobedience against my parents. It would have been all right to play basketball if I had finished hoeing the corn as I was commanded. But I disobeyed, stole that time, and, of course, lied about it to my parents. Choosing not to obey my dad and mom not only left me with guilt and fear of discovery, but it also hurt my heart and darkened my ability to be at ease with them.

Suppose that either then or later I confess my disobedience and receive my parents' forgiveness. Perhaps I even release all the resentments I may have harbored at having to work when I wanted to play basketball with my friends instead, and whatever sibling jealousies or other factors also lay behind my disobedience. Perhaps as a result of discussing my experience with a prayer minister, I lay at the foot of the cross all my practices of deceit or malingering and the fears of discovery that have built up in me. Perhaps years later in my heart I reconcile in full with my parents, beyond forgiveness to full acceptance and reinstatement in the family life.

All that is good, but it may not be enough. What more is needed in that example? What is full healing? It is comfort and healing for the guilt, estrangement, fear of rejection, perhaps fear of further punishment, and loneliness that have bruised my inner spirit and heart. Listen to Isaiah's description:

Where will you be stricken again,
As you continue in your rebellion?
The whole head is sick,
And the whole heart is faint.
From the sole of the foot even to the head
There is nothing sound in it,
Only bruises, welts, and raw wounds,
Not pressed out or bandaged,
Nor softened with oil.

—ISAIAH 1:5–6

That is not mere poetic expression. There are indeed "bruises, welts, and raw wounds" if we only had eyes to see our hearts and spirits.

The words of a hymn tell us: "There is a balm in Gilead to heal the sin sick soul."[1] That balm is the oil of the Spirit. The blood washes away guilt. The cross crucifies sinful desires. Christ's resurrection life restores our life, but we still have wounds and bruises that need His gentle touch. The *oil of the Spirit* is the comfort of His healing presence.

During biblical times, shepherds felt the faces and ears of their sheep at night for ticks. Finding some, they did not pluck them for fear of leaving a portion that could cause disease. Instead, they poured oil until the suffocating ticks were forced to back out. But the oil accomplished more than that. It also soothed their dry, sun-parched skin. It entered the wound and acted as an antiseptic balm. But most importantly, it simply comforted and healed.

How awful it would have been to call Lazarus forth and leave him bound! (See John 11:44.) Not only did Lazarus need to be unbound, but also, if we think practically for a moment, how dreadful it would have been to bring him back to life only to leave him still ravaged by whatever disease or condition brought him to death in the first place! He needed more than resurrection. He needed physical healing and comfort for whatever wounding his spirit suffered in death and loss of fellowship with his loved ones whom he had been forced to leave behind.

We rejoice, as we ought, when a lost soul finds salvation or a sin is discovered and forgiven or some ancient practice in the self is hauled to the cross. But have we perhaps rejoiced and resigned the task too soon? There may be wounds not yet "pressed out or bandaged, nor softened with oil," and we wonder why that fellow falls into the same sinful pattern again! There may be many reasons a man falls, but we need to take responsibility to comprehend and administer *in fullness* our commission from the Lord to do the works of healing.

I thank God that our Lord gave my (John's) father the wisdom to know the need to heal our wounded spirits—whether he ever consciously knew—and the grace to do it. My brother Hal and I could guess how many minutes—usually about a half hour—would lapse after a spanking before we would hear Dad's feet coming up the steps to take us in his arms, Hal on one knee and me on the other. "You know that hurt me more than it did you, don't you?"

And we would think, "Did not, y' mean ol' thing!"

Then he would hug us against himself and sometimes wet our brow with a tear. And despite our stubborn hearts, the balm of his presence would soothe us through and through. We not only had been hauled to account, forgiven, and restored, but we had also been healed in heart.

Had Dad not so healed our spirits, we would have known forgiveness and discipline, but something of the heart's ability to expand and relate in embrace would have remained crippled. We would still have retained sores and reticence, blocking openness between us and Dad and Mom. We could have functioned again in the family but with holes in us like Swiss cheese, areas in which a heart not fully healed would have engaged in role play to cover our inability to embrace honestly and uninhibitedly. But who could resist that warm heart and those big, gentle hands? So we were disciplined and forgiven, restored and healed.

Our hope is to call the body to heal in that sense—beyond confession, forgiveness, death on the cross, and a new heart—to make each believer aware that we need more of His healing touch and to teach how, in simple ways, to reach into and heal the depths of your own inner spirit and the inner spirit of each person to whom you minister.

YOUR PERSONAL SPIRIT

The first difficulty we encounter is that the body of Christ, and mankind generally, has nearly lost awareness that each person has a personal spirit and that it has particular functions and needs of its own, distinct from the heart, mind, and soul. In addition to that, there is much confusion and controversy about whether soul and spirit are indeed two different things, and if so, what is the correct theological or biblical interpretation or distinction between them?

Paula and I are neither particularly interested in nor concerned about settling biblical or theological debates, and we hope not to become entangled in them. We will use the words *soul* and *spirit* in a descriptive way to help people understand how to minister. If a scholar of Greek or Hebrew or doctrine or theology objects, let him transfer whatever words fit his theology into our meanings. We know we are solid in Christ and are concerned for fruits. Though we try to be as accurate and true as we can be theologically and doctrinally, we know we can't fit everyone's theological traditions. We define *soul* and *spirit* only to make clear our understanding

in order to focus this discussion on how to comfort and heal people—we
need to be on the same page.

> And the LORD God formed man of the dust of the ground, and
> *breathed* into his nostrils the breath of *life*; and man *became a living
> soul.*
> —GENESIS 2:7, KJV, EMPHASIS ADDED

That describes the process. First God breathes our spirit into us, and
then we *become* a soul. The word for "breath" in Hebrew is *ruach*, which
we take to mean that breath of God's life that is our own personal spirit.
What we see is that as our spirit experiences the events of life in our body
and reacts, our soul's character is formed. Our reactions form structures
within the heart and mind, temperament and personality, through which
our spirit continues to encounter life and expresses responsively according
to the way it has interpreted experiences. As we develop the structure of
our character, in which the mind and heart interplay, the soul becomes
in some areas a temple through which our spirit gloriously worships God
and meets others, or in other areas a prison, or worse yet, an armored
tank by which our spirit rushes out to attack others.

We do not see soul and spirit as separate in space, for our spirit perme-
ates every part of us. But we do see separate functions.

Throughout the Bible, from fig leaves and coats of skin in Genesis 3 to
fine linen as the righteous deeds of the saints in Revelation 19:8, the Lord
uses the metaphor of clothing to describe aspects of our soul. We see this
especially in Colossians 3 in the metaphor of putting off unrighteousness
and putting on righteousness as in putting garments off and on. Others
may call that nexus of practices our "old man" or our "unregenerate self."
Those terms are biblically correct. We simply see that "old man" as a part
of our soul, the total structure of us through which our spirit expresses
who we are in all of life. That old man died when we received Jesus as Lord
and Savior, but the problem is it won't stay dead.

> See to it that no one comes short of the grace of God; that no root of
> bitterness springing up causes trouble, and by it many be defiled.
> —HEBREWS 12:15

The old man springs back to life, which is why inner sanctification and
true foundation are needed. Every part of us—body, soul, and spirit—

needs redemption. In the end we who are in Christ will fulfill the clothing metaphor, as St. Paul predicted:

> For this perishable must put on the imperishable, and this mortal must put on immortality. But when this perishable will have put on the imperishable, and this mortal will have put on immortality, then will come about the saying that is written, "Death is swallowed up in victory."
>
> —1 CORINTHIANS 15:53–54

We shall then have become, fully and forever, the perfected soul we only wear and express imperfectly now. Our spirit, soul, and body will then be as St. Paul prayed: "…preserved complete, without blame at the coming of our Lord Jesus Christ" (1 Thess. 5:23).

Until and in preparation for that time, we are to be involved in the process of cleansing and healing the heart and spirit. We need to identify the three functions and needs of our spirit, that He may make us whole.

The first function of the spirit is to worship God.

We shall see, especially in chapter 2, "The Slumbering Spirit," what enables the spirit to worship *in truth*, and what prevents it from doing so.

The fact is that our spirit has many distinct functions. As the body must be fed to be healthy, so our personal spirit must be nurtured and disciplined, else it cannot sustain and perform as God intended. The horrifying fact is that almost no one now in the body of Christ, far less of course in the world, comprehends the stark reality that our spirit requires nurture!

A painful paradox is that parents who mean to be dutiful knowledgeably feed their children's bodies three balanced meals a day, see to it that their minds are well fed by means of schools and books and in many forms of training and discipline, and provide so that their souls are trained in the Word of God and Sunday school. Yet these same conscientious parents may have almost no awareness that the primary immortal aspect of man, his spirit, needs even more careful nurture and training.

Understand that though we speak of distinct functions of our spirit, we are not speaking in a docetic way, that is, as though only our spirits count and our bodies are of little import. Christ was not a discarnate being as some from the docetic (meaning "to seem" from the Greek *docein*) way of thinking may want to believe.[2]

Nor are our spirits apart from and separate from our bodies. What touches the body touches the spirit. We are incarnate beings. That means that we are not spirits *in* a body, as water fills a can. We are spiritual bodies. "And the Word *became* flesh, and dwelt among us" (John 1:14). It is not that our Lord came down from heaven, donned a body like putting on a suit of clothes, and then returned to heaven to be a spirit. He took on human form—spirit and body existing in unison.

The Word *became* flesh; it did not merely visit in a body. He arose in His body, nevermore to be without the human body. We *become* flesh; we *are* that body; spirit and body having become one, though remaining distinct. *Death is the divorce of the union of spirit and body.* When our spirit can no longer retain its union with the body to keep it alive as a functioning reality united to itself, it returns to God. Death then means that "the dust will return to the earth as it was, and the spirit will return to God who gave it" (Eccles. 12:7).

We were not designed for death. God built us so that body and spirit would sustain one another, and the spirit so healing and rejuvenating the body that the union need never have been broken. Sin fractured the ability of the personal spirit to sustain the body. Ezekiel 18:4 says, "The soul who sins will die." The Lord is very careful in His use of the words *soul* and *spirit*. When He says *soul*, we believe He speaks concerning our entire inner being—heart, mind, and soul, and within all that, our spirit. But sometimes He distinctly refers to our spirit, as in John 4:23, "True worshipers shall worship the Father in *spirit* and truth" (emphasis added), or in St. Paul's 1 Thessalonians 5:23, "May your *spirit* and *soul* and *body* be preserved *complete*, without blame at the coming of our Lord Jesus Christ" (emphasis added).

At times the Bible speaks of how our Lord felt in His soul.

- At the Last Supper: "Now My *soul* has become troubled" (John 12:27).

- In the garden of Gethsemane: "My *soul* is deeply grieved, to the point of death" (Matt. 26:38).

At other times the Word speaks distinctly of what He felt in His spirit.

- Before the tomb of Lazarus: "When Jesus therefore saw her weeping...He was deeply moved in *spirit*, and was troubled" (John 11:33).

- At the Last Supper, when He declared one would betray Him: "He became troubled in *spirit*" (John 13:21).

- On the cross: "Into Thy hands I commit My *spirit*" (Luke 23:46).

- After His resurrection: "A *spirit* does not have flesh and bones as you see that I have" (Luke 24:39).

The Word is as careful when speaking of others.

- St. Paul: "Now while Paul was waiting for them at Athens, his *spirit* was being provoked within him as he was beholding the city full of idols" (Acts 17:16).

- Mary, the mother of Jesus: "My *soul* exalts the Lord, and my *spirit* has rejoiced in God my Savior" (Luke 1:46–47).

This would imply that because her spirit *has* rejoiced, her soul is now able to exalt the Lord. In each case the Holy Spirit is incisive in the choice of words. Our Lord means to speak of the personal spirit as distinct from heart, mind, and soul.

When He says the soul that sins shall die, we understand it to mean that our spirit loses its capacity to seek and embrace God and others and therefore the structures and desires of our soul and heart no longer are enabled. They consequently tend to block. As a result, we die to the ability to relate as we were intended to God, man, nature, and ourselves. If sinful structures in the mind and heart and waning strength of spirit continue, the body is afflicted.

> When I kept silent about my sin, my body wasted away
> Through my groaning all day long.
> For day and night Thy hand was heavy upon me;
> My vitality was drained away as with the fever heat of summer.
> I acknowledged my sin to Thee,
> And my iniquity I did not hide;

I said, "I will confess my transgressions to the LORD";
And Thou didst forgive the guilt of my sin.

—PSALM 32:3–5

Physical death is the final result. When all mankind's redemption is finally consummated and sin is no more, "then will come about the saying that is written, 'Death is swallowed up in victory'" (1 Cor. 15:54).

Some are tempted to think that if any Christian were able to live purely in Christ, he would not have to die. But we are not capable of such perfection; furthermore, we are corporate creatures tempted by the sins of others. Therefore none shall live eternally without death until the consummation of Christ's purpose for all His own: "The *last* enemy that will be abolished is death" (1 Cor. 15:26, emphasis added). Enoch and Elijah were exceptions, but perhaps they were not perfect, only sanctified enough to be received into heaven.

The second function of the spirit is to keep our bodies alive and functioning.

Whatever medical definitions may be acceptable for death, Christians know that death occurs when our spirits can no longer abide in our bodies and leave them (Eccles. 12:7). Hundreds of testimonies are recorded in many life-after-death books that universally speak of the spirit leaving and returning to the body. Apparently our spirit requires a body that is capable of functioning in certain necessary ways, though it can suffer breakage and loss in others, or the unity of spirit and body is broken and the spirit must "return to God who gave it." How the spirit sustains and energizes the body and how the body houses and protects the spirit, no one knows. But the psychosomatic interrelation of the two is well documented both in the Scriptures and in psychosomatic medicine (though some medical researchers might not call that life force or "psyche" within us the "spirit," as Christians would). The fact that the body instantly begins to decay beyond natural repair the moment the spirit leaves ought to prove to us that it is our spirit that sustains the body and keeps it from death as long as it is able. Scripture describes clearly that our personal spirit sustains our body's health.

A joyful heart is good medicine,
But a broken spirit dries up the bones.

—PROVERBS 17:22

The spirit of a man can endure his sickness,
But a broken spirit who can bear?

—PROVERBS 18:14

The third function of the spirit is to interrelate and interact with others.

Our spirits reach out across space beyond the body and sometimes beyond the five senses to meet and interact with others. When a father holds his infant child in his arms, their spirits sense a flow of blessing one to another. That is what makes such moments so tender. That is what makes love a real and practical interchange of energies rather than an isolated feeling or attitude within the father or the baby alone. When St. Paul said, "Do you not know that the one who joins himself to a harlot *is one body with her*?" (1 Cor. 6:16, emphasis added), it is that meeting and uniting of personal spirits in and through human touch, beyond each one's skin into union with the other, that is the basis of his statement that a man becomes "one body with her."

All of us have at times felt the presence of another in a room, perhaps a moment before we turned to look to the exact place where our inner spiritual sense told us the other would be; or we may have felt the energy of peering eyes and looked to find someone staring at us. While we were in college, Paula and I returned from a weekend visit to my home, and though no one was in sight, we stepped into a gloom so heavy about the campus that the dullest, least mystically sensitive person could not have missed it. We learned then that earlier in the day four popular students had been killed in a car crash. The sadness in the spirits of all on the campus permeated the air everywhere. In an age accustomed to radio and TV waves invisibly filling the air, it should cause no wonderment at all that our spirits do something similar.

It is because our spirits can reach out and feel within another person that we can empathize and share deeply with each other. We commune with each other and communicate silently. We look for corroborative signs in the eyes, facial expressions, inflections, and words of the other. Sometimes we are puzzled or hurt when a friend is obviously grieved in spirit but so good an actor that his eyes, face, and voice mimic happiness. Once, while making rounds calling on parishioners in the hospital, I turned, as was my custom, to pray for a lady in the next bed, whom I did not know. When I began to pray, however, I found myself unaccountably checked by the Holy Spirit. I could not utter a word and found myself merely standing and praying silently for a long time, letting the Holy Spirit flow through me to her. Having said amen and being a little embarrassed, I was surprised to see her face radiant with pleasure and to hear her exclaim, "Oh, thank you! Thank you!"

"For what?" I replied.

"For giving me communion. I'm a Quaker, and you just gave me communion in the spirit. How did you know?"

Of course I hadn't known, though the Holy Spirit had. Quakers only consciously tune in to what we all feel in every kind of meeting of spirits—sometimes light and joyous, sometimes sad or filled with tension, sometimes bristling with dagger thrusts of animosity, sometimes refreshing, or sometimes filled with weariness. As one cannot step into the same river twice, so meeting any person is different each time because what emanates from the spirit moment by moment is different. Sensitivity through our spirit is what actually guides conversations in ways and subjects we seem merely to have tumbled into. It is a primary basic function of our spirit to enable us to meet and commune with others and with God.

In chapter 2 we will discuss more fully nine functions of our spirit. It is these three—worship, sustaining life in the body, and communing with others—that we regard as primary and basic. The first refers to our ability to meet, cherish, and adore God; the second to our ability to relate to ourselves; and the third to our ability to commune and communicate with God, others, and nature.

If we understand that our spirit acts within these basic functions and that we are incarnational—that is, that our spirit acts in and through all that our bodies are—we are ready to attempt to answer the crucial question of this book: "What nurture does the personal spirit require, and how does it receive it?"

NURTURING OUR SPIRIT

Our spirit finds nurture from its source—God. It is personal devotion and corporate worship that are the basics of nurture for our spirit. The Holy Spirit is by design the power of our life. "It is the Spirit who gives life" (John 6:63). But what can keep Him from nurturing us? Lack of devotion. What allows Him to nurture us? Devotional prayer. Children too young or who do not yet know how to pray are filled with His presence by the devotional life of their parents. The intercession of friends and even strangers fills us all with His life. Prayer is thus the key to life.

How often have we heard prayerful saints testify that if they go one day without prayer, they know it; if two days, their mate knows it; if three, the world knows it! We can tank up on Sunday or by the intercession of others, but all experienced Christians know that sooner or later they will have to return to His presence in their own devotions or run out of spiritual capacity to function as they ought. I know of no sound spiritual leader who does not know that his spirit absolutely requires daily momentary nurture in the presence of our loving Lord. The least Christian a few days old in the Lord is already learning that he can only walk His life if his own spirit is continually, regularly charged in private devotion and worship.

We all know that simple truth. The strange thing is twofold. First, we forget it so easily and so often. But stranger is the second; somehow we often fail to apply the same common sense to the needs of children! Did we think their spirits can run forever on a single initial charge from God's inexhaustible bank? Perhaps their natural vitality and ebullience beguile us. We are writing this book to reveal wounds and sins, and here lies the most common and grievous! When parents fail to pray regularly with and for their children, their children's spirits literally starve and wither. How often did Jesus try to tell us that He Himself is food and drink to our spirits?

> Jesus answered and said to her, "Everyone who drinks of this water shall thirst again; but whoever drinks of the water that I shall give him shall never thirst; but the water that I shall give him shall become in him a well of water springing up to eternal life."
>
> —JOHN 4:13–14

> I am the living bread that came down out of heaven; if anyone eats of this bread, he shall live forever; and the bread also which I shall give for the life of the world is My flesh.
>
> —JOHN 6:51

> Jesus therefore said to them, "Truly, truly, I say to you, unless you eat the flesh of the Son of Man and drink His blood, you have no life in yourselves. He who eats My flesh and drinks My blood has eternal life, and I will raise him up on the last day. For My flesh is true food, and My blood is true drink. He who eats My flesh and drinks My blood abides in Me, and I in him."
>
> —JOHN 6:53–56

Abide in Me, and I in you. As the branch cannot bear fruit of itself, unless it abides in the vine, so neither can you, unless you abide in Me. I am the vine, you are the branches; he who abides in Me, and I in him, he bears much fruit; for apart from Me you can do nothing. If anyone does not abide in Me, he is thrown away as a branch, and dries up; and they gather them, and cast them into the fire, and they are burned.

—JOHN 15:4–6

Oh, that the body of Christ might come to think as practically and truly about the spirit as it does of the body. No conscientious mother would fail to feed her children three balanced meals a day. Famine or poverty devastates her when she knows she cannot feed her loved ones. Pictures of starving children grieve our hearts. If only there were some way parents could see the spirits of their children in the same way as they see those photos. Can we not come to realize that our spirit needs feeding perhaps even more desperately than the body?

Once we see it, the remedy is so simple. Bedtime prayers. Mealtime thanksgiving. A short blessing before the children catch the bus to school. Flash prayers for the children during the day. Knowing our Lord as someone with whom we live and walk, not something we grab hold of in frantic times when all else fails. Sunday school. Regular worship service. Christ in all our life in the church (and out of it) as a loving presence who meets us, teaches, empowers, holds us accountable, forgives, disciplines, heals, restores. Never should we have formed law or religion without relationship.

So often when conducting prayer ministry with parents of errant teenagers, we hear, "I can't understand it. We gave them everything! A good home. Three square meals a day. They never lacked for a thing." A few moments of questioning reveals that the most important form of nurture had been almost totally lacking. They had never given their children's spirits a thought. Some even took the kids to Sunday school and church, thus feeding their souls, somewhat, and their spirits one quick meal a week. What parent would think his child could eat one physical meal a week and have the strength to be a normal child? But let the reader check his memory to see whether he knows of even a few parents who think and act in these terms, consciously and dutifully *nurturing and feeding* their children's *spirits* daily in the presence and power of the Holy Spirit. Do we see that we have not even thought in these terms, much less acted on them? Herein lies the first grievous wounding of most children to whom we will minister as adults.

The rule is (given that almost no one now thinks in terms of daily feeding the personal spirit), in those families where much prayer and tactile affection regularly occur, children are less starved or wounded. In those families where there is little of this, or none at all, children's spirits grieve and starve. Their inner spirits are angry and hurt, whether or not their minds and hearts are aware of it. The mind may know something of loss, but the spirit intuitively hungers.

> As the deer pants for the water brooks,
> So my soul [and the spirit within us] pants for Thee, O God.
> My soul thirsts for God, for the living God.
>
> —PSALM 42:1–2

Imagine a sunflower in a darkened room sadly and slowing turning its face to find tiny glimmers of light, gradually withering, slumping, and dying. That is a profoundly accurate picture of children's spirits in such homes. We will see later (in chapter 2) why that condition is directly the cause of rising crime rates and all manner of sexual perversion.

When we discover that the adult to whom we are ministering was raised in such a home, we ask the Lord to find that starving inner child and take him into His own loving arms. We ask Him to restore to him as many years as the cankerworm has eaten and the locust has destroyed (Joel 2:25, KJV). This prayer has full scriptural warrant: "For my father and my mother have forsaken me, but the LORD will take me up" (Ps. 27:10). We ask the Lord to come to him day after day, loving and wooing him to life. We tell the person after the prayer to become part of a prayer group and to plop himself into "the mercy seat" (where people gather around and pray with laying on of hands) every week for a while. A child needs many, many touches.

The greatest feeding place, all the way to the grave, is at the Lord's table. Did you ever wonder why the Lord commanded us as He did?

> For I received from the Lord that which I also delivered to you, that the Lord Jesus in the night in which He was betrayed took bread; and when He had given thanks, He broke it, and said, "This is My body, which is for you; do this in remembrance of Me." In the same way He took the cup also, after supper, saying, "This cup is the new covenant

in My blood; do this, as often as you drink it, in remembrance of
Me."

                                        —1 CORINTHIANS 11:23–25

There are many reasons why the Lord commanded us to feed at His
table; among them are forgiveness, remembrance, the unity of eating
together in worship, healing, and the like. But is it possible the Lord was
also responding to what He knew is the primary need for all of us? He
knew our souls, specifically our spirits, needed to feed on Him through a
simple act. From this vantage point can we see that it may be that Roman
Catholic and other liturgical churches are very wise to encourage daily
attendance at Mass? What a treasure you have, my Roman Catholic
friends! We Protestants feed the soul grandly on the Word of God, and
rightly. But sometimes I think we overlook the greatest feeding place for
our spirit. All segments of the Church would do well to learn from one
another that the banquet we enjoy in the presence of the Lord might be
more full and rich to nurture both soul and spirit. This is not to say that
Catholics and Protestants alike are not fed in spirit by all other aspects of
worship, but only that I personally treasure and know that the Lord's table
feeds my spirit more fully and directly than anything else I know. I believe
that is so for every one of us.

Other things feed the spirit. God's laughter is in the chuckle of a friend.
His Spirit touches us in the flit of a monarch butterfly on the wing. God
is "through all and in all" (Eph. 4:6) touching us. But the key is this: only
as we commune with Him directly do we retain the capacity to let His
Spirit touch ours meaningfully through the creation. I have wept in spirit
as I watched my dead-in-spirit friends crush a lily without a thought or a
spark of awareness. Haven't we all, who can still be profoundly moved by
beauty, grieved in similar situations?

Beauty seems all but lost to so many in this calloused generation. God
created beauty to feed our weary hearts and souls and spirits. There was
a time when artists and musicians thought that their highest aim was
to create beauty. Theirs are still the great works on which our souls and
spirits feed. Today, strident nonsense struts itself across canvases and
musical scores, witnessing to the world of the death of starving spirits
who can no longer sing beauty's refreshing song of creation. How this
generation needs its new John Talbots to create songs for the rejuvenation
of the spirits of God's children! Few people know how much most rock

concerts and weird forms on canvas jangle spirits. How many parents today take their children to something like Tchaikovsky's beautiful *Nutcracker* ballet? I used to spend my Sunday afternoons as a child flat on my back with my head below the sounding board of the grand piano while my mother played music by Chopin, Debussy, and others, and my spirit soared. It seemed the notes played themselves up and down my body in glory. Where does spiritual stamina come from but in such moments? Even today as I write, my stereo is on and Beethoven's Sonata for Piano No. 14 in C-sharp Minor ("Moonlight Sonata") and Piano Sonata No. 18 in E-flat Major, op. 31, no. 3 ("The Hunt") have been bathing my spirit with inspiration.

I have scriptural precedent for how I feel. King Jehoram of Israel enlisted King Jehoshaphat of Judah in his war against Moab. For three days they sought water and, finding none, searched for a prophet. When someone recommended Elisha, he responded that he would act for the sake of Jehoshaphat and said, "'But now bring me a minstrel.' And it came about, when the minstrel played, that the hand of the LORD came upon him" (2 Kings 3:15). Elisha told them water would come without rain, to dig trenches and be ready, and it did (vv. 16–20).

Devotional music is the soaring vehicle of the spirit and a place of power. At the dedication of Solomon's temple, the musicians and the singers were designated and trained to make music to the Lord, and such glory fell that none could stand:

> When the priests came forth from the holy place (for all the priests who were present had sanctified themselves, without regard to divisions), and all the Levitical singers...and their sons and kinsmen, clothed in fine linen, with cymbals, harps, and lyres, standing east of the altar, and with them one hundred and twenty priests blowing trumpets in unison when the trumpeters and the singers were to make themselves heard with one voice to praise and to glorify the LORD, and when they lifted up their voice accompanied by trumpets and cymbals and instruments of music, and when they praised the LORD saying, "He indeed is good for His lovingkindness is everlasting," then the house, the house of the LORD, was filled with a cloud, so that the priests could not stand to minister because of the cloud, for the glory of the LORD filled the house of God.
>
> —2 CHRONICLES 5:11–14

Music fuels our spirit; it is itself power. When the "evil spirit from God" was upon Saul, he called for David, and when he played and sang, that evil spirit would leave him for a while (1 Sam. 16:14–23). When Jehoshaphat went forth to battle:

> They rose early in the morning and went out to the wilderness of Tekoa; and when they went out, Jehoshaphat stood and said, "Listen to me, O Judah and inhabitants of Jerusalem, put your trust in the LORD your God, and you will be established. Put your trust in His prophets and succeed." And when he had consulted with the people, he appointed those who sang to the LORD and those who praised Him in holy attire, as they went out before the army and said, "Give thanks to the LORD, for His lovingkindness is everlasting." And when they began singing and praising, the LORD set ambushes against the sons of Ammon, Moab, and Mount Seir, who had come against Judah; so they were routed. For the sons of Ammon and Moab rose up against the inhabitants of Mount Seir destroying them completely, and when they had finished with the inhabitants of Seir, they helped to destroy one another.
>
> —2 CHRONICLES 20:20–23

How often do we parents consciously feed our children's spirits on devotional music? Paula's mother played the piano as her children gathered around and sang the grand old hymns of faith. My mother and I spent hours together as she played and I sang the hymns of God. Our grown family now gathers at holidays to sit around to sing choruses or the familiar old Christmas carols.

Reading feeds the heart and soul and spirit, depending on what we read. The Word of God is a complete diet; it does feed our heart and soul *and spirit.* In Ephesians 3:16 St. Paul prayed that the Ephesians might be "strengthened with power through His Spirit in the inner man." It is strength in our spirit we need to stand for Christ in the world. We have found that if people find every other kind of nurture for their spirits so that they should be strong in Him but fail to feed daily on God's Word, their spirits do not retain long whatever strength has been gained elsewhere. Reading God's Word is like building strong banks for the flow of God's Spirit in our spirit, without which our life's strength ebbs away as a river is lost in desert sands.

Who among us did not find his spirit soaring in dreams of glory when as children we read the grand stories of heroes and heroines? I am sure that the stories of knightly chivalry and of the sacrificial lives of the saints fed my spirit with determination to serve God beyond the call of duty. My mother read Wordsworth, Tennyson, Keats, and Shelly to me and taught me to love and understand poetry, which still feeds my spirit today. My parents provided several sets of children's books, among which was *Journeys Through Bookland*, which took me from simplest nursery rhymes into Greek mythology and the great fables and legends of all the world's peoples. That training and provision has nurtured my spirit well throughout my life. I still find refreshment by the habit of good reading.

At mealtimes, my father demanded that we all be washed and dressed nicely for supper, *together*, around the dining room table. We joked and teased and bantered and sometimes laughed so hard we wound up rolling on the floor. Far more than our bodies were fed. Our spirits drank family fun and fellowship. Our own children's friends' eyes sometimes have widened in surprise when they have sat at supper with us. "You people actually eat together and have fun," they say. "My family never eats together. We just all grab a bite here or there." Their spirits lagged from lack of nurture in the family.

So far we have been speaking mainly of how God feeds our spirit through worship and beauty and music. But since we have begun to speak of the family, let us turn to how He would feed us through others, most especially the family.

OUR SPIRITS NURTURED BY THE FAMILY

In child raising one thing is more important than all others. Parents can succeed in feeding their children's bodies nourishing food, their minds with good schooling, and their souls with sound teaching in the Word, yet still fail miserably. If they do not give copious amounts of simple affection, their children starve. Affection is the "without which nothing" in child raising. Every child needs to be held in loving arms many times daily. Because we are incarnational beings, spirit touches spirit in every hug, and His Spirit touches each in the embrace. Jesus said, "To the extent that you did it to one of these brothers of Mine, even the least of them, you did it to Me" (Matt. 25:40). He was speaking of every person. His influence is made weak in the lives of many by their neglect or denial. He expresses

Himself in power in others. But He is there in all. His life is love. When we act in love, His life flows in ours and nourishes each person in every embrace.

Think of the nature of Jesus in each person. Can He pour who He is through us when we are yelling abuse? Will He love through us when we are kissing our neighbor's mate? Will His strength energize us when we want to beat up on someone in jealousy? Of course not. He is there, in us, but He can only grieve and pray.

But suppose we want to nuzzle a baby against us. The sluice gates open, and His own person flows in what we do, and both the baby and we are refreshed. If a father reads a bedtime Bible story, the Holy Spirit joins the father and penetrates to the child's spirit in the sound of his voice. When a mother sets a lovely table and bows her head to take her children's hands in her own as Papa prays, whose love pours through her hands and his voice but that of the Lord? God's Spirit pours forth healing power when a mother's hand touches a fevered brow. Even the hands of discipline bear the loving touch of God. In all that is right and true, the love of God refreshes.

Dogs will nose and push against hands to ask for petting and stroking. I have often wondered why they become so insistent. What did it mean to them, or do for them, that made them press us for more and more? Then the Lord reminded me that He had given them a spirit (yes, animals do have spirits; see Ecclesiastes 3:21) that can feel our spirits' love cascading in heaping waves of glory through their bodies when our hands stroke them.

Infants and young children still retain that same sensitivity. Their little spirits are still open and vulnerable, present and able to melt into us or drink our presence through our touch. Every nursing mother knows that her baby drinks far more than milk from her.

Unfortunately, most people, especially fathers, do not know their worth to children. In a world of materialistic science and hard objects, the world of the personal spirit has seemed abstruse and far remote from reality. In a secular world that demands practicality identified and measured by the five senses, too many fathers have lost track of the *most* practical and real—the power of the spirit through human touch.

The remedy is so simple as to seem inconsequential in a world of technology and computers. A little conscious effort to remember is enough. Merely hug family members each night upon arrival home. Take a child on the lap while watching TV. Put a hand on a shoulder or give a pat on the back. Give a light kiss at bedtime. Engage in a romp on the floor occasionally. Hold hands at prayer times. Sit with a child nestled under the crook of an arm in the car or at the movies or even in church.

Hear a simple maxim: when affection is given in normal, healthy ways, people's spirits stay whole and seek normal, healthy ways of expression. When affection is not given, drives and urges express themselves in wrong ways, and the spirit sickens, seeking wrong answers for right needs. True affection does not lead to improper sexual touch and embrace but away from it. It is the rare touches of inadequate affection that turn into lust. In wholesomely affectionate homes, all the forms of child abuse almost never manifest themselves. We do not need to fear touch, only the absence of it.

When children have not received enough affectionate touch, it is the task of prayer ministers and the body of Christ to heal. Affection given to fifty-year-olds can warm the hearts of five-year-olds within. When questions reveal starvation diets of affection, prayer ministers need to pray with the person, enabling their heart to forgive. Never mind that the person's mind may never have consciously identified resentment or anger. Our personal spirit has a mind of its own; it has desires that, when it is thwarted, turn to anger. It is to that inner spirit we minister when we ask the grown one to say, "I forgive you, Dad and Mom, for not holding me enough." When the hurting one says the words of forgiveness, we should then pronounce that he is forgiven that sin of dishonoring his parents. Never mind that in all his outward attitude he may have honored to the best of his ability. It is for the sins of the heart our Lord holds us accountable.

> God sees not as man sees, for man looks at the outward appearance, but the LORD looks at the heart.
>
> —1 SAMUEL 16:7

> For out of the heart come evil thoughts, murders, adulteries, fornications, thefts, false witness, slanders.
>
> —MATTHEW 15:19

Anger in the heart toward parents may be so well controlled, suppressed, forgotten, and overlaid with love and loyalty that it is thought not to be there, but this same anger may fuel perplexing explosions in other areas of our lives—toward our mate, children, friends, employers, pastors, and so on. Having forgiven, we need to pray that the bruised and starved spirit be healed and nurtured by our Lord.

Finally, nurture comes to us by our cherishing of our own person. In this, we are not advocating narcissism. Rather, here is another true maxim: when we disobey the great commandment to love our neighbor *as ourselves* and cannot truly love being who we are, our spirit becomes so drained and empty we develop ways to puff ourselves up in pride, braggadocio, and false love to fill the vacuum. Whoever loves himself as he ought need not fear pride or selfishness. True love of oneself will overflow to others as naturally as a creek may begin to form a pond but, overfilling its banks, spill out to bless the earth beyond. We only love ourselves wrongly when we fail to love ourselves rightly.

True love of self manifests itself most directly in the way we think of our bodies. We need to stop cursing and blaming our bodies: "What a fat slob I am!" "I'd forget my own brain if it weren't attached!" "What a klutz! I can stumble over the linoleum!" "I detest the way I look!" Our spirit manifests itself in and through every part of the body and takes every railing as hurt and rejection. Being grateful for our body, and expressing that gratitude, blesses and invigorates our spirit.

Devotion to God, Bible reading, loving relationships and services to others—all the ways that emulate our Lord—bless the body and spirit, for we flow in His Spirit as He intended. Imagine a man dragging burning feet across sun-fired sands mile after mile, thirsting after water that he cannot find, while in fact green grasses stretch in lanes beside rivers not ten feet away, parallel to him. That is an accurate description of the condition of our spirit when we walk apart from Christ and His way. Our spirit was not made to walk apart from our Lord. We force it to starve in alien, darkened alleyways when we walk any other path than that for which He created us.

Enough. It is enough if we see that our spirits are not amorphous, foggy things somewhere inside of us. Our spirits suffuse and reach beyond every cell of our being. They require nurture of their own. The main import of this chapter is to awaken us all to the simple fact that not only do our spirits have specific functions of their own, but also they need to be fed daily, in as practical and disciplined a manner as we feed our bodies.

CHAPTER 2

THE SLUMBERING SPIRIT

His watchmen are blind, all of them know nothing. All of them are dumb dogs unable to bark, dreamers lying down, *who love to slumber.*

—ISAIAH 56:10, EMPHASIS ADDED

Many years ago, Paula and I were ministering to a number of Spirit-filled people who, no matter how much help they received, remained incapable of walking straight in the Lord. One was a young man who loved the Lord, had been born anew and filled with the Spirit, attended church regularly, loved his wife and children, but seemed unable to discipline himself to pay his bills. When bill collectors sent overdue notices, he was furious at them for bothering him! At the same time he kept falling into adultery, with no apparent conscience about either the adulteries or the overdue bills. He seemed to spend life caught in the temptations and gratifications of the moment, unable to understand how his actions robbed and hurt others. He learned no lessons from past hard experiences and had no real awareness that there would come a day of reckoning.

We wore ourselves out discovering and praying about fractures and sinful practices in his character, but he could not take hold of life and walk uprightly. We kept asking God, "What's missing? Why doesn't he have a functioning conscience?"

Another was a minister who seemed devoted to hurling hard words at his people. No matter how we prayed, he could not understand how his hearers could be hurt by what he said. He related to the plan of salvation and to letter and law, but not to people's hearts. I would make him aware logically that his sermons were unloving, lacking both humanity and hope, and were genuinely harming his people. But next Sunday he would be at it again. Prayer ministry sessions revealed that though he had gone through the ritual of inviting Jesus into his heart and of being filled with the Holy Spirit, he had never experienced His presence or heard His voice or known Him in any other than an intellectual way. We finally came to the end of our rope with him, crying out to the Lord, "What is missing? Why can't he come to know You personally?"

At the same time, traveling as teachers and prayer ministers across the country, we crossed the tracks of many other Christian leaders. People came to us for ministry, wounded and angry with more than half a dozen itinerant Spirit-filled teachers of God's Word who had had sexual affairs with relatives and friends of theirs! One traveling miracle-working evangelist had caused a pregnancy, forced the girl to have an abortion, and subsequently denied ever having known her. At that time, there were no ways to establish paternity, as there are today, so the parents were both angry and frustrated. We were ministering to them, trying to explain how God can continue to work through fractured, sinful vessels. We attempted to persuade them to forgive both the evangelist and God. But inside ourselves, questions were tumbling. "How can this happen, Lord? Why don't these men have a conscience strong enough to keep them out of trouble? They love You and preach a true word; why can't they live it? How can they wound Your heart like that? What's the matter? What's missing?" So we said our usual fervent, intellectual, and righteous prayer, "*Help!*" And God answered.

First, He said, "John, these people do not have an alert and functioning personal spirit. Their own personal spirit is not awake. They have a slumbering spirit."

Immediately I wanted to know what that meant. Over several weeks of meditating, searching the hearts and histories of the persons to whom we ministered, and seeking the Lord, He laid it out for me.

We are born with an alive and awake personal spirit. But that spirit needs to be met, welcomed, loved, and nurtured through warm physical affection. If a baby growing from infanthood into childhood does not receive enough human touch, to that degree his spirit is not kept awake or drawn forth into full functioning ability. If he responds by closing his heart, then he becomes a slumberer.

It was soon revealed that there are two kinds of slumbering spirits:

1.   Those who never have been drawn forth to life, who early in infancy have fallen asleep and can no longer function spiritually

2.   Those who did receive parental and other nurture and so were awake and functioning spiritually, but turned away from worship services, prayer, and affection until their spirits fell asleep, or who fell into sins that soon quenched their spirits

In both, the heart has hardened as well.

If their spirits were totally inert, such people would of course be physically dead. It is in the areas of relationship to God and man and nature or to their own beings that these sleepers cannot function in their spirits. That means that they come to God mentally and emotionally but never really meet Him. They relate to the forms, to liturgy, doctrine, theology, law, or the plan of salvation, but not to His person. They can share in emotions, weeping over the lost, and about their own sins through remorse, but they are not able to commune with Jesus or share His sufferings as St. Paul related in Philippians 3:10. They have no ability to empathize with Him or others. They are relegated and confined to the necessity of calculating and estimating with their minds what others think and feel.

One might ask, "What about the Holy Spirit? He is the very giver of life. His task is to make us alive. Why didn't such people come awake when the Holy Spirit came in?" Some did. But when I asked the Lord that question, He answered by telling me to picture a river. "That represents the Holy Spirit," He said, "truly flowing through a man's life." Then He said to picture a rock in the middle of the river, unmoved, the water cascading against it and around it. That rock represents the personal spirit of some people, hardened and incapable of participating in the flow of the Spirit's life. The Holy Spirit is there, flowing through the man's mind and heart, emotions and body, so he can preach brilliantly, work miracles, and say mighty prophecies. But the man's own spirit cannot participate. It lies asleep, encased and nonfunctioning. Sadly, if the condition continues, it may demonstrate what Jesus meant when He said:

Many will say to Me on that day, "Lord, Lord, did we not prophesy in Your name, and in Your name cast out demons, and in Your name perform many miracles?" And then I will declare to them, "I never knew you; depart from Me, you who practice lawlessness."

—MATTHEW 7:22–23

The word *knew* in "I never knew you," is in Greek the same as the marriage word: Adam "knew" Eve. Jesus is saying, "I never fully *met* you."

The more we thought, the more this revelation made sense, and we could see it clearly in the lives of those to whom we ministered.

THE NINE FUNCTIONS OF THE PERSON SPIRIT

We proceeded to teach about the slumbering spirit, but we were shocked to discover the appalling fact that very few people in the body of Christ knew what each person's spirit is supposed to do! It had not occurred to many that we have a spirit with specific definable functions. That drove us to seek and find what are the peculiar, distinct capacities and operations of our personal spirit.

We have come to see that the condition of having a slumbering spirit is one of the epidemic illnesses of our generation, increasing constantly as nurture dwindles and marriages and homes break apart. Everyone's spirit is asleep to some degree. Some fail to function in all of the nine areas we will shortly outline. Some function in only one or two. None of us are fully awake, nor are we fully slumbering.

1. Corporate worship

The first function of our personal spirit is corporate worship.

But an hour is coming, and now is, when the true worshipers shall worship the Father in spirit and truth; for such people the Father seeks to be His worshipers. God is spirit, and those who worship Him must worship in spirit and truth.

—JOHN 4:23–24

Those whose spirits are awake feel the uplifting presence of the Lord in a worship service. They feel His anointing pouring over them. Their spirit is touched and filled anew with His. Such joy and love well up that their soul sings praises to God. They can *abide* in His presence in great "joy inexpressible and full of glory" (1 Pet. 1:8).

Note "soul" and "spirit" and the tense in the first lines of the Magnificat: "And Mary said, '*My soul exalts* the Lord, and my *spirit has rejoiced* in God my Savior'" (Luke 1:46–47, emphasis added). When God moves upon us, He moves first upon our spirits. Our spirits rejoice in His love. That enables us to praise Him with a full heart, so the soul can then exalt Him. Because the spirit "*has* rejoiced," the soul *can* exalt.

Awakened people not only are carried by Him into worship, but they also sense and feel the swell of other people's spirits and hearts. They become suffused not only with His love but also in the love of all the fellowship. True worship knits hearts together because spirits are melted into one fire of love.

People who have slumbering spirits have often said to us, "I don't know what they are talking about. I never feel God's presence." Some feel momentary flickers but have no power to abide. They don't know how to bathe their needy spirits in His river, though surely "there is a river whose streams make glad the city of God" (Ps. 46:4). We may ask a person whom we suspect has a slumbering spirit, "When you are in a worship service or a prayer meeting and others are raising their hands and praising God, do you feel His presence, or do you just know by faith that He is there?" The answer slumberers invariably give is, "Oh, I just know He is there." One thinks of Jesus's words to Thomas, "Blessed are they who did not see, and yet believed" (John 20:29). These people do not experience the fullness of worship and perhaps never have. At least they believe.

2. Private devotions

The second function of our personal spirit is to enable us to have satisfying private devotions. Awakened people can enter His presence, bask in His love, and soar. They "mount up with wings like eagles" (Isa. 40:31). Words leap by inspiration off the pages of the Bible, and thoughts and images flow into their minds, unbidden, by the gentle power of the Holy Spirit. Slumbering people, on the other hand, tell us, "I try to have devotions, but it always runs dry. I run out of words. I never feel anything." Sometimes they may decide, "If I can't pray very well, at least I can read the Bible." So they try to establish a discipline, perhaps to follow a lexicon through the Scriptures. But that too becomes a desert. Fairly soon they realize they have read the same sentences several times and not yet caught

the meaning, even on the surface. Job 32:8 says that it is the *spirit* in a man
that gives him understanding. In awakened people, the Holy Spirit moves
through their spirits to cause understanding to spring forth in His Word;
meanings and excitement leap off the pages. But for sleepers, reading is
mechanical and barren because their spirits cannot respond to the Holy
Spirit. If they continue with private devotions, it remains a duty without
blessing.

We are accustomed to think that when a person receives the Holy
Spirit, he immediately understands the things of the Spirit. But there is no
magic, only anointing, to those who have ears to hear and eyes to see. In
this context, let us read:

> But a natural man does not accept the things of the Spirit of God; for
> they are foolishness to him, and he cannot understand them, because
> they are spiritually appraised.
>
> —1 CORINTHIANS 2:14

Comprehension is not a matter of brilliance or intellect. We know
hundreds of brilliant spiritually asleep men who, like Nicodemus, can't
grasp the simplest things of the Spirit, though technically they are filled
with the Holy Spirit.

3. Hearing God

The third function of our personal spirit is to enable us to hear God.
Turned-on and tuned-in people have dreams or visions, or they hear the
Lord speak directly, as Numbers 12:6–8 says of His prophets. Awakened
people may have intuitive hunches (empowered by the Holy Spirit). They
receive revelations and thrill to walk hand in hand with God by His direction. Somnolent people say to us, "It's all Greek to me. I guess I have to
believe these people who are always saying God keeps telling them things,
but it never happens to me. I never have a dream or see a vision. I guess
I just plod along." It is by our spirit that God communes with us. He speaks
into the ears of our spirit. These who "just plod along" have deafened ears
and blind eyes because their spirit does not function.

4. Inspiration

The fourth function of our spirit is inspiration. Quickened people find
ideas blossoming in their minds. They are creative. They discover new
ways to do things. If they write poetry or compose music, it is redolent

with the quality of life and blesses those who see and hear. Those in spiritual torpor do not often have fresh insights to share. If they write poetry, it is likely to be doggerel, or so perfectly scanned, metered, and rhymed that it has no song; it is just metered, rhymed words.

I was alone in a church in our southland when the violinist who was at that time concertmaster of the local symphony came in to practice a piece he was to perform that night in the service. I didn't see him. Suddenly sounds burst the silence. They were technically perfect. The music was magnificent! But something was missing. It did not take long to sense that his violin was singing, but his spirit wasn't singing through it. Later I saw reviews of his performances as a concert soloist across the country. They were all the same. Technically perfect. Marvelous finger work. Impeccable interpretation. But no spirit. His music didn't sing. His spirit was not awake; it couldn't sing the composer's songs through the instrument. He had technique without inspiration.

A friend speaks of two kinds of engineers in his office. Some, he says, have new ideas that carry the company forward in the excitement and thrill of the work. But others he calls "drones." They never have an original idea. They copy what others originate. Some are awake. Some sleep.

5. Transcending time

The fifth function of our personal spirit is to enable us to transcend time. Lest that seem mystical or mysterious, let's illustrate it by example. Two kinds of couples come to our office for marital prayer ministry. The first possesses awakened, functioning spirits. They are not confined to the pain of the moment. Their spirits enable them to remember lovely memories of the past and to think of happy times to come. They have roots and hopes. They reach beyond present time to nourishing events of the past and dreams of the future. But the second class is dead to all that. Their spirits cannot project them backward or forward. They are enmeshed and confined to the pains of the moment. Present affliction is all they can think about, and they want to flee.

The young man of whom I spoke in the beginning, who did not pay his bills, had this problem. If he wanted something in the moment, he charged it. But there was no way he could project into the future to see that there would be a time when bill collectors would insist on payment. He had no sense whatsoever of unfolding time. When bills arrived, those charges were so much a part of the unrecallable past that to him creditors were nuisances who had no right to bother his present moment rather than those trying to collect legitimate debts.

Perhaps our readers have wondered, as Paula and I have many times, how parishioners can sit under powerful preaching that warns of judgment coming for sin, say (and seem to mean) "Amen" again and again, and then so quickly and easily forget and go out to sin as though Judgment Day had nothing to do with them at all! When I examined this in prayer ministry, I found that these people did truly believe that we will all be held accountable for our deeds (Rom. 14:12; 1 Pet. 4:5). The puzzling question is, Why did that not have the force to convince them not to knowingly sin? They acted as though there would be no record of anything they ever did. When the Lord opened my eyes to see spiritual slumber, I understood. Their minds could understand logically about final judgment, but their spirits could not receive that as anything more than words. It held no reality for them because they could not grasp any real sense of the future. Paula and I now see that no matter how anointed a teaching may be about the end times, to the slumbering spirit it is no more effective than putting a coin in a vending machine, only to have it fall through into the coin return slot. We need to remember at this point that we are not speaking in an accusatory manner. We are simply describing the condition and its results. Perhaps if we can truly understand, we will find compassion. These people are simply incapable. It is not a matter of willpower or trying harder. They just don't have that part of their inner machine working to catch the coin when it is inserted!

6. Communion and communication with others

The sixth function of our personal spirit is one of the three basic ones discussed in the first chapter, to enable us to commune with and communicate with others. Spiritually alert people meet each other through their spirits. We tune in to one another by empathy. Our spirit identifies with the other and feels what he feels. Many of us have had the experience of meeting someone for the first time and feeling like we have known him all our life. With that person we soon discover that we resonate. We hardly have to complete some sentences because the other has identified with us and has already leaped accurately to our meaning. Conversations leapfrog joyfully, quickly. It's fun. We come away refreshed, and we want to be with that one again.

On the other hand, we may have worked with a fellow for years and have to admit in the end that we don't know him any better than we did the first day! We have just never "clicked." Conversations remained meticulous and guarded because he never seems able to catch our meanings unless we spell them out tediously. It was tiring to be around him. We were never able to develop friendship.

I am sure that we have all had the experience of visiting with someone, thinking that person was tracking with us, only to have him say something totally irrelevant, like out of left field somewhere. Perhaps we can see what happened by referring to spiritual slumber. He wasn't able to read our spirit. He was figuring out with his mind what to answer, and when the conversation entered an area he had to "read" to respond to, he couldn't. His mind was unable to track there, so he missed us.

People who have slumbering spirits are reduced to mental games. They never really can meet anyone. Their spirit isn't able to function in that way.

This leads to a corollary fact relative to so many divorces today. People whose spirits slumber cannot sustain relationships. Living with a slumberer is not only lonely, but it is also galling. For me to have sustained my half of more than fifty years of marriage with Paula, I needed to be able to read where Paula is emotionally. I need each day to be able to sense when she wants a hug, or when physical closeness would be jarring to her. I need to stop chattering happily if my spirit senses her sorrow and ask, "What is it, sweetheart?" I need to know when not to be silent and withdrawn when her spirit sends signals of needing to share. Often I have become so preoccupied and absentminded, I've still missed that more times than I've responded! On the other hand, she needs to be able to sense when my spirit is a thousand miles away, so as not to take my silence as a personal rebuff. She needs to know how to come after me in my spirit and call me to be present to her. The fact that we can do such things is one of the things that makes our marriage a blessing rather than a grind.

In prayer ministry we hear so often how people whose spirits slumber miss each other. Out of their isolated, unperceptive mental guesses, they do and say those things that are inappropriate to the other. After a while, that afflicts again and again. Living with a mate who tries to be nice but cannot relate sensitively to us can become painfully lonely and more excruciating because we know the other was truly making an effort. We can see as more and more homes break up that they will produce more and more fractured people whose spirits never have been nurtured to life. More and

more people are less and less equipped to make a go of marriage! Such
unfortunates are reduced to impersonal, temporary encounters, because
they cannot enter and sustain the inner sanctum of holiness between the
spirits of a couple. We used to sing the lyrics from "Stranger in Paradise"
and little knew the potency of what we sang! So many people are trying
to live and have good marriages and families, but they are so woefully
unequipped.

7. Creating the glory of marital sexual union

The seventh function of our spirit is to create the glory of marital sexual
union. We learn from St. Paul that when a man lies with a woman he
becomes one with her (1 Cor. 6:16).

> And don't you know that if a man joins himself to a prostitute she
> becomes a part of him and he becomes a part of her? For God tells
> us in the Scripture that in his sight the two become one person. But
> if you give yourself to the Lord, you and Christ are joined together
> as one person. That is why I say to run from sex sin. No other sin
> affects the body as this one does. When you sin this sin it is against
> your own body.
>   —1 CORINTHIANS 6:16–18, TLB

Those are not mere poetic words. St. Paul was describing the fact of
union. Those who have awakened spirits and who have been consecrated
to one another in a Christian wedding ceremony can discover in their
union a glory especially designed by the Lord for them to enjoy. In true
union, the spirits of a couple interflow through their bodies, exhilarating
and blessing one another. For this reason the Scripture says, "Adam *knew*
Eve" (Gen. 4:1, KJV, emphasis added). In marital sex rightly shared there
is an intimate and precious knowing of one another, a cherishing and
fulfilling meeting of whole being to whole being. That meeting depends
upon the ability of the personal spirit of each to feel the other's presence
and interpenetration of spirit.

Some couples have testified that while they were hugging and caressing
the other, it seemed as though they could feel their own hands stroking
their own chests through the other! Some men have testified to being exhilarated by great swirls of loving energy flowing from their wife's breasts,
filling them with exalted love and cherishing for her. For this reason
Proverbs 5:19 says, "As a loving hind and a graceful doe, let her *breasts*

satisfy you at all times; be *exhilarated* always with her love" (emphasis added).

Paula and I have been blessed to know, in all of our more than fifty years of marriage, the holiness and refreshment God created marital sex to be. It is my firm belief that if a man discovers the glory of the gift God has given to him in his own wife, which none other can have, he is greatly shielded from sexual temptation. The glory of marital sex happens by the fact that the Holy Spirit sings the love song of creation, for example, through my spirit to Paula and through Paula's spirit to mine. Our spirits alone cannot fully enrapture us to and in each other, but God can and does. When His Spirit flows through mine to hers and hers to mine, we are blessed and fulfilled and caused to love and cherish each other more than words or actions can express. That being a fact (to us because we know and experience it), then by logic alone we know that no sexual union outside of marriage can ever participate in the glory of sexual union! Our God is holy. The Holy Spirit will not flow into or participate in unholiness. Therefore there absolutely cannot be glory in any union outside the marriage bed! Sex outside of marriage is strictly forbidden (Deut. 5:18; Exod. 20:14). The Holy Spirit will not thrill another's being through the spirit of an adulterer!

It is part of every Christian's protection to know that God's law is absolute.

> The advantage of knowledge is that wisdom preserves the lives of its possessors.
> —ECCLESIASTES 7:12

No matter how lovely in face, figure, and character a woman may be who is not one's mate, she positively cannot have or be glory, despite whatever feelings a married man may think he has toward her. Sexual union outside of marriage defiles both and confuses their souls. A wife tells her husband who he is by entering into union with him. Any other woman, however attractive, can only tell him a lie and confuse his identity. For this reason, Scripture says of those who have committed incest (applicable also to any other unlawful union), "they have committed incest, their bloodguiltiness is upon them" (Lev. 20:12). And he who commits adultery "destroyeth his own soul" (Prov. 6:32, KJV).

To our great sorrow, not everyone believes and adheres to God's laws as absolute. They throw their glory away. To prevent that tragedy, St. Paul wrote:

> For this is the will of God, your sanctification; that is, that you abstain from sexual immorality; that each of you know how to possess his own vessel [make love to his own wife] in sanctification and honor, not in lustful passion, like the Gentiles who do not know God; and that no man transgress and defraud his brother in the matter because the Lord is the avenger in all these things, just as we also told you before and solemnly warned you. For God has not called us for the purpose of impurity, but in sanctification.
>
> —1 THESSALONIANS 4:3–7

Not many understand and experience the glory even if they believe and have kept themselves only to each other. Couples may be blinded and prevented through simple lack of knowledge that sex can be a blessed meeting. Worse, many cannot enter that glory because their spirits are asleep.

People whose spirits have slumbered throughout their marriage have often expressed to us during ministry sessions lack of interest in sex after a while. When early romantic zest wanes and newness wears off, they may lose sexual desire. For every one man who comes to our office to complain that his wife will not open to him sexually, we hear at least fifty women complain that their husband will not "fulfill his duty to his wife" (1 Cor. 7:3). Why? Because if women's spirits are asleep, they tend to remain dutiful and will give themselves, whereas men who have never discovered the glory of their wives commonly think it is a wife's duty to give to her husband but have little or no awareness that a husband has a duty to give to his wife. Trained in a sick culture, men too often think of their own sexual needs as a nasty bother to their wives, who may put up with it, but who would probably be just as happy if their husbands desisted it. What a tragedy!

Whether male or female, slumbering spirits miss the glory of marriage. Having missed it, they become vulnerable to whatever person may entice them. All they know is physical titillation and emotional arousal. When someone comes along who seems to promise a little excitement, they fall prey to the attractions of sinful opportunity. Conscience, as we shall see, does not prevent them from committing sin. No memories of glory exist to call out warnings of loss. In the adultery, they may strike sparks to emotional tinder, starting romantic fires long since dead in their relationship with their mate. That kind of illicit union may seem so much better than what they have at home that they become thoroughly confused, thinking themselves alive again, whereas in fact their soul and spirit are dying. They do not know that Proverbs 7:27 says of the adulteress, "Her house is the way to Sheol, descending to the chambers of death."

I think of a pastor I ministered to. He was evangelical and a fundamentalist. But his spirit had never been awakened. He failed to find glory with his wife, not only in the marriage bed but also in every other area of married life. The vacuum in his heart was inevitably filled by his secretary. He came to me in fear that the adultery he had already committed would be discovered. I explained that when a husband and wife fail to keep each other alive emotionally, the vacuum can be filled by a love that is not real mate love but only confusion. After we prayed for forgiveness, I told him he not only had to break it off completely with the secretary, but also he could never be around her again in any kind of relationship. There was too much danger that he would fall again into sin. His response was, "Oh, I can't, John. This woman is life to me! I can't live without her."

I implored him, "That's delusion, my friend! She is death to you! You can't live *because* of her."

"But I've tried it, John," he argued. "I sink into emotional death without her. I can't let her go."

I persisted, "Your own wife was given to you to keep you alive emotionally. You have to find your life with her. It is there that your spirit really wants to find life. This woman is only a poor substitute."

He insisted, "This woman is in my guts, John."

I insisted, "The love you have with her is not real. You will lose your family, your church, your ministry—"

We went around and around. Neither I nor the Lord won. He would not break free. He lost his church. For years his wife tried to stay with him, but she finally left him. Since then he has been a broken man, wandering around looking for a place to serve. Truly "the way of transgressors is hard" (Prov. 13:15, KJV).

Were this case isolated, we could grieve less. Unfortunately we have ministered to literally hundreds of such cases. In 1983 we came across more instances of pastors in adultery than in all our previous thirty years of ministry!

The most common root we see behind such adulteries among Christians is the condition of the slumbering spirit. When we do not discover the glory of what God intended marriage to be, we also never know why God gave the Law. Some even think God unfair, as though He does not want mankind to enjoy life. In fact, God wants the highest and best joys in life for us and has designed the marriage bed as one of His highest fulfillments of that purpose. The law is to protect. But spiritually slumbering people are like people behind high wooden fences who have no awareness of what wonderful life is happening beyond the fence.

8. Protection from disease and granting buoyancy in recovering quickly

The eighth function of our personal spirit is to protect us from disease and to grant us buoyancy to throw it off quickly when we do have an illness.

> The spirit of a man can endure his sickness,
> But a broken spirit who can bear?
> —PROVERBS 18:14

> A joyful heart is good medicine,
> But a broken spirit dries up the bones.
> —PROVERBS 17:22

We have all known people who are seldom ill, or who, if ill, bear it well. Disease has no power over the emotions of such people. They soon throw it off, or if beset by a crippling or terminal condition, they remain vibrant and glowing. Their spirit sustains and overcomes. They never remain "*under* the circumstances." They bounce. On the other hand, we have all grieved for and been irritated at people who go down *under* every illness or setback. Flu or colds that hit the community and knock others down for a day or two last weeks with them. Crippling accidents or terminal illnesses destroy them. They wilt. Their trouble becomes the dominating center of their lives and the lives of everyone else around them. Without the vibrancy of a functioning spirit, they have no see-through ability, no staying power, no stamina, no perseverance, no lasting joy.

9. Providing a good conscience

The ninth function of our spirit is a good conscience, which works *before* the event to keep us out of trouble, not merely afterward to make us aware of sin. Conscience works by the ability of our personal spirit to empathize with others so that we are informed about their feelings, especially what may wound them. For example, if I see a brother my size wearing a jacket I like, what keeps me from stealing that jacket if he leaves it and no one is watching? The Ten Commandments tell me not to steal (Deut. 5:19), but the commandments are not designed so much to keep me from sinning as to convict me.

> Now we know that whatever the Law says, it speaks to those who are under the Law, that every mouth may be closed, and all the world may become accountable to God; because by the works of the Law no flesh will be justified in His sight; for through the Law comes the knowledge of sin.
>
> —ROMANS 3:19–20

At no time in Israel's history or ours has knowledge of the Law alone been able to keep men from sinning. Israel knew God's laws—and failed. So do we all, if law is all we have.

Fear does not deter; people fall to adultery despite fear of discovery.

Love of the Lord should prevent sin, but servants on fire with love for Him sin anyway.

What keeps me from stealing my brother's jacket is that my spirit informs me how much I would grieve the Holy Spirit (Eph. 4:30), and it pains me in advance by causing me to know my brother's hurt.

There are two kinds of conscience. Slumberers may well possess an active conscience that causes remorse *after* they sin. It operates by the law. It works well through the mind, by recall and emotions. But it seldom, if ever, works powerfully enough *before* the event to prevent it. It reminds us that *we* have failed the Lord and ourselves; it rarely makes us aware *of our brother's hurt*. It makes us aware only that we failed to be what we set out to be. It seldom moves us to real repentance. Repentance happens when we are hurt for the sake of the Lord and others. Remorse remains self-centered and is seen only in terms of our own failure to perform. Real repentance is a result of the gift of love. If I love someone, and my spirit is awake and alert, it checks me *before* I do a potentially harmful deed. Love constrains me because I cannot stand to hurt the one I love. If the brother is a stranger to me, the Lord in me loves him and sends warning signals through my spirit not to do what might grieve the Lord and him.

If a man's spirit is in a stupor, it cannot warn him. It is as though that man wears blinders. If possible hurt to others begins to rise to consciousness, greed and desire block that out. But an awakened spirit sings out too loudly to be silenced without considerable effort. Perhaps it is for this reason 1 John 3:6 says, "No one who abides in Him sins; no one who sins has seen Him or knows Him." Really knowing Jesus in our spirit awakens such love in us for all others that we cannot bear to cause injury to another. If a man does sin, it is because in that area he does not actually in his spirit know and abide in Jesus.

> No one who is born of God practices sin, because His seed abides in
> him; and he cannot sin, because he is born of God.
> —1 JOHN 3:9

Christians have long puzzled over that Scripture, knowing that Christians do sin. Perhaps understanding slumbering spirits may help to explain the mystery. When we were converted we were positionally born anew. But what we are seeing here is that in some areas of the inner being, we have not yet responded to that new birth. We haven't yet worked out that salvation "with fear and trembling" (Phil. 2:12). Though St. John did not qualify being born of God by speaking of differing areas inside of us, we do see by our years of experience in prayer ministry that every aspect in which a person's spirit slumbers is actually an area in which his spirit has not yet received the good news and the new birth. In those parts of his being, though positionally he is born anew once for all, he has not yet felt the affect. Thus he can and does sin because his conscience does not function in certain areas. On the other hand, in all aspects in which a person's spirit is truly awake, indeed he cannot consciously choose to sin. His spirit will not let him. He makes plenty of blunders, and too often leaves undone what ought to be done. He still is plagued by wrong thoughts and feelings, but in the sense of willful wrong choosing, he cannot sin. His awakened spirit has too powerful a tool through his conscience to suffer him to fall. Love overcomes him through his spirit and will not let him choose to wound the Lord or other people.

However, if a man falls away from the discipline of the way—worship, study of the Word, self-sacrificial giving to others, affection, and so forth— his spirit can fall asleep. Conscience then fails. Most of the promises of

God are conditional, dependent on our staying in position to receive them.

Perhaps we can begin to see the dreadfully sick condition of mankind. As more and more homes have broken, increasingly fewer people possess fully awakened, functioning spirits. Conscience therefore fails, and all manner of ills increase, among them adulteries, crimes, divorce rates, and Christians speaking honor with their lips while their lives are far from His way. Truly, when a nation has turned from God "their foolish heart was darkened" (Rom. 1:21) and "God gave them over in the lusts of their hearts to impurity" (v. 24). A people whose spirit cannot function devolve generation by generation to more inhumane, bestial behavior.

As Paula and I began to see and grieve more and more, we cried out to the Lord the second question: "Why are people's spirits slumbering?" The Lord gave us the second answer: "These people have never yet become human beings."

Let us immediately make one disclaimer: we are not talking about humanism. Satan tries to copy all the glories of God. Humanism is Satan's copy of what God is accomplishing in mankind. Humanism is mankind, urged on by hell, attempting to set itself at the center of the universe, trying by flesh (and by hidden powers of darkness) to become all that it thinks it should be. In short, humanism is nothing more or less than the first sin all over again—man trying to be good without God. Humanism is an attempt to raise men to mankind's highest potential. In itself this is a lofty ideal, but by flesh without God, it is nothing but sin and idolatry.

We must, however, guard against letting our reaction against error turn us away from what truth is. Why should Satan try so hard through humanism to copy God's works unless something very important and right exists about being human? Something most important does exist. What are all of creation and Jesus's death and resurrection for? What is God's ultimate purpose? God is raising sons and daughters with whom to have fellowship (1 John 1:1–4)! God already had plenty of angels—beings without human bodies. The one new and abiding element that shall remain when all of creation is destroyed is the redeemed and glorified human body. Think about it. Heaven and Earth will pass away. When fire has burned up and dissolved everything else in all creation (2 Pet. 3:10), only two things that were part of that creation will remain. One, His words. "Heaven and earth will pass away, but My words shall not pass away" (Matt. 24:35). Two, His own redeemed people. His words came

from heaven (John 14:10) and passed through Him to us. They were not
born of Earth but of heaven. In this sense, like the angels, they were not
part of this creation.

That leaves us, the only residue, born in but outlasting creation! Note
the crucial factor. None of the material of this creation will abide—all
matter will be burned up and destroyed—except the redeemed and resurrected human body! Elijah and Jesus took the earth of their human bodies
into heaven forever and so will we! All of this is one way to say that it is
humanity, not discarnate spirits, whom God is raising up as the new order
of creation, the end of the entire project of creation.

So I asked Him what He meant by "human beings." As a man trained in
anthropology, sociology, and psychology, I know the definitions of *Homo
sapiens* that those fields propose. Here is the Christian definition the Lord
gave to me: "A human being is a person who has an alive and functioning
spirit by which he empathizes with others and cherishes what is in others
more than his own life or interests."

> Greater love has no one than this, that one lay down his life for his
> friends.
>
> —JOHN 15:13

> Do not merely look out for your own personal interests, but also for
> the interests of others.
>
> —PHILIPPIANS 2:4

By years of training and prayer ministry experience, I knew what
He meant by "These people have never yet become human beings." He
was saying that such people are inhuman, "inhumane," because in their
upbringing as children when they did not receive that most essential
nurture that was designed to make them human, they chose to close their
hearts. *God placed us in families, knowing the risk, because only there,
from fathers and mothers, brothers and sisters, relatives and friends, could
we receive the nurture that alone could bring our spirit to fullness of life
and function.* It is affectionate, gentle touch that interpenetrates another
through the physical body. It is rocking, cradling, nuzzling, and fondling
that awaken, draw forth, and train each spirit to function socially. The
love of God for us is as Spirit to spirit. That alone is not enough to make
us human, wonderful as it is. If it were, why should He send us to Earth
at all? *The very purpose of our being here on Earth is that right here, in*

the body, we may be loved to life in a way heaven could not provide. God designed that we should find His love person-to-person, body-to-body, and so be drawn forth and trained to become humans.

Human beings are the only species in all creation that will not become its own kind if not raised by its own kind. Raise a horse among cattle, and it will still run and whinny like a horse, not like a cow. If a cat is raised by dogs (as our loving dog raised our kitten when its mother died), the cat will not become confused and try to bark or lift its leg to urinate. It will meow and act in every way like a cat. But let a human baby lose its mother and be raised by wolves, as has happened in history, and the human will in most effects act like a wolf, running on all fours and baying at the moon. We do not become human by instinct, as other animals become what they are no matter where they are raised. Other animals, like dogs, may be helpless in the woods if raised in the city, but if they survive long enough, they regain by instinct what they were. But human beings do not. Mankind is necessarily tribal. He is dependent on his parents and society longer than any other species in all of creation. Human beings must be talked to in order to be able to talk, walked to walk, loved to love. We are culturally dependent.

We want to make it very clear that if our parents fail to give nurture, we are set into patterns of sin by our sinful responses. We can never be said not to be responsible. We will be held accountable for our responses to those people who wounded us, but we are not accountable for the wounds themselves. The remedy for sinful response is forgiveness. The remedy for wounds is healing. If parents fail to provide affection, wounding happens, regardless of whatever good responses. Desperately needed faculties are crippled and dormant. That calls for healing with resurrection life in it.

No nurture is so vitally important to the human spirit as affection. Immediately after birth, we need holding and cuddling. A baby's spirit reaches out to nestle through that tiny body into the one who holds him. That nurture is as necessary as food and drink. Without food and drink the body dies. Without touch the human spirit starves. With touch the spirit expands, learns who and what it is, relishes life, cherishes others, and becomes strong. Without touch, the spirit recoils as from cold walls or metal bars and finds no place to take hold of life. It shrivels and withdraws inside and closes its eyes.

God designed that the nurture we need should come through the primary people who called us to life, our fathers and mothers. Both are essential to full, balanced nurture. Mothers have carried us inside themselves and fed us with more than milk on their own breasts (hopefully). Fathers need to be actively present for the sake of their children during this time as well. From mothers we receive a special feminine quality of warmth, softness, and sensitivity without which we would be bulls in china shops. But fathers are primary in building structure and strength of character through which that warmth and sensitivity of spirit may flow.[1] He is the one who is designed to call the spirit forth with courage and vision to be, and the mother is to balance, support, and encourage that process. Note: We do not say that the mother supplies *all* of the warmth and sensitivity and the father *all* of the structure and strength. We are speaking of *primary* giftings and responsibilities, which, when exercised according to the beautiful and perfect plan of God, are designed to equip and empower us to grow into the most of what we were created to be.

Scripture again and again addresses both fathers and mothers but consistently gives fathers primary responsibility for raising children.

> And, ye fathers, provoke not your children to wrath: but bring them up in the nurture and admonition of the Lord.
> —EPHESIANS 6:4, KJV

"Bring them up" in the Greek is *ektrepho*. It literally means "nurture," which can include but is not confined to discipline and instruction. Notice that the Word does not say "mothers…bring them up…" Nor does it say, "Parents…" The command is given specifically to fathers, perhaps because mothers would have done so anyway, and it is fathers who have to be reminded. More likely because it is fathers who are primary in the raising of children.

> Behold, I am going to send you Elijah the prophet before the coming of the great and terrible day of the LORD. And he will restore the hearts of the fathers to their children, and the hearts of the children to their fathers, lest I come and smite the land with a curse.
> —MALACHI 4:5–6

Notice again that the Lord addressed fathers. If fathers and children are not reconciled to each other, the earth will be smitten with a curse. But the promise is positive. He does not say all fathers will be turned to all their children, but enough, apparently, that the earth will not be fully smitten with a curse.

We founded Elijah House Ministries, teach around the world, and write books because we know beyond a shadow of a doubt the crucial importance of fathers. Fathers must be awakened to know who they are to their children. Christians, and the world, must hear and respond to the many Elijah messengers who call fathers to their children or the curse will come, or the promise of Malachi will remain for a later generation with ears to hear.

> Hear, O Israel! The LORD is our God, the LORD is one! And you shall love the LORD your God with all your heart and with all your soul and with all your might. And these words, which I am commanding you today, shall be on your heart; and *you shall teach them diligently to your sons* and shall talk of them when you sit in your house and when you walk by the way and when you lie down and when you rise up.
> —DEUTERONOMY 6:4–7, EMPHASIS ADDED

Notice how often the Lord says the same thing concerning both fathers and mothers, but especially to fathers, since in each case He lists fathers first, and sometimes mentions fathers only.

> Hear, my son, your father's instruction, and do not forsake your mother's teaching; indeed, they are a graceful wreath to your head, and ornaments about your neck.
> —PROVERBS 1:8–9

> My son, if you will receive my sayings, and treasure my commandments within you, make your ear attentive to wisdom, incline your heart to understanding… Then you will discern the fear of the LORD.
> —PROVERBS 2:1–2, 5

Note how often the teaching of parents, especially of fathers, is directly related to "life."

> My son, do not forget my teaching, but let your heart keep my commandments; for length of days and years of *life*, and peace they will add to you.
> —PROVERBS 3:1–2, EMPHASIS ADDED

Hear, O sons, the instruction of a father, and give attention that you may gain understanding, for I give you sound teaching; do not abandon my instruction. When I was a son to my father, tender and the only son in the sight of my mother, then he taught me and said to me, "Let your heart hold fast my words; keep my commandments and *live*."

—PROVERBS 4:1–4, EMPHASIS ADDED

My son, give attention to my words; incline your ear to my sayings. Do not let them depart from your sight; keep them in the midst of your heart. For they are *life* to those who find them, and health to all their whole body. Watch over your heart with all diligence, for from it flow the springs of *life*.

—PROVERBS 4:20–23, EMPHASIS ADDED

My son, keep my words, and treasure my commandments within you. Keep my commandments and *live*.

—PROVERBS 7:1–2

It is clear that by God's command, by His plan and provision, it is fathers and mothers who are commissioned to train children in the way. Sunday schools never existed before the nineteenth century. We do not say they should be discontinued. They need to be strengthened and improved. But parents are not to relegate all teaching to Sunday schools and thus abdicate their responsibilities. Sunday schools can be one delegated arm of parental teaching for the *mind* and *soul*. But children's *spirits* learn more from life than by rote. What children learn in Sunday school and church may have little or great consequence, depending solely on how the personal spirit is nurtured and taught by experiencing life in the home. Hugs teach. Kisses instruct. Discipline forms. Reproof harnesses rampaging energies. Admonition builds checks upon emotions. Instruction forms guidelines and channels for the flow of energies and emotions. Without primal early training in the home, Sunday schools merely weave inconsequential doilies over volcanoes. "Foolishness is bound up in the heart of a child; the rod of discipline will remove it far from him" (Prov. 22:15). Children become by experience what parents are, not what they say, nor what Sunday school teachers or anyone else says.

The moment a baby is conceived, his spirit needs his father's presence beside the mother. A fetus is a person who knows by his spirit whether the father welcomes him. Infants in utero know what sex the father desires them to be. They hear what the father says to the mother and react to the way he approaches her. The spirit and character of a father affect the formation of the character of the child already in the womb.

The moment a baby is born, he/she needs his/her father. Thank God modern medical practice encourages the presence of fathers at birth and allows the father to hold the newborn child as soon as possible. Immediately the father's spirit and strength encompass the child and draw his spirit to open, trust, and risk, to venture vulnerability, to share, to nestle into another, to give and take. That is vital, basic training. A baby needs both the mother's sweetness and the father's warmth and strength. He needs to be made to feel welcome, secure in his belonging, at ease and at home in the earth.

Such touch brings healing. Many are the wounds of every person's spirit in becoming part of this sickened world. A baby immediately experiences loneliness and lostness from the wholeness of the Creator. Every trauma of mother and father for nine months have been his. Already he has known the shock of being cast out of the warm safety of the womb into the harshness of life. Touch is balm. Holding is healing.

Babies need fathers to walk and burp them in the night, to sing lullabies, to talk softly, lovingly, reassuringly. Fathers should feed, change diapers, rock, and cuddle; everything that mothers do, fathers should do as well, except breast-feed—and had they been so equipped, they ought to have done that, too! Infants need fathers to romp on the floor, play and laugh with them. Mothers are needed for all of this, too, but most mothers do these things naturally. It is fathers who must be told how crucial their presence is. Mothers alone cannot fully draw children's spirits forth to life.

Marshall L. Hamilton, in his book *Father's Influence on Children*, said:

> Studies of father absence report detrimental effects on children's aggression, dependency, degree of adjustment or "psychopathology," delinquency rates, moral behavior, success in the Peace Corps or military, premarital pregnancy rates, masculinity in males, and intellectual performance…
>
> A number of psychological problems and disorders, initially viewed as a result of inadequacies in the mother's behavior, appear to be influenced at least as much by the father's behavior in those studies where investigators have made the effort to study the father's influence.…

It is also clear that the model the father provides of political views, religious beliefs, and attitudes toward people of varied ethnic characteristics or national origins helps to determine at least the initial and often the lifelong attitudes of his children on these topics...

The failure of the father to establish and effectively enforce guidelines has been related in varying degrees to male homosexuality, delinquency, schizophrenia, low self-esteem, lower levels of competence, and unsuccessfulness.[2]

From a study by Tess Forrest in 1966:

She must learn paternal trust during infancy when she learns maternal trust. Especially from her father does the infant girl need confirmation of her desirability as a female and affirmation of her value as a different and separate person. His gentle tenderness communicates to her his pleasure in her femininity. Father, by comparison with mother, has a sharper eye, a firmer grip, a rougher cheek, a deeper voice. He is nonetheless equally tender, loving, warm and safe, and the infant girl can feel herself lovingly cradled by a man's arms and comforted by a man's voice. Contact with the father opens the door of the mother-infant dyad to the possibility and pleasure of triadic union and secondary dependency....

To become like the father who is reasonably admirable and desirable is regularly associated with appropriate masculinity, popularity, and general good adjustment for the boy. If the father fails in any of these aspects, the risks of the son's incurring such problems as homosexuality, psychological disorders, or a delinquent pattern are increased, although there remain many ways in which adequate adjustments for the boy can be achieved.[3]

Boys and girls look to their fathers for their philosophy of life. From relating to fathers comes much of our zest for life, creativity, ambition, destiny, and purpose. When children cannot drink life from their fathers, they are starving and crippled in spirit. To the degree of parents' failure, most especially fathers', children's spirits fall asleep. From then on they live by half emotions and brittle thoughts, much like having good sails unfurled to catch the winds, only to flap listlessly without breath from then on, a ship hung in irons. They *cannot function*. The body of Christ must come to comprehend the fullness of this tragedy. Children bereft of affection, most especially from their fathers, *cannot* meet God or embrace people or life or themselves fully. In this sense they have never become human. They cannot enter into another's heart by their spirit. They cannot love by spiritual sensitivity to the other. They are isolated, going through life's motions like zombies. Many are unaware that there is more to life than they have known. They are like eight-cylinder engines that have never run on more than two.

Since conscience cannot function except by remorse or fear, the result becomes callous disregard for life and progressively less and less regard for law. Before WWI, the nuclear family was not isolated. Aunts, uncles, grandparents, and cousins took up the slack when fathers were called to war and mothers went to work in war plants. Infants born then could still receive affection from primary relatives. It was a romantic and affectionate age.

Then increasing industrialization and mobility dehumanized and decentralized the family. By the time of WWII, many nuclear families had become isolated. Heads of families had gone to war and their infants did not know them at all. An entire generation fell asleep spiritually. Religion was still popular, but more and more by rote and rite, less in true piety.

What is wrong is so simple: slumbering spirits cannot truly meet God until healed by the body of Christ. How to heal slumbering spirits is the missing key.

Consider that now entire generations of incapable people have filled divorce courts. Their children have less spirit yet and exhibit more and more openly rebellion and debauchery. Crime rates soar. Perhaps now we can understand St. Paul's prophecy:

> But realize this, that in the last days difficult times will come. For men will be lovers of self, lovers of money, boastful, arrogant, revilers, disobedient to parents, ungrateful, unholy, unloving, irreconcilable, malicious gossips, without self-control, brutal, haters of good, treacherous, reckless, conceited, lovers of pleasure rather than lovers of God; holding to a form of godliness, although they have denied its power; and avoid such men as these.
>
> —2 TIMOTHY 3:1–5

As we see it, the curse is already coming. "A curse without cause does not alight" (Prov. 26:2). We fathers must shoulder the blame and act to save our families before it is too late. Note "holding to a *form* of godliness, although they have denied its power." These people can mentally relate to doctrine and teaching. They can find comfort emotionally and logically in liturgy and the plan of salvation. These are "forms." Laws and rituals appeal to mind and heart. But they cannot embrace Him personally, for that requires a functioning spirit. When St. Paul advised, "Avoid such men," we are sure he meant not to trust such people in closest fellowship and not to place them in positions of influence or authority. Paul's command in Galatians 6:1 is:

> Brethren, even if a man is caught in any trespass, you who are spiritual, restore such a one in a spirit of gentleness; each one looking to yourself, lest you too be tempted.

Spiritually asleep people are not helped by making pariahs of them. They need welcome and embrace, holding and resurrection life. Perhaps there is no greater cry in our generation than to "clear the way for the LORD" (Isa. 40:3) in the desert of the hearts and spirits of the slumbering.

In a moment we will share what can be done to awaken slumbering spirits, but let's first see how universally mankind knows this truth in heart if not in mind.

MANKIND'S UNIVERSAL TRUTH

Our most beloved fairy tales tell the story of slumbering and captive spirits. *Snow White and the Seven Dwarfs* appeals to generation after generation because we know deep within that it is about us. Snow White eats the poisoned apple—the poisoned fruit of life without affection—and falls asleep! The seven dwarfs represent our dwarfed talents. Who needs to be told who the wicked queen represents? Or Prince Charming—Jesus! And how does Prince Charming bring Snow White to life? By a kiss! It is love alone that can wake us from sleep.

How about *Sleeping Beauty*? The princess pricks her finger on the distaff—work without expressions of love becomes drudgery—and falls asleep. All the servants and creatures in the castle fall asleep for a hundred years (as do all our talents and capabilities). Hedges and thorns surround the castle (much as we grow defensive prickly walls around our inner being). Prince Charming (Jesus) hacks his way through the thorns with his flaming sword (of truth), slays the dragon (Satan), and enters our castle. Again, it is by the kiss of love that the princess and all her court awaken.

Think about the frog who tricks a princess into keeping him by her bedside and feeding him until he bursts forth as a handsome prince—when he is kissed! We only hop and croak until our spirits are awakened by love to be the sons and daughters of the King. It is this sick world with its devils who have bewitched (put us to sleep) and turned us into frogs, caricatures of what we were meant to be.

Soon after the Lord taught us this key, Walt Disney produced a renewed version of *Sleeping Beauty*, and I wept through the whole thing! "Oh, God, come!" I cried. How we need that kind of revival!

How can we cause it to happen? How can we love slumbering spirits to life? First we need to discover the condition. It takes only a few incisive questions to discover, and the questions come from the list of nine functions of the spirit:

1. When you are in a worship service or a prayer meeting, do you feel the anointing of God flowing over you and through you, or do you only know He is there by faith?

2. When you have private devotions, can you enter easily into His presence? Can you abide in His presence? When you read the Bible, do the words leap with meaning off the page at times? Or does Bible reading run dry?

3. Do you ever hear the Lord or have spiritual dreams or visions? Can you hear God talking to you? (I am not talking about receiving words for the church. Not everyone has the gift of prophecy [1 Cor. 12:7, 10]. But every Christian should be able to receive personal words of guidance [Job 33:13–14].)

4. When you are in conversation, do you enter in and feel what the other person feels, or do you have to figure out with your mind what to say?

5. Are you a creative person? Do you have new ideas? Or do you always have to follow the manual?

6. Have you experienced a glory in marital sex in which you feel your mate's spirit flowing into yours?

7. Does your conscience warn you strongly before you do anything and keep you out of trouble, or does it only work by remorse afterward?

We seldom have to ask more than the first four questions to know.

When we see the condition, we explain what it is, and what its causes are. Almost every time, people readily and easily understand. They begin to exclaim, "Oh this is why I could never..." and, "No wonder..." and, "How do I get this healed?"

We ask then, or review if we have already covered that ground, what their history was with their parents, particularly during earliest childhood. We look for the father's presence or absence in the first two or three years; affection, or lack of it; discipline, or lack of it; teaching and example, good or bad. We can then reveal to the person how his spirit thrived or starved, expanded or fell asleep.

It may be necessary to explain how his spirit can hold resentment and judgments toward his parents when he is unaware of it. We help him to identify the fruits in his life, which necessarily have roots. We assure him that just as he received salvation by faith, not by feeling, so he need not try to feel again what his spirit actually felt toward his parents; he needs only by faith to acknowledge that, because the fruit is evident, sins of resentment may be there and receive forgiveness by faith. St. Paul said, "I am conscious of nothing against myself, yet I am not by this acquitted" (1 Cor. 4:4). Job said, "How many are my iniquities and sins?" (Job 13:23). David said, "Acquit me of hidden faults" (Ps. 19:12). And, "Search me, O God, and know my heart; try me and know my anxious thoughts; and see if there be any hurtful way in me" (Ps. 139:23–24). We may quote some of these scriptures in prayer ministry sessions.

In prayer we do not pray for such a person apart from him or silently. We kneel beside him as he sits or kneels. We put an arm about his shoulders and hold a hand; we know he needs human touch through which God's Spirit will do the work. Through touch the Lord supplies love that the person missed in infancy. We ask the Lord to minister to the child within. We ask the person to repent and pray aloud concerning resentments. We pronounce forgiveness. We have him renounce inner vows he has made out of resentment toward those who did not nurture. Such inner vows pull him away from life. For instance, "I will not need love." "I will not feel." "I will not share my heart." "I will not trust." Renouncing these is one of the most important steps in healing. For no one ever becomes a slumberer instantly. Sleep is induced by a series of decisions not to remain awake. Most importantly, we ask the Lord to enter and woo him to life in his spirit, to fill the vacuum. We pray that the Lord may restore to him as many years as the locust has eaten and the cankerworm destroyed (Joel 2:25). We ask specifically that the Lord awaken and draw his spirit forth to function with liveliness and enthusiasm. Sometimes we have to haul to death whatever death wishes and bitter-root judgments and expectancies have resulted from his being rejected or starved for affection.

After the prayer comes the most crucial part of healing. Other conditions may be overcome by a single prayer, or several. The prayer minister or intercessor may or may not be much involved in the process. And *perhaps* the other may recover whether or not he is in a good church or small group. Not so for the spiritually slumbering. The healing of this condition requires that the Church be the Church! Some branch of the Church must be there as family to incubate that child in love, to provide what his natural family was not able to give him. It is not enough for slumberers to have what the churches usually call *Christian fellowship*. Sitting in rows fellowshiping with the backs of each other's necks on Sunday morning will not resurrect anyone. Church suppers, pastoral calls, church meetings, and study groups will not get the job done. These are too detached, too distant, too unengaged at deep heart levels. It is good to have these as background and filler. But only rich personal encounter and involvement that reaches beyond secondary relationships to become immediate and primary can touch that slumbering spirit with life-giving power.

We need more fathers and mothers in the body of Christ. Suffice it to say here that in the case of slumbering spirits, reparenting is not just a nice option; it is the "without which nothing." It does not always need to be consciously attempted, named, or discussed. Sometimes it just happens. It is helpful if the one in the parent role sees what is happening and quietly allows and checks and guards until the other is whole enough to detach and go his way. Sometimes it is best to do it consciously as St. Paul did, to make the other aware that "I am again in labor until Christ is formed in you" (Gal. 4:19). It may be that the knowledge of a friend's willingness to risk and bear so much to carry us in love is the very thing that acts as a wedge to pry the heart's door open to receive.

Reparenters come to know such love for their "child"; they experience firsthand what St. Paul meant when he said:

For who is our hope or joy or crown of exultation? Is it not even you, in the presence of our Lord Jesus at His coming? For you are our glory and joy.

—1 THESSALONIANS 2:19–20

Therefore, my beloved brethren whom I long to see, my joy and crown, so stand firm in the Lord, my beloved.

—PHILIPPIANS 4:1

…for this reason, brethren, in all our distress and affliction we were comforted about you through your faith; for now we really live, if you stand firm in the Lord.

—1 THESSALONIANS 3:7–8

For this reason, when I could endure it no longer, I also sent to find out about your faith, for fear that the tempter might have tempted you, and our labor should be in vain.

—1 THESSALONIANS 3:5

One who struggles in love to reparent another finally comes to see the Lord's tremendous love for him as He wooed him so patiently. Until then, one can give hardly more than lip service to the sacrifices of Jesus in loving us to life. But when we discover the cost to Him by wringing our own hearts for others, we fall on our knees, bursting with gratitude He did not give up on us. The healer is more healed in resurrecting the slumbering than the slumberer. Truly, "It is more blessed to give than to receive."

We must be aware of the limits and pitfalls, the clues when to enter and when to desist in such relationships. This work is not without danger and confusions. Nevertheless, though the Lord did call us to be righteous and circumspect, He did not call us to be self-righteously safe; rather, He called us to lay down our lives sacrificially for others.

Slumbering spirits are awakened by the sacrificial love of a few and the support of the body. Without the body, the labor is too heavy and the dangers of fastening idolatrously too great. In one and the same chapter (Eph. 4), St. Paul spoke both of the importance of the few, the fivefold ministry of apostles, prophets, evangelists, pastors, and teachers, and of the "whole body…building up of itself in love" (Eph. 4:16). Prayer ministers should not work alone to resurrect the spiritually asleep, nor should the body think it can do without those soldier specialists who risk themselves as prayer ministers.

Those who deal with this issue should be aware that when people realize they are slumbering spirits, they often fall into despair. As children, many were forbidden to feel. In order to please, they shut down their emotions and, with them, their spirits. When they discover that they are slumbering, they often find themselves in a worse predicament than they did as children. For, as members of the body of Christ, they are now expected to feel and sense, but this time they cannot please. This brings a sense of shame, for it makes them feel different from others. Therefore, it is wise to be careful about using labels such as "slumbering spirit" that can emphasize differences. In many cases, it is better to describe traits rather than use labels.

Slumbering spirits also need to be reassured that God has His own time-table and that in His eyes, they are not behind schedule. One reason they fell asleep in the first place is because, as children, there was no comfort. They had to learn to rely on themselves. Therefore, if God awakens their spirits too soon, they might rely too much on their own ability to hear God, to sense, and to feel. They need to be told that God will indeed restore the functions of their spirits—but only after their hearts have learned to trust in the hearts of others.

For that reason, slumbering spirits often report that they are enabled to feel God's presence when worshiping or fellowshiping with others, long before being made able to sense His presence while alone or to hear Him on their own. They may need to be told that this is good, that to learn to rely on God through others is an even more important step in healing than learning to experience the spiritual gifts. For what is the purpose of such gifts, except to increase reliance on God and fellow believers through mutual edification. (See 1 Corinthians 12.)

Understanding the All-Important Role of the Prayer Minister

We cannot leave this subject without pleading to the entire body to comprehend the level of risk such prayer ministers endure. Many a prayer minister has fallen to confusion. We cannot afford to fail them. We must watch over and consult with our burden-bearing saints. We must protect them in prayer. We must see to it that when people misquote them or repeat things about them that ought not to have gone past closed doors, our prayer ministers are defended and murmurers squelched.

Perhaps there is no more crucial finger to be placed in the dike that holds back the waters of destruction over our entire society than this work of awakening slumbering spirits. We, the Church, must wake up to our task, or Satan will continue to rule a society filled with crime and divorce. Church, take the cry "Maranatha" (even so, come, Lord) out of the mystical future. Here is where the King comes now, immediately, practically, to kiss His own to life—or we sleep on.

> Awake, awake, clothe yourself in your strength, O Zion; clothe your-
> self in your beautiful garments, O Jerusalem, the holy city.
> —ISAIAH 52:1

Obviously we can't rush out to wake up the whole world. John and I (Paula) tried to take on the burden of that for a short time. We flattened ourselves before we realized that truly that was a job the Lord already came to do. It was a relief to know that we are to take responsibility only for those whom the Lord either points out or brings to us.

People may not be ready for intense ministry, neither are they even aware that they need it. Often we have been called to soak them with general prayer apart from them while we quietly make ourselves available. The Lord will prepare hearts. We must never "accuse" a person of being needy or crash through his closed doors in a way that will cause ministry to appear as an attack.

Not all of us are called to intense prayer ministries. Not all are called to reparent. But every Christian is a part of the family of God. In that family relationship we are all called to share the life we have been given. The Lord "comforts us in all our affliction so that we may be able to comfort those who are in any affliction with the comfort with which we ourselves are comforted by God" (2 Cor. 1:4).

We all slumber to a degree in some areas. We all have areas in which we have been quickened to life. As the body shares in close relationship and unity, we will effectively impart life to one another. The Lord in us is the power. He has *only* imperfect vessels through whom to work, and yet His work is perfect.

Resurrection ministry does not have to be complicated. The following are testimonies of simple but tremendously powerful happenings we have seen in the body of Christ.

In our community in the Baptist church is a retired couple who will never retire from active service for the Lord because service describes *who* they *are* more than *what* they *do*. I doubt that they have any intellectual knowledge about slumbering spirits, but they have warmed and sparked untold numbers. They know and love the Lord and have made it a way of life to involve themselves in doing what He is doing. They have been Mom and Dad to many of the young couples in the church who are in the area without supportive families. Their home is open, and they know how to make people feel at ease and welcome. Every month they host birthday parties for people in the church, many of whom would have no other celebration on their special day. They have been concerned for the increasing number of children from broken homes whose fathers are gone and whose mothers are too burdened to spend quality time with them. Every day they go to the nearby elementary school to *be* there in the lunchroom or on the playground as loving grandparents for the children to identify with, to talk to, to drink from. Everett and Bernice know from deep inside that Jesus becomes flesh again and again through His people, so that when they hug a child or speak a word of love and encouragement, Jesus's life and healing flow in immeasurable quantity, quality, and power. They give themselves in other ways too numerous to mention. And they do so with joy.

In Cornerstone, the church our oldest son pastored in the 1980s, there was a young woman who conceived a child out of wedlock. When the time arrived for her infant son to be dedicated, Loren said to the congregation, "You all know the circumstances of this baby's birth. We don't know how long it will be before he has a daddy, and every little boy needs a daddy. If there is any man in the congregation who will promise to uphold this mother as she promises to raise her child in the nurture and admonition of the Lord, let him come forward now." Not *one* man came, but *every* man in the congregation! That promise was and is being fulfilled in simple ways: prayer for healing, support, provision, prayer that he be brought into the fullness of his life, watchful sensitivity to hug the little fellow whenever possible, to admire his person and his achievements, to extend a firm, quiet hand of discipline when needed, to communicate to him that his belonging to the family is a blessing and delight, and to be available for counsel and help should the mother seek it. That little boy has grown up to be a solid, awakened citizen, as is his mother.

In Cornerstone, there were home fellowship groups that included all ages. They were for the purpose of worship, Bible study, sharing, body ministry, and fun, but especially for a sense of belonging in the family of

God. Every single parent who consented was a part of one of the small group families. As a part of this group, they were no longer in isolation as they carried their heavy loads. Many churches are beginning to discover this anointed way of providing. Care extends beyond the meeting times. We have heard grateful testimony again and again along the line of, "I can't begin to say how much it meant when you came to help me with my children, to clean my house, to bring food, to hug me, to pray with me. I never knew what it was like to have a family before." The Lord awakens spirits and establishes them in love and strength through the personal involvement of those who lay down their lives for others.

One of the most astounding stories of growth under the Lord's anointing comes from Kansas. A professor who was head of his department at a state university was concerned for the large number of students who were far away from home, many of them having broken family ties because of rebellion or because homes had simply shattered beneath them, a good number of them looking for comfort and answers in wrong places and ways. He quietly let it be known that his home was open to anyone who just wanted a place to come and relax, have a cup of coffee, and visit a while. A few students came. Soon they were so at home they were talking about things that mattered. Sensitively the professor and his wife offered counsel and prayer. Those students brought friends. Soon the household took on the shape of a home fellowship, and groups were sharing counsel and prayer and Bible study. Many still came only for coffee and hugs. The home group overflowed into a school building and began to look more like a church. In a short while it was necessary for them to find a building to call their own. The professor found himself so busy pastoring he had to drop his job as department head at the university; then he dropped half of his teaching load and was finally ordained as full-time pastor of a full-fledged church. Many of the young people who began as emotional basket cases are now the ones who have a basket full to overflowing to share with others. Some of the original group stayed with the church, but we have met a number around the country who, when we have related this story, have said, "Oh! You're talking about the Mustard Seed! That's where the Lord saved my life!"

This beginning of resurrection ministry really can be so simple as saying, "I care. My door is open. My home is yours. Come on over and have a cup of coffee. We can talk if you like."

CHAPTER 3

SPIRITUAL IMPRISONMENT

I waited patiently for the LORD; and He inclined to me and heard my cry. He brought me up out of the pit of destruction, out of the miry clay; and He set my feet upon a rock making my footsteps firm. And He put a new song in my mouth, a song of praise to our God; many will see and fear, and will trust in the LORD.

—PSALM 40:1–3

Spiritual imprisonment is a condition akin to, but in some ways different from, spiritual slumber. We discovered this condition while ministering to a lovely lady who is now one of our friends and co-workers. Mary* came to us distraught because she could not enjoy the fullness of life. As the wife of a man in the military, Mary felt obliged to host parties and to attend social functions on base. She felt awkward and uncertain because she found herself unable to feel what other people felt. She seemed like a square tire in tandem with all the round ones, jarring everyone with out-of-place sentiments and statements.

At the chapel she had become filled with the Holy Spirit, but she still had all the incapabilities slumbering spirits suffer. Nothing helped. Private devotions ran dry. Corporate worship was either only mildly enjoyable or boring, but they were never full of His presence. She thought of herself as

---
* Fictitious name

59

a constant embarrassment to her husband and couldn't imagine why he continued to appreciate and love her.

Worst of all, she said, was the fact that sex meant little or nothing to her. She would rather not have been bothered. Her husband persisted in being a gentle and considerate lover, amazingly patient with her. It hurt that she could not respond to such a wonderful man. If he hadn't been so kind and patient, she could have found some self-justification for turning away. But she couldn't fault him at all, and that filled her with self-disgust and remorse.

It was not that Mary had any physical problems. She was, and still is, one of the most beautiful women of face and figure Paula and I have ever known. "Disgustingly healthy," as Mary used to say. Never a headache or physical problem on which to blame her resistance to sex. She simply could not get into the act and feel anything but physical sensations, which after a while by themselves became boring and bothersome.

She wanted to find out what was blocking her. We asked our usual questions and found lack of parental affection, especially from her father. After a while, the Holy Spirit revealed a suppressed and forgotten molestation. So we brought to forgiveness every hurtful experience of any kind that we could find and to the cross every practice in her character. But Mary always returned to say, "I'm not any better, John. I still can't feel a thing."

In those days we knew nothing about spiritual slumber. We discovered spiritual imprisonment some months before slumber. Probably that history was the Lord's providence, for if we had known of spiritual slumber, we most likely would have leaped to the conclusion that it was the cause, and we would have missed what was actually the problem, because the two conditions are somewhat similar. Failing to produce results, we would have become even more confused. We mention this because a number who have become aware of slumbering spirits have tried to set imprisoned spirits free as though slumber were all that was the matter, and consequent failure has caused them to doubt themselves and the key.

There came a day when Mary and I (John, ministering to her that day) were totally stumped. We couldn't think of another moment of her biography we hadn't looked at from a dozen angles. We couldn't imagine why she couldn't find any joy and zest in life.

I felt led to try an experiment. The Lord sometimes enables me by my spirit to identify with another's being by empathy so as to feel what the person feels inside, and so find clues that could not be discovered otherwise. For a while, by the power of the Holy Spirit and permission of the other, I become as the other one is. I know him or her intimately, from within, as if I had lived their life. Not knowing anything else to do, Mary and I tried it.

When I have experienced that with others, I have been able to feel the presence of their spirit, their hurts and joys, through the Holy Spirit, obtaining a strong sense of the character and personality of the other.

When I identified spiritually with Mary, it felt like nobody was home! It was like stepping into a vacant hall. We have all felt the emptiness of great buildings when we have entered alone. To me, Mary felt as empty as a vacant cave! Her own spirit did not seem to be there (although, of course, it was). It was not that Mary was inhabited by any foreign spirit; I would have sensed the presence of evil. Her Christian life and the Holy Spirit, whose presence I *could* feel, had kept demonic things from attacking her. It was the opposite of demonic inhabitation. Other than the Holy Spirit, nobody seemed to be there, not even Mary!

I exclaimed, "Mary, where are you? I can't find you."

"You tell me, John. You're the prayer minister. I don't know."

Again I was stumped, more so than before. I had never experienced anything like this.

Sometimes help comes from strange places. I had been reading J. R. R. Tolkien's *The Lord of the Rings,* a three-volume series. In the third book, *The Return of the King,* Merry, a friend of Strider (who had by then been revealed as the returning king), had been struck down by one of the black wraiths, servants of Sauron (the Satan of that fantasy). Merry's spirit was wandering in nether glooms, more and more lost, as he slipped into a coma from which none had been known to awaken. Calling for the herb athelas, crushing it in boiling water until its fragrance filled the room, Strider, now become King Elessar Evenstar, took hold of Merry's hand and sent his own spirit seeking Merry's. At length he found him in the visions of his inner spirit and escorted him back to life. (Let those who have reservations about such fantasies hold them in check; they merely gave me an inspiration. The Lord can use anything for His own purposes.)

Recalling that story gave me an idea. I sought and gained permission from the Lord (our returning King) to set out to "find" Mary. He showed me a vision of a place where I saw our wonderful Lord walking down a steeply sloping dark tunnel. He did not carry a torch or lantern. He was Himself the light. My eyes followed Him. The experience was much like following a car down a narrow lane at night, watching the headlights momentarily shine on walls or bushes, leaving darkness behind. I "watched" the light of Jesus illuminate the walls as He passed.

When we came to a huge dungeon door, ancient and rusted, locked, it opened before the Lord all by itself. Scriptures raced through my mind, "…behold, I am alive forevermore, and I have the keys of death and of Hades" (Rev. 1:18). I knew we were entering a place very similar to that! "He who is holy, who is true, who has the key of David, who opens and no one will shut, and who shuts and no one opens" (Rev. 3:7). "All authority has been given to Me in heaven and on earth" (Matt. 28:18). He hadn't needed to insert a key; He Himself is the key! The door flew open at His authority. "The gates of hell shall not prevail against it" (Matt. 16:18, KJV). It was confirmed to me in a flash that Jesus meant to speak of the Church on the attack, not on the defensive, breaking open the gates of hell to invade and set its captives free!

I watched as He walked across a dirty floor. Phantasmagoria of hell fled before His presence. There, in a corner, huddled in a fetal position, manacled by wrists and ankles attached by chains to a wall, was Mary. She appeared ghastly white and blue, emaciated and starved, tiny as a child. With His beautiful, nail-scarred, brown hands, He deftly, gently broke the shackles off of Mary. He picked her up, cradling her softly against His chest, and I thought, "He shall feed his flock like a shepherd: he shall gather the lambs with his arm, and carry them in his bosom, and shall gently lead those that are with young" (Isa. 40:11, KJV). I wept for joy and at the beauty of it.

The Lord carried Mary out of that place. I described aloud for her what I was seeing. Later she told me that she felt every moment of it in indescribable joy and anticipation.

As He carried her, He breathed His own breath into her, while Genesis 2:7 (God breathed life into Adam) and countless scriptures about the wind of the Holy Spirit (as in John 3) and Elisha breathing his breath into the Shunammite woman's dead son (2 Kings 4:18–37) cascaded through my mind. Then He set her on her feet, and, taking her left hand in His right, began to walk out of the tunnel with her. As they walked, Mary began to grow, like the Wonder Bread advertisement of years ago, from a little girl to the grown woman she is. Then He passed His hands over her body, and wherever I could see skin, it turned from deathly pale to glowing pink.

The vision ended as I saw Him turn her loose to frolic in a lovely meadow as He watched, beaming with joy and pride.

After several minutes of silent basking in the glow of His presence, I said, "Mary, I don't pretend to understand all that, but I know something wonderful has happened. Let's wait and see."

Mary left for a two-week trip. The next time I saw her, she was beaming! She could hardly wait to tell me. "John, guess what! I'm out, and I'm alive. I can feel! People on the airplane started pouring out their troubles to me, and for the first time I felt like I had something to say to them. I felt what they felt. I knew what to say. I don't feel like a stranger anymore. I enjoy visiting with people. Best of all, I really enjoy sex now. Sometimes I even go after my husband. And," she said with a chuckle and a gleam in her eye, "he can't believe it. He's wearing himself out!"

Twice Mary fell back, not fully into prison but into slumber and incapability. It was a simple matter to call her to life again. She learned to exercise a discipline of saying each day, "Lord, I choose life." People began to stream to her door. Of course, the Lord brought to her person after person who had suffered the same kind of imprisonment. She delighted in seeing the Lord set them free one by one. Mary came on staff as one of our prayer ministers. She formed prayer groups and started Bible study classes. She was on fire for the Lord, so glad to be free and whole.

Despite the obvious good fruit, all this drove me to the Scriptures. By then I had been down so many seemingly good blind alleys, I wasn't going to have anything if it contradicted the Word of God. Although spiritual captivity is not "outlined" in all its particulars, captivity in general is a common scriptural theme. Jesus said it in Luke 4:18 (quoting Isaiah 60:1). This was one of the very purposes for which He had come!

> The Spirit of the Lord is upon Me,
> Because He anointed Me to preach the gospel to the poor.
> He has sent Me to proclaim release to the captives,
> And recovery of sight to the blind,
> To set free those who are downtrodden.

What was Mary but that—captive and downtrodden?

Then He revealed many other scriptures, one of which is listed at the beginning of this chapter. Note, however, how precisely Psalm 88 describes what Mary was feeling:

1. "My life has drawn near to Sheol" (v. 3).

2. "I am reckoned among those who go down to the pit" (v. 4). This is not merely our expression "It's the pits," but a very real literal pit for our spirit.

3. "I have become like a man without strength" (v. 4). This was exactly Mary's condition.

4. "They are cut off from Thy hand" (v. 5), aptly describing the way Mary felt.

5. "Thou hast put me in the lowest pit, in dark places, in the depths" (v. 6). Mary knew that as real, not poetic.

6. "Thou hast removed my acquaintances far from me; Thou hast made me an object of loathing to them" (v. 8). This was the social condition Mary had lived in all her life.

7. "I am shut up and cannot go out" (v. 8). This was Mary's prison. She was shut up, and unable to get out.

8. "My eye has wasted away because of affliction" (v. 9). Mary grieved every day because she couldn't live.

9. "I have called upon Thee every day, O LORD; I have spread out my hands to Thee" (v. 9). The reference is that God didn't seem to hear and didn't answer the psalmist, nor did He seem to hear Mary.

10. "Wilt Thou perform wonders for the dead? Will the departed spirits rise and praise Thee?" (v. 10). Whatever that scripture means literally, to Mary it described how dead she felt, how vacant and "departed."

The entire psalm described how she felt.

Seeing that it was compatible with Scripture was not enough. I knew by then I could read into Scripture what I wanted to see. So I asked God both to teach me more and to give me so many undeniable experiences of undying fruit that it would be much further around the barn to deny this revelation than to accept it.

He began to teach me. In His still, small voice, He explained that when a person experiences overwhelming trauma early in life, that person may rebel against God. The person then turns back from life, wanting to flee and hide, not wanting to be born, not wanting to have to come out of the womb and risk life. He reminded me that when we bury our talent, even what we think we have is taken from us (Matt. 25:14–30). Then He quoted the scripture "The thief comes only to steal, and kill, and destroy; I came that they might have life, and might have it abundantly" (John 10:10). In a still, small voice, He said, "John, you and so many others in My body have fastened on the words *kill* and *destroy* because you could understand these from your own experience. But have you ever considered, what does Satan want to steal? It is my sheep he wants to steal. Many have understood that and thought it meant only to carry their souls into hell in the end. But that is not all he can do. When children rebel against Me, they open doors to Satan. His minions can then come about that person in the womb, or sometime later in life, and imprison his spirit. From then on he cannot live and function, as you saw with Mary."

He went on to explain that there is a hidden meaning in another familiar scripture: "If you have not been faithful in the use of that which is another's, who will give you that which is your own?" (Luke 16:12). He said, "John, did you ever stop to think, what is it that is your own, which is to be given to you?" The answer was many things, of course. But He applied it in this instance this way, "Turn that scripture around. If a man is faithful in that which is another's, he will be given that which is his own. Mary, imprisoned as she was, was trying her best to be faithful with that which was not hers, My kingdom. She was trying to serve. By her faith and obedience, then, I could give her what was hers, her own spirit set free to live life."

How to Know if Someone Is Spiritually Imprisoned

Spiritual imprisonment is discerned both by observing symptoms and by the operation of the gifts of knowledge and perception. We ask the following questions:

1. Do you often feel hollow, empty, or vacant, like something is missing?

2. Do you often feel deeply lonely, alone, way off somewhere, even when you are with others?

3. Do you feel tormented or afflicted when on the surface no one is bothering you? (Demonic spirits often torment the spirits of captive people, and they feel it like a subcurrent river of pain without knowing what it is.)

4. Do you suffer from the sense that there are talents and abilities in you that you can't reach, as though they are locked away from you?

5. Do you often feel desperate and lost and futile inside when on the surface everything seems to be going fine?

6. Do you have unaccountable inner rages? Do you get furiously angry with something, when actually there is nothing to be angry at? (The spirits of imprisoned people rage against the chains that bind them.)

7. In the midst of a powerful time of worship, do you feel at peace and joyous, or nervous and unaccountably upset? Do you feel agitated or calmed when others around you pray and thank God for being present?

    Perhaps this reaction happens because they can sense the glory of God at a distance but cannot participate. Like blind Bartimaeus, they call out all the louder when Jesus passes close by (Mark 10:46–52), but they do not experience His healing touch. Or perhaps their demonic captors are made nervous and fearful by His presence, and they feel it.

8. Do you feel like there is a film or a fog over life, as if everything is dimmed or muted? Does light not seem light enough? Do colors not seem colorful enough? Do sounds seem muffled, even if your hearing is perfect? Since captives

have made inner vows to disconnect from life, they feel distanced from what their five senses tell them.

9. Is your mind frequently vacant or blank? This is caused by disconnection between mind and heart.

10. Are you often forgetful? Captives are so used to disconnecting from life that the mind sometimes automatically disconnects from whatever information is put into it.

11. Do you feel as if an imaginary glass wall separates you from life? Whether or not you imagine it as an actual wall, do you feel held back? Can you sense the life out there, while being unable to experience it firsthand?

If we still are not certain or want other corroborations, we may ask a few other questions. (These symptoms are less common.)

12. Do you often feel like trouble is all around when everything seems all right, or that danger is all around when everyone is perfectly safe? (Captive spirits can sense trouble around them, but because they have disconnected heart from mind, they often cannot identify it.)

13. Do you, or did you, ever suffer vertigo (dizziness)? In the presence of the power of the Lord in a worship service, have you felt weak or dizzy? (We do not know why this phenomenon occurs, but it is common for imprisoned people to break out in a cold sweat and/or become dizzy when others feel uplifted, warmed, and joyous under the Lord's anointing.)

14. Have you ever suffered any dyslexia? (Imprisoned people commonly, but not always, have had some degree of dyslexia in childhood or currently suffer from it.)

Frequently, the answers of the people to whom we minister reveal quite clearly whether or not they suffer imprisonment. Sometimes, however, questions and answers remain inconclusive. For some are so used to being captive that they cannot contrast what they feel with what is normative, so they cannot answer in the affirmative. It is then that we enter into prayer and wait upon the Lord for discernment. Sometimes He reveals the condition instantly, sometimes not. In His wisdom, He may know it is not time to answer clearly. He may want us to discuss the biography of the person more fully; there may be clues He wants us to have in mind that we would not bother to seek were He to answer too soon. So we visit some more, asking the Lord to reveal in our sharing what He wants us to see.

SETTING THE CAPTIVE FREE

Once we discover that a person is captive, we need to understand the process of setting him free from his prison. Subsequent to the ministry to Mary, we found that there are two ways a person can become captive.

1. In the womb: The powers of darkness come about them and imprison them as early as the womb, causing them to recoil from life.

2. Step-by-step: In reaction to harsh treatment or neglect, a person becomes imprisoned step-by-step through a series of inner vows made to disconnect from life.

The first way is what happened to Mary. She recoiled from life once and for all as early as the womb, and from then on she could be likened to an eight-cylinder car, unable to run on eight, trying to function on only two.

In the second way a person, as a result of mistreatment or abuse, makes inner vows to disconnect from life. "I'll not open my heart again; that hurt too much." "I'll not share again what I feel; nobody understands." "See if I ever trust him again." "I'll keep things to myself." And so on. Inner vows can take many forms, whereas the results are the same: the person becomes locked up within his own walls, inside his own heart of stone. Each inner vow is like another bar on the prison. The cumulative effect is inability to connect with life.

With the first way, one begins life in captivity. Since disconnecting has become his mode of operation, he may continue to make inner vows to disconnect, reinforcing the prison he is already in. With the second way, one starts out life still connected. Then, through a series of inner vows to disconnect, at some later time in life, he finally arrives at the point where he becomes truly captive.

Demons often take advantage of all this to increase the hold of the prison, so that though the person made inner vows to withdraw and thus became imprisoned, repenting about these will not by itself be effective. Deliverance will also be needed. Wounding must also be healed before the person gains courage to come out and risk life. Many inner vows may need to be broken, along with much healing, to emancipate from the prison.

In a few words, here are the steps someone must walk through to come out of captivity.

1. Repent of rebellious choices.
2. Accept forgiveness from God for burying self.
3. Renounce inner vows to disconnect from life.
4. Decide to stubbornly resist passivity.

Once a person repents of rebellious choices, is forgiven his sins of burying self, and has renounced inner vows to disconnect from life, the cumulative effect of all these reconnections is that he comes out of captivity. However, this is not where healing ends. God will not do all the work. Passivity got the captive into his prison. Often, demons have taken advantage of that passivity. The antidote to passivity is to become a fighter. One must decide emphatically that he truly wants to come out and risk life, lest captivity, and the demons that enforce it, return.

Resist the devil, and he will flee from you.

—JAMES 4:7, NIV

One lovely lady to whom I ministered had renounced enough inner vows to bring her to the edge of freedom. So I told her that in order to stay free, she would have to choose life.

She said, "John, I know if I come out, I'm going to be hurt."

I said, "Yes, you will be. Life is full of joys and hurts. But are you willing to come out anyway?"

Because healing and repentance had enabled her to trust God, she emphatically answered, "Yes!"

So I prayed to set her free.

A few weeks later, I came to see her. She brought me coffee and then said, "John, you remember I told you that if I come out I'll get hurt?"

I thought, "Uh oh, I'm going to get it now."

But she only exclaimed, wreathed in smiles, "Well, I did get hurt—but it was worth it!" She needed no further ministry. She was out of prison to stay.

But many imprisoned people seem to slip backward off and on along the way to full healing. Prayer ministers need to persist in the love of the Lord and not get discouraged at this or if several times the person seems to flee back into captivity before finally coming out to stay. Understand that the relapses often herald the fact that another inner vow to disconnect is coming to the surface to be removed like another bar on the prison being dismantled.

Some people come out of captivity more quickly and easily than others, as was the case with Mary. Once I saw the in utero withdrawal and the consequent onslaught of demonic affliction, one dramatic prayer was all that was needed to set her free. However, even she fell back a few times and needed more ministry to make her freedom secure. Since then, I have ministered to many who, like Mary, were similarly imprisoned by an early urge to flee. They had subsequently resisted the urge and so had made few further inner vows to disconnect. And I have ministered to others who had done more to embrace their own imprisonment and built their prison step-by-step, making far more inner vows to disconnect. The first kind is relatively easy to free. The second require a more progressive labor of seeing and setting free.

If we suspect imprisonment of either kind, we will search out as much as can be discovered about the circumstances surrounding conception. Was the person invited, or did he happen by accident? Were the parents happy to be expecting and happy with each other? Was the mother a smoker or a drinker at the time of the pregnancy? What number child was the person? Did the parents have strong desires for a baby of either sex? Were there separations due to business or war? These can be clues to when and why a person has made inner vows to disconnect.

As I said before, there are distinct differences between spiritual slumber and spiritual imprisonment. One we have not yet mentioned is that people tend to gravitate toward one or the other according to their temperament. People who are innately analytical tend to shut off their spirits and live in their heads, becoming slumbering spirits. People who are innately intuitive and spiritually attuned cannot shut off their spirits easily, but they can decide to disconnect from life. So they can become spiritually captive without becoming slumbering spirits. Like Mary, some people who are both innately analytical and innately spiritually attuned become slumberers and captives. One who is captive but not slumbering might suffer more than one who is both, or only slumbering. They feel and sense many things keenly in their spirit, which only increases bafflement and pain when they find themselves locked away from ability to live life. Satan being the hypnotist he is, they may fight against their own inner vows, trying to connect with life, becoming more and more fatigued and strained.

When spiritual imprisonment seems certain to us, we explain the condition and what causes it. Before prayer, we make the person aware that his own sins are involved. We discuss rebellion, shrinking back, amniosis (a condition of fleeing back to the womb), and the necessity to "forgive" Father God and be forgiven for resentments against God and life on Earth. We insist on verbal statements in reply to the questions: "Do you choose life? Are you willing to pay the price of pain and vulnerability in order to choose and risk life anew every day?"

Prayer begins with simple petitions for inner healing. We make sure that full prayers of forgiveness are said, both for the person to forgive and to be forgiven, to accomplish fullness of reconciliation to being a person on Earth.

We have the person renounce any inner vows he might have made to disconnect from life. In the process, we lead him to forgive parents and others who tempted him to disconnect by treating him harshly or neglecting him. As he does this, one by one, the demons connected to these issues are exposed, and we command them to leave in the name of Jesus.

Sometimes after that the Lord will accomplish final freedom, usually in my ministry, by means of a vision. After I ministered to Mary, the Lord brought case after case of imprisoned spirits. The scenes of captivity varied from person to person. In one vision, I saw one person in an old ramshackle cabin, locked in and chained to a bunk bed in a corner. It turned out that the man had experienced such a cabin and still feared it irrationally. He simultaneously saw the same scene I saw, sometimes in advance of my describing it. In another vision, I saw another man frozen in an iceberg. His heart was indeed frozen. Paula once saw in vision a woman in a birdcage, unable to sing. In another vision, she saw a man in a hole in the ground, covered over by grass. He called out again and

again in a weak voice, but none of those who walked by could hear. Such
prisons I take as parables, though it seemed to me that in Mary's case I was
seeing something much closer to actual reality. The fact that the pictures
seemed appropriate and that many could see and experience even while
I described it was not enough. I knew the powers of suggestion.

What became more and more convincing was lasting and undeniable
fruit. Hard-shell cases began to change before my eyes. More importantly,
like Mary, they came back to exclaim, "I heard a beautiful symphony this
week. I thrilled to it! I could always sense the life in it from a distance, but
now I felt and experienced it!" or, "I saw a sunset! For the first time I really
experienced it. I felt it." "I never knew how much of life I have been plod-
ding through—dead!" "John and Paula, visiting with people has stopped
being a weariness. I can really connect with people now. It's refreshing
to visit." "Hallelujah! I can experience God's presence firsthand, not just
sense Him from a distance. He's real! I can feel Him."

On the other hand, God does not work in the same way with everyone.
Often, He elects to free someone by other means than by vision. If we
assume that we must have visions in order to set people free, we may
attempt to force God's hand and concoct "visions" not of His making.
Understand that many persons are freed simply by the cumulative process
of reconnecting to life through forgiveness and repenting of their inner
vows to disconnect. There comes a day when they just "know" they have
reached freedom, and the fruit of their lives confirms it. Know also that the
frequency of visions as a part of the process varies not only from person to
person but also from prayer minister to prayer minister.

Most often, when people are freed from inner prisons, it is as though
they set out to make up for lost time. They are often more on fire for the
Lord than others are. They find themselves ministering with great faith
and joy. Others seek them out until they wonder where all the people are
coming from.

Mary served with us in Elijah House Ministries until her husband was
transferred to another military base. Mary had become as a daughter to
us and was heartbroken at first. "All the way across the country!" she said.
"Even if we were stationed somewhere still in Idaho, it would have been
too far already."

But we said, "It's time you were on your own, Mary. The Lord will go
with you."

Soon after she arrived at the new base, a women's group invited her to give her testimony. It turned out to be electrifying. Women and men swamped her for prayer ministry. She phoned, "John and Paula, I can't do this."

"Yes, you can, Mary. The Lord will be with you."

She started study and prayer groups. Then a local pastor, leaving town for a while, asked her to fill his pulpit. Again she phoned, "I can't do that, John and Paula. I'm no preacher. How can I, a woman, step into a pulpit as a preacher?"

We asked her, "What does your husband say?"

"Oh, he's all for it. Says he'll be right there to support me."

"Well, then, go for it; the Lord will be with you." Again the Lord blessed her, and everyone was pleased, including Mary's family.

Somehow a family across the country whose husband and father was dying of cancer heard that this woman nearby could pray and God would answer. They called Mary, pleading with her to go there to heal their father. "John and Paula, I can't do that. What if nothing happens? I'm no magic faith healer. What will I do?"

"What does your husband say?"

"He says to go on; my prayers can't hurt anything."

"Give it a try, Mary. The Lord will go with you."

When she arrived, she found the family gathered in the house, already bickering over distribution of the estate. The man, who had been large and strong, now lay withered and frail. Mary thought, "Oh, what can I do?" There was no way to phone us, and she could hear the refrain inside her head anyway, "The Lord will be with you." She sat by the bed and began to pray. Then, led by the Holy Spirit, she cradled the man in her arms and sang to him in the Spirit as she rocked him like a baby. After a while, he fell sound asleep, the first real rest he had been able to find in days.

The next morning Mary returned to find the man much improved; he had eaten a meal and was sitting up in bed. But the family was gathered in the next room, still fussing audibly with one another. The Lord said to her clearly, "Call them to repentance. They are killing their father."

"No, Lord, I can't do that."

"Tell them, Mary!"

She called them all to his bedside and said, "You are killing your father by your continual fighting with one another. The Lord wants you to repent." They got down on their knees, and she led them through prayers of repentance, forgiveness, and reconciliation. As they said amen, the sick man exclaimed, "The fire is gone! There is no more pain!" Several of the family received the Lord.

Mary wished she could report that the man fully recovered and that everyone lived happily ever after, but that didn't happen. Mary returned home. Some in the family returned to their old ways. The man died several weeks later. *But he never suffered pain again!*

The Lord continues to use Mary and her family. The military sent them to Africa, where they know, "The Lord goes with you."

We tell Mary's story because we know that many who have been imprisoned feel ineffectual, as though they have already blown the mission of their life. Far from it, their experience and the glory of being set free has equipped them as few others. They *know* the reality of evil. They *know* the mercy and grace of our Lord. They do not have to strive to believe. They know *whom* they have believed. People are drawn to their fire.

Our spirits may have known this key all along. As the fairytales *Snow White* and *Sleeping Beauty* tell the story of slumberers, there are many fantasy stories of princes and princesses who are held captive, Rapunzel and the story of Bluebeard being two examples. Such stories seem fresh to every generation. They hold a fascination for us. It could be that our spirits know about imprisonment while our minds remain unaware or tend to scoff.

In grade school, we never tired of playing a game variously called Stink Base or Prisoner's Base. Two teams faced each other across a field. Each had its own line and its own prison. Combatants dashed across the field toward each other, attempting to lure the other side into chasing them. Whoever came most recently from behind his own line had the "power." Whomever he touched became his prisoner. No one could interfere as he conducted his prisoner to the area blocked out as the prison. Now the other team sought to set their teammates free. If someone could run through without being touched and grab the hand of a prisoner, both could walk back to their line unharmed. Whichever team held the most prisoners at the end of the game was declared the winner.

Even as a child, though I was admittedly more mystical than most, I "knew" there was something more to that game than met the eye. It spoke to something deep within me. I knew something was true about it.

Whoever comes freshest off the baseline of prayer truly does have the "power." There *are* real captives. We do run into enemy territory to grab captives' hands to set them free. Since Jesus is with us, in us, we are safe to walk with them hand in hand to freedom. One difference: there will be no Christian captives in Satan's camp when the warfare is ended! We win, because the Lord Jesus Christ has already won!

Perhaps some cautions need to be voiced.

1. This work is not for beginners in the faith. One must have such trust in the lordship of Jesus that he is neither afraid of nor distracted by powers of darkness, nor foolhardy. The prayer warrior must know obedience to our Lord, so as to walk in and out with Him leading, not running off to fight irrelevant battles.

2. The prayer warrior must have an ability to see in the spirit and one disciplined by experience in Christ. He must on the one hand be able to receive whatever impressions the Lord would give him, and on the other be disciplined as a soldier not to add to or become entangled in any other pursuits than the one at hand (2 Tim. 2:3–4). His imagination must be firmly under the control of the Lord Jesus Christ and none other. It is all too easy to make up visions out of our own imagination.

3. Emotions, as well as the mind, must be disciplined not to run amok. Paula and I have never experienced harm or encountered any real danger to ourselves in this work, but we also know that our Lord did not engage us in it until we possessed that kind of self-control and discipline.

4. We want also to be wary of leaping to conclusions that this or that person is imprisoned. Time is a friend. If the person has been imprisoned for a number of years, one more day may not hurt much as we wait and observe, pray and think. The Lord can confirm and will do so.

    On the other hand, if the person is not imprisoned, I doubt that our prayers could damage much more than our pride. No one wants to appear foolish. But it is possible the person could become more turned off and wounded in the end if what we prayed about was not his condition after all.

All cautions observed, nothing ought to deter us. How many people are there who are leading strangled lives—who know there is something more if they could only get to it? Such people would rather we try than guard our reputation. So what if we miss? At least we loved enough to risk, and though superficially some may be frustrated if we fail because we wrongly identified the problem, they know at heart level at least we loved enough to attempt something for their sake.

This is the very work for which Jesus came to Earth, to "set the captives free." Let us respond and serve, and let the Lord, who is foolish enough to use us cracked vessels, live with the results! He is big enough to do that, only we do not want to use our freedom as a pretext for evil or foolishness. God's children—so very, very many of them—need to be set free.

CHAPTER 4

DEPRESSION

Rejoice with those who rejoice, and weep with those who weep.

—ROMANS 12:15

Like one who takes off a garment on a cold day, or like vinegar on soda, is he who sings songs to a troubled heart.

—PROVERBS 25:20

nfortunately, in zeal to heal while remaining woefully unin-formed, Christians have often unwittingly done those things that torment rather than ease depressed people. The body of Christ needs to learn first of all what *not* to do in their efforts to help those suffering in depressive states, and, second, what *can* be done that will complement whatever professional treatment may have been prescribed.

We need to understand what depression is and what it is not. Though we recommend that the reader acquaint himself with the many valid medical definitions of depression, we do not intend to present those here. Our purpose is not medical. We do want to say emphatically that there are very real, medically discernible, chemical factors involved in depression, and that all who minister without medical qualifications need to respect and observe medical counsel, advice, and prescription. No Christian nonmedical counselor or prayer minister should ever say, "Throw your pills down the drain," or "Quit seeing that psychiatrist." If a depressive under our ministry begins to improve, and we suspect that drugs may hinder more than help, we can send him or her to the doctor to describe the improvement and ask the doctor about the advisability of reducing the dosage. Or, if we have opportunity, we ourselves can consult with the physician. No one should ever practice medicine without a license. To give medical counsel without training and licensing is legally reprehensible, to say nothing of being theologically erroneous.

It is not lack of faith to take medicine! Ecclesiasticus 38:1–8 (though as a part of the Apocrypha and not regarded by Protestant churches as part of the scriptural canon, it's still regarded by all of Christendom as inspired by the Holy Spirit and to be respected) says:

> Honor the physician with the honor due him, according to your need of him, for the Lord created him; for healing comes from the Most High, and he will receive a gift from the king. The skill of the physician lifts up his head, and in the presence of great men he is admired. The Lord created medicines from the earth, and a sensible man will not despise them. Was not water made sweet with a tree in order that his power might be known? And he gave skill to men that he might be glorified in his marvelous works. By them he heals and takes away pain; the pharmacist makes of them a compound. His works will never be finished; and from him health is upon the face of the earth.

We do not think it shows lack of faith to ask a mechanic to overhaul our car engine or a lack of trust to follow a recipe in baking. Neither should we, having prayed for a healing, fear to take whatever medicines a doctor may have prescribed. If the Lord has power to heal, then He has equal power to work through a medication until it is no longer needed. Most physicians are happy to reduce dosages. Let the body of Christ hear! The first caveat is *not* to give medical advice! Few readers can imagine how many times we have heard of Christians arrogantly bragging about how they told someone to flush their medicines down the toilet and to have faith, and how often we have heard of consequent damage, only to hear those same self-important prayer ministers blame the results on the person's "lack of faith." That kind of arrogant foolishness needs to be repented of and firmly abandoned.

Depression is both physical and emotional. In each case, however psychosomatically it may have been induced, depression is a very real physical condition. On the other hand, whether the depression originated in something chemical, was induced by organic shock to the system, or originated in some purely emotional cause, it is tremendously intense with emotional realities. Later on we will list many emotional causes for depression. It needs to be held firmly in mind that such a list does not overlook or rule out simple chemical imbalance. These things overlap and interact.

We do intend to present a Christian definition of depression. It is our intention to equip Christians to minister to depressives in those ways in which every common layperson can minister, without impinging upon any professional medical field. It needs also to be remembered that in presenting a spiritual definition of depression, we are not intending to invalidate or treat any other definition as of lesser value. Many psychiatrists whom we have taught in our prayer ministry seminars have been able to lay our Christian definition of depression alongside their medical perspectives with no apparent conflict or difficulty.

In short, *depression* is a condition in which our personal spirit has died to its capacity to sustain the person fully, either emotionally or physically. Were the death of a spirit's capacity to function complete, death would be the result. In depression a person's spirit still sustains the body, though far less successfully than normally; it has no capacity to sustain the person emotionally. No matter how stridently duty calls, the depressive has little or no energy to perform. He cannot feel joy. Conversations that once were refreshment become tiresome. "Oughts" and "shoulds" impel him to make responses he can no longer feel or possess inner drive to accomplish.

> What strength do I have, that I should still hope?…Do I have any power to help myself, now that success has been driven from me?
> —Job 6:11–13, NIV

When not in depression, he may have been able to reach into inner reservoirs and call up reserve energy to make himself feel and act. Now the reservoir is empty. He is emotionally bankrupt. There are no more emotional energy funds in the account. There is only perplexity, guilt, despair, bleakness, and blackness.

Moodiness is not the same as depression. We all have highs and lows. Normal people know that tomorrow they will feel better. They know they can still call upon inner reserve funds by listening to music, hiking in the fields, or going to a party or a prayer meeting—whatever they have learned to do that refreshes. Even if the normal "pick-me-ups" fail, they know that a night or two of rest will renew them. The key factor is that they still possess *hope*. The most telling fact of depression is *despair*. Depressed people are not only without hope; they *know* that tomorrow will not be better. "Knowledge" gained by bitter experience has taught them that tomorrow will be as bleak as today. It is not a matter of valid or invalid reasoning or positive or negative thoughts. "Facts"—solid "irrefutable" events—nail the feet of tomorrow's bird of hope to the floor. There is no way to think or reason that something good will someday appear. The candle of hope is totally extinguished.

The first fact every ministering Christian must hold constantly in mind is that a depressed person *cannot* help himself. Recovery is not a matter of thinking more positively, making a series of positive confessions, making oneself feel better, getting rid of a demon, getting enough rest, or changing one's diet. Recovery is a matter of rekindling and resurrecting that deadened spirit. No person in depression can kindle his own fire. He must be brought out of the pit by others or not at all. He must be resurrected by the prayers of others. He *cannot do it alone.*

Sometimes depression mysteriously lifts, seemingly unaccountably. One wonders who may have been pumping the handle of prayer unseen and unknown, whether some chemical lack or imbalance was suddenly overcome, or whether the Lord, who moves in mysterious ways, simply sent a ray of light. For whatever reason, depression sometimes slowly or suddenly unaccountably departs, but the point is that the depressive had nothing to do with it and knows he didn't. Overcoming depression is not a matter of willpower.

Once we see that a depressive cannot do anything to move himself out of his condition, we will have the key to stop most of the mistaken ways by which we may have been trying to help depressives.

In a moment we will list many important things that should not be done, but first let us consider some clues that will help to determine at least on a lay level whether or not a person is in fact in depression. Neurotic depression is not the same as bipolar depression. Bipolar depressives often exhibit what is called a mixed condition. They can swing from euphoric highs to depressive lows. The condition is extremely complex. Our advice to laypeople is to avoid ministry to bipolar depressives. Refer such people to acknowledged medical authorities.

In either case, depression is distinguished by lack of energy. The skin is often flaccid and gray, and the eyes commonly appear vapid and flat. Looking into the eyes of a depressive is to look into a sea of nothingness. One sees no drive, no flickers of interest, no sparks of emotion, no lust, no greed, no joy, no humor, no sparkle. Only emptiness.

Depression is also a matter of deepening degrees. Toward the depths, shoulders sag and steps shuffle haltingly. Hearing is not impaired but appears so, due to slowness or entire lack of response. Hair loses its shine and body and finally hangs in greasy streamers. Sometimes stale body odors are present.

Depressives often require little or no diagnostic skill on the part of the one ministering to them. They know they are depressed and can usually express that fact most clearly. Sometimes, having said they are depressed, they will volunteer enough symptoms to confirm easily the accuracy of their own self-diagnosis. If not, a few simple questions will quickly confirm the diagnosis:

1. How long have you felt this way?

2. Do you wake up every morning feeling impossible?

3. Is every little decision a major burden to you these days?

4. Do you find that you can't make yourself do the simplest household chores (or tasks on the job) that you used to do easily?

5. Do you hate yourself for it and sink further?

6. Do people tell you to cheer up, and you don't know how, and then hate yourself for hating them?

Often, most depressives will unhesitatingly say, "Oh, yes," to all or most of these questions, grateful that you understand. Depressives are usually emotionally honest.

Depression is not a sign of weakness. Strong people fall into it. People who are determined not to hurt others find the pit of depression far more often than aggressively hurtful people. It is as though they were strong enough to prevent themselves from attacking others until unexpressed emotions rebounded to attack their own energies. Depressives are usually people who have had the emotional strength to face reality as it is, though they have tended to see the cup as half empty rather than half full. They are not in delusion. Their perceptions may be out of balance, full of the negative, but they have not lost track of reality. A psychotic may happily pronounce that two and two are five, but a neurotic depressive says, "Two and two are four, and I can't stand it another minute!"

Once diagnosis of depression is corroborated, by a medically qualified person if at all possible, ministry is totally different from the ministry that would be used for a nondepressed person. (It should be restated carefully here that we are addressing the matter of ministering to the neurotic depressive person, *not* the bipolar. As said above, bipolar depressives belong in the hands of medical people or professionally trained counselors.) One must do everything in reverse to what one would do in relation to a nondepressive. The key scripture is, "Rejoice with those who rejoice, and weep with those who weep" (Rom. 12:15). To weep with those who weep means to empathize, to enter in and feel with, to walk where the other is. What might benefit a person who is not depressed, one must *not* say to a depressive. What encourages a person who is not depressed will further depress a depressive. What lifts the heart of the nondepressed will crush one already in the pits. All the techniques or personality charms we have found effective elsewhere belong nowhere in ministry to depressives. We have entered an entirely different ball game, one with its own rules. Ministering to the depressed calls us to death on the cross so that none of our practiced ways for general ministry intrude and interfere.

This means that the body of Christ must most importantly learn what *not* to do in proximity to persons in depression. Having taught in many seminars the following list of things not to do when ministering to depressives, we are sad to report that the universal response has been, "Oh, my, I've done all the wrong things. I see I have meant to help, and I've actually been cruel. God forgive me." Let us hope we can at least lessen the burden we have unwittingly been to those in depression by being careful to observe the following:

Do not say, "Cheer up!" A depressed person is totally unable to cheer himself or to respond to cheer. It is not a matter of willpower. He is simply incapable of doing so! Trying to brighten and then failing depresses him more. Your command not only tells him you fail to understand, but also it plunges him further into isolation.

Do not take a depressed person to a party. Parties may be good antidotes for momentarily moody people. The fellowship and fun may refresh them. But that same comradeship and enjoyment only inundate a depressed person with feelings of guilt for being a wet blanket. Then perhaps the environment pushes him into jealousies and angers that others can enjoy life while he can't, thence further he goes into guilt and anger at himself. We see from this why Scripture says, "Like one who takes off a garment on a cold day, or like vinegar on soda, is he who sings songs to a troubled heart" (Prov. 25:20). Again, joining the party is not a matter of willpower; it is not blameworthy that he can't put on a face so as not to hamper the merriment. Your taking him to a party has put the depressive in an untenable position, which only caused his differentness to stand out like a thistle bush among the daisies.

Do not take a depressed person to a comedy, or for a hike in the woods, or a picnic, or for a swim at the beach for all the same reasons that parties are taboo.

Do not take a depressive to a worship service, theater, ballet, opera, ball game, or other sporting event.

Do not preach to, scold, or teach a depressed person. Depressives know they cannot do what you preach because they know, as St. Paul did, "that nothing good dwells in me, that is, in my flesh; for the wishing is present in me, but the doing of the good is not" (Rom. 7:18). Failing energies drastically limit a depressed person's attention span. Words become tiresome. "Excessive devotion to books is wearying to the body" (Eccles. 12:12). Even nondepressed people tire of wordiness; to depressives, wordiness becomes oppressive by fatigue. Exhortations prove to him that you fail utterly to understand. You still think there is something he could and should do to help himself if he would only try. You fail to grasp that his spirit's ability to cope is gone. He is incapable of functioning. He can turn all the knobs on his gas range, and no burners will turn on. Your words show that you do not fully believe that his pilot has gone out. He feels condemned.

Do not give advice. "Have you tried this? Well, if you would only…" All such well-meant remedies drive the depressive further into blackness. Most likely he has tried everything his advisors can think of and more. Advice participates in the same delusion as exhortation. Nothing a person in the pits can do will propel him out of it, and he knows that. The telling mark of depression is helplessness and hopelessness. Only someone who has experienced depression can fully appreciate the futility, the total blackness of the pit of despair. "I am reckoned among those who go down to the pit; I have become like a man without strength, forsaken among the dead, like the slain who lie in the grave" (Ps. 88:4–5). Exhorters and advisors are to depressives what Proverbs 28:3 says: "A poor man who oppresses the lowly is like a driving rain which leaves no food."

In most cases, do not attempt to exorcise a depressive. Depression is not first demonic. It is not primarily a matter of invasion by a foreign entity. Since it is a psychological and spiritual condition in which one's own personal spirit has sunk close to death in its ability to function, attended by all manner of concomitant fears, anxieties, guilts, and frustrations, a demonic spirit of *oppression* may take advantage of the lassitude of mind and heart to oppress a depressive into further darkness. But usually the depressed person does not need even to be made aware of that possibility. One can silently bind and/or cast away any oppressive spirits and call for the Lord's angels to surround and protect him. "For He will give His angels charge concerning you, to guard you in all your ways" (Ps. 91:11). "The angel of the LORD encamps around those who fear Him, and rescues them" (Ps. 34:7). If someone treats the condition loudly and overtly as a demon and pronounces an exorcism, that spirit of oppression is cast away. For a short duration, perhaps for a day, or even a week, the person may seem to be out of depression and may give such testimony that the church rejoices in another seeming victory. But such a victory seldom lasts. If the condition in the heart and mind that invited the oppressive spirit still remains, the person will soon plunge into the full depths again. The depressive will eventually feel worse than ever, and when nothing good persists, he may conclude, "There, I knew it. Even God can't help me. The devil's got me for sure. I'm doomed." He may well identify with the words of Jeremiah 6:14: "And they have healed the brokenness of My people superficially, saying, 'Peace, peace,' but there is no peace." To make the depressive aware of demonic presences can increase fear. Such people already know they are helpless. They know they have no power. To tell them that demons are present can be like saying to a paper hanger busily slapping paper to the ceiling that malaria-carrying mosquitoes are buzzing around him and he had better mash them or else, or like shouting warnings to a hog-tied man that he is about to be thrown into the water.

Do not take a depressed person to a prayer meeting. We all fall into the pits occasionally, and prayer meetings are usually great medicine for weary hearts. A good worship service lifts us. "Like apples of gold in settings of silver is a word spoken in right circumstances" (Prov. 25:11), and "Like the cold of snow in the time of harvest is a faithful messenger to those who send him, for he refreshes the soul of his masters" (Prov. 25:13).

In the days when Proverbs 25 was written, a particular fruit called the kitchilika was grown in backyard gardens. It was somewhat like a cross between an orange and a grapefruit, looked in color like an apple, and was commonly squeezed for juice as a refreshing drink for weary traveling guests. Snow at the right time brings forth flavor, as frost is needed in the state of Washington to give its apples their sweet and delicious flavor. Just so, the Word of God and prayer refresh nondepressive people. But depressives no longer possess a functioning spirit with which to catch and hold either the Word or the presence of God. They are incapable of joining the corporate worship that lifts everyone else. It only depresses them further because they cannot help seeing the benefit others receive while they feel nothing but increased sadness, anger, and jealousy.

Do not exhort a depressive to find help in private devotions. Do not expect him to be able to leap into the arms of the Lord for comfort and healing. Devotional practices are first and best helps for a person who is not depressed, but for the depressed they are torture. Depressives no longer feel that they can pray, especially for themselves. In first states of depression, one accomplished prayer minister I knew could still pray for others and they would be healed, but she had absolutely no faith in her prayers for herself.

> O LORD, the God of my salvation,
> I have cried out by day and in the night before Thee.
> Let my prayer come before Thee;
> Incline Thine ear to my cry!
> For my soul has had enough troubles,
> And my life has drawn near to Sheol....
> Thy wrath has rested upon me,
> And Thou hast afflicted me with all Thy waves....
> My eye has wasted away because of affliction;
> I have called upon Thee every day, O LORD;
> I have spread out my hands to Thee....
> But I, O LORD, have cried out to Thee for help,
> And in the morning my prayer comes before Thee.
> O LORD, why dost Thou reject my soul?
> Why dost Thou hide Thy face from me?
> —PSALM 88:1–3, 7, 9, 13–14

Depressives have become convinced God will not hear their prayers. Again, therefore, to subject them to meetings in which their eyes can see the faces of others suffused with His presence while they feel only the blackness of apparent rejection is to them nothing but torment. To expect that they will be able to enjoy the Lord's presence in private devotions reveals that you fail to comprehend they can no longer abide in His presence. The powerful presence of the Lord, which refreshes others, oppresses them.

> How long, O LORD? Wilt Thou forget me forever?
> How long wilt Thou hide Thy face from me?
> How long shall I take counsel in my soul,
> Having sorrow in my heart all the day?
> How long will my enemy be exalted over me?
> Consider and answer me, O LORD, my God;
> Enlighten my eyes, lest I sleep the sleep of death,
> Lest my enemy say, "I have overcome him,"
> Lest my adversaries rejoice when I am shaken.
>   —PSALM 13:1–4

One might ask, "How could His perfect and gentle presence ever oppress anyone?" The Lord's presence in reality never oppresses, but depressives are fully capable of perceiving blessings as oppressive. This is the closest depressives come to delusion.

> With the pure Thou dost show Thyself pure;
> And with the crooked Thou dost show Thyself astute.
>   —PSALM 18:26

I (John) can remember being so foolishly angry a number of times at my parents or brothers or sister that when one or all of them with a fully good heart came to offer affection to me, it seemed full of guile and oppression, something not at all to be received, until the anger had run its course. Just so, the eyes of a depressive wear glasses that see rejection and "I ought to be rejected" when love is purely poured. They cannot receive His goodness and mercy when they most need it, often thinking perversely that they don't deserve it because obviously they have failed. However, when not in depression, they would have grasped easily that they never did have to deserve His love. Jealousy of others who obviously enjoy His favor continually attacks and oppresses depressives. When the depressive is in crowds and groups, his energies are too low to withstand the impressing energies of others around him.

I can remember that when I suffered migraine headaches, I could not stand Paula's presence. I wanted her nearby. But under the pain, my spirit was somehow more sensitive to movements around me. Sounds strummed on the nerves of my body as if raking me with briars. People under depression have lost energy to respond, but the energies of others crash like high and demanding waves on their shores. They cannot stand to be in crowds, especially under the powerful energies of prayer or high emotions. For that reason:

Do not attempt to heal the memories of a person in depression until the person is ready. Often ancient and unhealed memories are a primary cause for the depression, but they can only be healed *after* the subject is at least part way out of depression. Inner transformation is death and rebirth in the inner man. At best, it requires strength of spirit as we undergo whatever degree of trauma such change by inner death and rebirth requires. (See chapter 6, "Breaking the Cycle," in *Transforming the Inner Man* for a fuller exposition of the process of death and rebirth in inner healing.) Depressives cannot withstand the pressures of inner transformation done too early. We must lift the depressive far enough out of the pit that he is able to respond. Then we must not fail to heal the inner heart so that guilt, anger, hate, rejection, or other wounds and sins do not entangle and imprison him again in depression.

Do not visit too long with a depressive. Be sensitive to his energy level and attention span.

You might ask, "Well, then, what is left that I *can* do for a person in depression?" A great deal. But you must know what and be confident in the Lord that you truly can "do all things through Him who strengthens me" (Phil. 4:13).

In the process of revealing what can be done, we will also continue to list what one should not do.

Do not smile. Wipe the smile off your face. "Weep with those who weep." Smiles tell him that we are not where he is and, more cogently, that we fail to commiserate, and probably cannot, and are therefore to be avoided. There are inner steel doors that when shut are not likely to open again for a while.

Do commiserate. Sit down and begin to share all the *worst* things: "I know how you feel. Every morning the sky is black. Every decision is too much. You can't make yourself do the little things you used to do easily. You hate yourself, and then you hate others because they can do everything so easily, and then you hate yourself for hating them. And nobody understands. They say, 'Cheer up,' and try to make you feel better, and you can't. You know tomorrow isn't going to be any better. You've tried everything and nothing works." We must enter in where the other is before we can carry him out. We do not have to become what he is, but we must empathize until he knows that we know and that we can share what he feels without judgment or blame.

By now the depressive will be sitting in the palm of your hand. He knows you are not in depression, because he can see it. And he believes you have been there because you understand and you aren't saying and doing all the foolish things everyone else has tried on him. At least some of his loneliness is eased. You aren't likely to reject him by being stupidly unaware of where he is. And since you are obviously out of depression, a tiniest glimmer of hope may for the first time enter his mind.

A psychiatrist friend, Dr. John Lefsrud of Edmonton, Alberta, knowing how vital hope is to the depressed, greets depressives at the entrance to his clinic with his own firm and compassionate presence, addresses them by name, and says, "Well, what are you going to do when you get out of here?" He doesn't demand or wait for an answer. By his professional status and the question, he is purposefully implanting a seed of hope.

Within the above paragraphs were several other implicit recommendations.

Do not stand when the other is sitting. You may not be aware of posture relative to status, but a depressive most likely will be. Your standing will elevate your presence as a weight over him. Sitting relaxedly in a chair on the same level with him says you are entering sensitively, on his level. I (John) learned this the hard way. A woman brought her husband, who was in the early stages of depression and whom I had never met. He was a proud man; for him to have any emotional problem was already demeaning, and it was downright insulting to be expected to talk to a prayer minister. Only the pressure of his wife forced him to come at all. We had recently left the pastorate to begin a prayer ministry center on faith and were using some low-slung chairs a friend had given us for people who came for ministry, while I used a rickety old high-backed thing for an office chair. Already needing something to pounce on to justify anger so he could escape, that was his opening. "He who separates himself seeks his own desire, he quarrels against all sound wisdom." (Prov. 18:1). To him it was patent that I had purposely chosen such chairs and such a seating arrangement to debase the people to whom I ministered and elevate myself. After telling me all about that in no uncertain terms, he flounced out, leaving his mystified wife wringing her hands. While, to me, there was no mystery at all, only regret.

Do not sit too close. Do not invade his space. With nondepressed people I like to be close. In prayer, especially, I will kneel beside the other and place an arm over the other's shoulders. Such closeness is to be avoided when ministering to depressives. Their jangled nerves cannot stand such proximity.

Do not minister to a depressive in a group or even two by two. If more than one ministers, let one sit in front, holding whatever attention is required, and let others sit behind the person, present but out of demanding consciousness. When ministering to people who are not depressed, it is wise to remember that the Lord sent them out two by two (Luke 10:1). Ecclesiastes 4:9–10 says, "Two are better than one because they have a good return for their labor." Nondepressed people are best helped by many. "But in abundance of counselors there is victory" (Prov. 11:14). The presence of many avoids confusing romantic notions; it avoids latching onto one person as healer rather than the Lord. But the depressive cannot stand the freight of too many people's unconscious demand for response simply by being visibly present. If more than one ministers to a depressed person, try to arrange things so that assistants are comfortably out of range. Depressives can only handle one, and that usually not for too long.

Do be sensitive about whether or not to close the door. A depressive can feel reassured by a closed door with a "do not disturb" sign. This shields him from the slightest possibility of being seen by unwanted passers-by that he feels incapable of responding to. On the other hand, to another depressive, a closed door may spell entrapment. He may need to feel that he can get out if he needs to flee. Your leaving the door open says you will respect that. And it also tells him you do not intend to put him through a spate of internal searches he can't now stand. That open door is a mark of your sensitivity to him. It relaxes him.

Do not be "humble." Do not say, "I *may* be able to help you." Do not say, "Is this how you sometimes feel?" With nondepressed people we do not want to seem presumptuous or prideful. We ask rather than state. We try to show respect for the other's privacy and initiative. We may mask our own inner confidence behind "may" and "I think I can," for humility's sake. Depressives, contrariwise, need to hear nothing humble, no "I think I know how you feel," no "ifs" whatsoever.

One prayer minister who went through a depression told us the thoughts she had when a young man came to minister to her: "If this young man says one 'if,' I know I'll never get well." The depressive at that moment is like a man being rolled into an operating room about to undergo surgery, totally dependent on the doctor. If the doctor were to try to be "humble," saying, "I don't know whether I can take this gallbladder out or not," I guarantee most pre-ops would be on their feet running bare-bottomed, pell-mell out the hospital door! We want absolute sureness in our doctor any time our life is dependent on his skill. Depressives know they can't revive themselves. If you offer to help, it will be all up to you or not at all. Knowing that, they want to hear no lack of confidence, no "ifs," no lack of positive assurance of success. They want to know that you know you can help them before they venture one iota of trust in you. Your assertion and your proof that you do know is tonic to their tortured soul. They have borne the burden of trying to make others understand them and failed often so completely that your assertion that you already know you can help them and then the fact that you proceed to prove it is restful beyond measure.

Do establish trust. It is vital to the other to establish trust and confidence. When the time is appropriate, a prayer minister can say, "*I can get you out of there,*" not "I think..." or "I may..." or "It is possible that..." Tell him you know how to pray over him in such a way that he will be healed, but immediately hasten to add, "By my faith, not yours." A depressed person knows that if anything is up to him, it won't work. Explain to him that he is like the paralytic who was let down before Jesus and that you will pray over him by your faith, not his.

Do not explain or talk too long. Once you commiserate enough to see that the person is willing to place himself or herself in your hands because you understand, stop talking and say, "I can get you out of there."

Do not say, "You can get out of depression," or "I can tell you how to get out of your depression." That is the surest way to blow the whole mission and slam the doors shut. Their healing must rest squarely and solely on your shoulders. A depressive is emotionally paralyzed. When the four men let down the paralyzed man in front of Jesus, He looked up, and "seeing their faith, He said...'Rise...'" (Luke 5:20–23). A depressed person will be resurrected from the pit by the rope of your faith, not at all his. He and you must be assured of that from the beginning.

Do not let him think for a moment that you think he must do something, anything at all, to claim his own healing. With nondepressed people we want to minister in such a way that their own faith is so involved that in the end we can say as Jesus did, "Your faith has saved you; go in peace" (Luke 7:50).

Do not lay hands on his head. He cannot withstand the weight of your hand physically; his nerves are too battered.

Do lay hands lightly on his shoulders while standing behind him. Standing behind gives closeness while respecting distance.

Do not pray too long. Remember not to say, "If it be Thy will." This is not the time for uncertainty. Nothing is surer in Jesus than that the Lord came precisely to set us free from such inner prisons, as He said in Luke 4:18: "The Spirit of the Lord is upon Me, because He anointed Me to preach the gospel to the poor. He has sent Me to proclaim release to the captives, and recovery of sight to the blind, to set free those who are downtrodden, to proclaim the favorable year of the Lord."

Do pray vividly, imaginatively, and positively. For instance, sometimes I pray seeing and describing the frame of the other as transparent, seeing through to envision the candle of his spirit as having gone out, now being rekindled by the Lord.

Do not let the other measure success or failure by feelings or any immediate signs. I hasten to say, "I know, Lord, that [name] may not feel anything at present. We are not doing this on the basis of feelings but on the basis of my faith, and I know it will work. Sooner or later, maybe today, maybe next week, but certainly in the near future, this person will begin to feel better, like suddenly seeing a blade of grass popping up through the snow. I'm going to hold him in my heart, Lord, and I will keep on praying until he is totally free and out of depression. I know it will work, Lord, and I thank and praise You for it."

Do not hand the person over to God in your prayer. Agnes Sanford was known the world over as the pioneer of rediscovering healing among mainline churches, the discoverer and forerunner of healing the inner man, postgraduate depressive, and authority on how to minister to depressives. When her husband, Ted, died, she promptly sank into another depression herself. She came to Paula and me, then pastor and wife of the little First Congregational Church, United Church of Christ, in the small town of

Council Grove, Kansas. We were overawed that this great pioneering saint would come to little us wanting help. We thought it humble and appropriate to say in prayer, "We place Agnes in your hands, Lord. We release her to You. We know You will care for her, Lord Jesus, because You love her." Agnes sank immediately into the blackest pits of depression. When I next saw her, she let me know how Paula and I had failed her. Agnes could still pray for others, and they would be healed. She could still teach and be powerfully effective. She had faith for others and not one whit for herself! She had already tried God alone for herself, and she and He (in her thinking) had failed. To hand her over to God was to doom her to failure. She needed to be carried by others and had come to us for that and that alone, which was the very thing our false humility and fear prevented us from doing for her. I immediately repented and said, "Oh, Agnes, we'll be glad to do it for you. We'll be glad to carry you in our hearts. We'll love you to life. That's a delight. You're not a burden. You're a joy." Agnes quickly rose out of depression. I continued to carry her in a heart of love. (See chapters 21–22 of her autobiography *Sealed Orders*.) Agnes not only was delivered from depression, but she also mellowed and became freer and wiser, happier and more relaxed as the years passed. (Unfortunately, the ministry of Agnes Sanford has been incorrectly judged by today's apologists. Failing to check with any of us who truly knew where she stood, they misunderstood some of her statements and have labeled [actually libeled] her as a demonically guided occultist. Nothing could be further from the truth!)

Never release people who have been depressed into God's hand alone too soon. You must carry them even as St. Paul wrote in Galatians 4:19: "…with whom I am again in labor until Christ is formed in you." Note the "again." People, strong and sure in Jesus, ministering saints as Agnes was, can temporarily lose it and need to be carried awhile. Do not give up. Persevere. Resurrecting the other may take a long time. One woman whose relatives called me (John) for help was so depressed she had been in bed two long years, with bedsores on her body. Her mother-in-law was running her household and caring for her and the children. I ministered to her as we have outlined. It took persistent visits, two a week at first, then once a week for over six months, before she rallied enough to rise out of her bed and begin to assume her position as a wife and mother. It took many more months of prayer ministry to discover and heal the many hidden roots behind the depression.

Do not end the session with the prayer.

Do end the session after prayer by immediately saying, "I want to see you again."

Do not say, "Can you come to see me again?" or "Would you like to see me another time?" With nondepressed people we assure respect of their wishes by such questions. Depressives are sure that no one could love them (or ought to), and certainly no one wants to be around them.

Do say, "I want to see you again." This is healing to their expectancy and to their dread of rejection.

Explain that sometimes we need to pray several times for the inner pilot light to come on and stay on. I sometimes say, "Our inner being is like an old Ford motor on a cold day. Sometimes it coughs and conks out again several times before it keeps running by itself. We may need to pray several times, but in the end I know it will work." Make another appointment.

Do not leave anything indeterminate. If you say, "Come when you can," he won't.

Do make a specific time and date. "I would like to see you on Wednesday at 2:00." Nail it down.

Do not expect the depressive to come to you. If the miracle has not already happened, he won't. To get dressed to go somewhere is too much, let alone the fear of failure. Rather, you go to him. If you don't already know, say, "Where do you live? I'll come and get you." Nondepressed people want to be given some latitude and privacy to feel free to keep an appointment or not. Depressives must have assurance that you will take full responsibility to come after them and that you want to. They may say, "Oh, don't put yourself out for me," but do not believe them. Put yourself on the line for them.

Do not fail to keep the appointment. That is an absolute imperative. If grandmother dies, bury her next week. That depressive's life now hangs on your dependability. If you fail to show up, no matter how valid the reason or how reasonably his *mind* says, "I understand, it couldn't be helped," his *heart* will conclude, "I knew it. It isn't going to work. I'm let down and rejected again, as I deserve to be."

Do not carry the burden of the other alone. You must minister one on one, but apart from the person in depression, call friends and prayer warriors to help you carry the burden. Wisdom may dictate whether to tell the depressive or not. Some already feel guilty that you have to expend so much effort and reproach themselves if they do not quickly arise. They do not want to burden anybody, which is a part of why they went into depression in the first place, and which must be unlearned eventually. Because of such wrong thinking, you may not feel it wise to inform the other of the many who are praying. On the other hand, some persons would take such information as a mark of love and be encouraged. We should act as we sense each individual needs. In any case, unless the depressive gives written permission to share his name or condition, keep him anonymous.

Do not enlist the prayer help of the "wailers." We do not need the moaners and the groaners whose stressful energies may afflict the person.

Do draft prayer warriors who are bright, positive, and happy.

Do not overlook simple practical matters as a depressive begins to come out of it. "Oh, you have a new hairdo." "You look better today." Body language, dress, sparkles in the eyes, many things will be clues as the other begins to resurrect. We can help that process of healing in two ways:

1. Notice, affirm, and compliment when a tiny practical step has been taken—"You're wearing a shirt and tie and a nice suit again. You look great. That's good to see."

2. We can encourage the person to try his wings again in many little ways.

A young man (not myself) ministering to Agnes years ago, seeing that she was beginning to come alive, said, "Agnes, what did you use to like to do before you became depressed?"

"Oh, I used to like to write. I'm an author."

"Well, try your hand at it again. Don't knock yourself out, but see if you can get some enjoyment out of it again."

Agnes wrote a full three-act play, the story of Saul, Jonathan, and David. Behind her depression had been many angers no Episcopal rector's wife "ought" to express. The more people she slew on stage, the better she felt, until entire armies had been slaughtered! Some people play piano, guitar, garden, hike, bird watch, or fish. Whatever practical interest is there, encourage renewal.

If the person begins to fall into transference, thinking that he or she is falling in love with you do not cut off the person to whom you are minis-

tering. With some, you can explain what a transference is. Some are not willing to hear that their love for you has unreal or confused elements. That places the burden squarely on your heart. Keep your own heart clear. Know that that kind of love from the other is not romantic or mate love no matter how convinced the person may be that it is. Know most surely that your own love for the other is neither romance nor mate love, that yours is that of the Lord for one being redeemed, or like that of a parent for a child, and that the other's love is a temporary, overly intense fastening upon you as the umbilical cord of their life's blood. Someday that cord will be cut and you may become the best of friends, but never lovers.

There is great danger in this area. More prayer ministers have fallen by not recognizing and handling transferences than any way Paula and I know of. So much so, one could almost say, "Flee the battle in the first place." However, Christ does not call us to be safe but rather to minister and risk ourselves as His own example showed. One *rhema* application of a word from Scripture has been of great assurance to us: "Where no oxen are, the manger is clean, but much increase comes by the strength of the ox" (Prov. 14:4). Things may get messy and fraught with danger as we serve, but the Lord would not have us be Pharisees who guard our own untouchableness, but servants who bear the burden and the heat of the day.

Be sure to persist until the other is free from depression, its root causes discovered, and the other fully transformed and walking in his new life. Do not terminate either the prayer ministry or the relationship until the person is able to stay free by himself. Our minds can grasp quickly that we are loved, but the heart must test and try and be assured again and again and again before it settles, firmly fixed and a question not needing to be raised again, that it is loved. Security becomes courage to live when the question of love is settled.

In transferences the person places his prayer minister in a seemingly idolatrous position, for temporarily he drinks from the prayer minister what normally ought to be obtained only directly from God. In or out of transference, a person rising out of depression walks for a while not in his own spiritual strength but in the piety of his helper. One could liken this to being born. In physical birth we are encased in our mother's body and life. During that time we are not idolatrous, though all our life's sustenance is mediated through our mother's being. We are not responsible for ourselves; another is. But to surrender such control of ourselves when we are adults *is* idolatrous, for our Lord wants us to stand on our own feet, dependent only on Him. But it needs to be understood that people in depression are no longer capable of functioning as responsible adults. This is not to say they have regressed to become as little children again, only that they have become currently incapable. They need to be carried for a time within the ambience of another.

The relationship is thus not idolatrous. But therein lies danger, for the prayer minister may so enjoy carrying the other—for ego, power, lust, the need to be needed, possessiveness, the idolatry of being like God to another—that he may unconsciously, even consciously, be unwilling to release when the time is ripe. Or the reverse may be true: the prayer minister may be so worried, wearied, or bothered by the responsibility that he cuts off the relationship too soon, and the person feels rejected and plummets again. Or the person being ministered to may be tempted to hang on too long or cut off too soon. Most often, it is the person receiving ministry who becomes confused. Prayer ministers must hold the line, informed and aware.

The worst and most common danger is sexual. Whether men minister to women or the reverse, or persons of the same sex minister to one another, either or both may become sexually or romantically aroused and confused. Mates of either or both may feel that spiritual adultery is going on, which is when either spouse drinks the kind of love and sharing (apart from sexual concerns) that properly belong only to each other. That may in fact be happening. Society, looking on, may impute scandal into an innocent love relationship or rightly see spiritual and/or physical adultery and react. Tragically, it often happens that the couples do become sexually involved.

The Lord sent me one time into a hospital room where I found a lady tardily recovering from a heart attack. Whether the depression caused the attack or came afterward, the result was that she no longer wanted to live. I assisted the medical people by ministering to the physical heart by prayer, and then I began the longer task of resurrecting her from depression. Several months later she was nearly free of depression and had overcome many of the original causes for both.

I was escorting her in my car to a prayer meeting. She was a physically beautiful woman, about the age of my mother, married, and a grandmother. I could sense that she was summoning courage to ask me an embarrassing question. Finally she drew a deep breath, and blurted out, "Pastor, if I asked you to go to bed with me, would you deny me?"

Hurt for her, for the pain and confusion she had put herself through, and ashamed that I had not spared her by wiser counsel, I thought awhile and finally said, "You know that I care for you, but it's not that kind of love, my friend. As the Lord's servant, I must not, so I would have to deny you, but I would not reject you." Though she was shocked by my answer and by my manner, I was trying in my own immature way to tell her that I would hold the line for her, that I did in fact have a love for her, and that I still accepted her and did not disrespect her for asking. I knew something was going on that was not really sexual at all. I wanted to keep the door open for further ministry. She would need to talk about it. There was a depth of transference and confusion.

I knew that something powerful had so impelled her as to overcome the great propriety with which she had always conducted herself. It was later discovered that though she might actually have seduced me had I been less secure in Christ and in my love for Paula, at a deeper level she was testing me. If she threw off the ladylike performing mask and appeared seductive, would I still be able to love, like, and respect her? My answer satisfied her deeper questions. I would not let the relationship go astray; she could rest about her feelings. She concluded then (it was later revealed) that she was indeed loved truly, and properly, and could risk becoming whole and free.

I share this story so that others may see that sometimes when relationships seem to be going the wrong way, underneath they may not be at all—and certainly need not. At that moment her life hung both on my determination to live righteously in Christ and upon my willingness to let Jesus find and minister behind seeming wrongness to the reality emerging within her. It was later disclosed that a stepfather she trusted and loved had made sexual advances toward her. Though twenty years older than me, she had put me in his place and was testing: Was it safe to let any father figure love her? Could her love seduce a father figure? Could she be loved without that love improperly turning to sex? That matrix of never answered questions had lain causally below every depression to which she had fallen prey. All of that was what was actually behind what seemed on the surface to be only sexual lust.

By this story I would advise prayer ministers, especially in ministering to depressives, *not* to react to what *seems* to be happening.

And He will delight in the fear of the LORD,
And He will not judge by what His eyes see,
Nor make a decision by what His ears hear.

—ISAIAH 11:3

Equal errors could have been made in the above story. On the one hand, an error could have been made and all concerned could have fallen into full temptation. On the other I could have acted self-righteously as though that person were reprehensible and only to be scolded, rejected, and condemned. Both would have missed what was actually happening. We must hold circumspectly to the way of the Lord concerning our own life, but we minister compassionately and patiently toward the other that the Lord may have opportunity to reveal the actual heart's song.

CAUSES OF DEPRESSION

We approach the causes of depression by that story for the reason that the most common and basic causes of depression are performance orientation and hidden unresolved emotional factors of guilt, fear, resentment, and rejection. Most likely, if a person had been able to elevate that nexus of sores to conscious awareness, depression would not have happened. As depression lifts, the heart begins to seek ways to send to the surface signals of the original causal hurts and sins. Performance orientation, as it did before the depression, still prevents simple open admission of guilt or trauma. So the inner spirit finds gambits, such as dreams, stories, or seeming seduction. It is the prayer minister's task to catch the clues, and the Holy Spirit's task is to reveal what they mean.

Performance orientation

Performance orientation can best be understood by reading chapter 3 in our book *Transforming the Inner Man*. In short, performance orientation occurs when a person does not receive enough unconditional love and affection, taking into the heart instead the message, "Only if you measure up to the standards around here will you be loved or belong." Since we all need love in order to live, fear rules the heart, fear of failure and fear of rejection. The result is either compliance—"I will do whatever seems to gain your approval because I understand that I must do so to win your love"—or rebellion—"If I have to perform for love, I won't at all, and that will punish you."

If the person is one who tries to perform for love, then he is filled with striving. He is never sure he has done enough to merit love. He is always measuring and judging how well he has done. Whatever affection does come his way never fully convinces him he is loved, because he thinks, "If they knew what I'm really like, they couldn't love me." Since being loved has become equated with being "good," every performance-oriented person fears discovery. He cannot let others see what is repulsive or reprehensible, either on the outside in behavior or on the inside in his character, for fear of rejection. This locks him into playing roles while inwardly feeling more and more isolated. The longer he performs, the more subconscious anger is fomented; he is angry that he has to perform for love instead of being loved simply because he exists. He develops an inner need to blow the good-guy image in order to discover whether he will be loved anyway (which is what was behind the grandmother's seductive proposal to me.)

In relation to depression, this means that performance-oriented people strive too long too hard to perform, until the inner being gets tired of the game. The unrecognized thought of the heart is, "This isn't working. I don't feel a bit more loved than when I began (to do whatever the person set out to accomplish). I quit." The spirit goes on a sit-down strike and dies to willingness to perform at all. Depressions of this type can happen seemingly overnight, though observant people could have seen the signs long before. "I quit" depressions are never as sudden as they seem.

A performance-oriented person can also try to win love by performing—and failing. Perhaps not at all in the eyes of others, but in his own eyes he feels dejected and unlovable. If loved ones give affection, he feels guilty. He feels as if he doesn't deserve it, or he says to himself, "They couldn't really mean it," because then he would have to live up to it, and he feels unable and unworthy. Under that kind of inner turmoil, he performs badly, feels worse, so performs less well and fails again, and so sinks stage by stage into the pit of depression.

A performance-oriented person can plummet into depression from either end of the scale. Overachievers get tired of the effort, and successes threaten to reveal to them that they don't feel a bit more loved or secure. The result is inner capitulation. On the other hand, failure is seen as tantamount to lack of love and rejection, which creates more failure, which in turn becomes the downward spiral of failure and feelings of ineptitude until depression becomes the bottom of the pit.

Performance-oriented people also fall prey to depression by dint of isolation and guilt. If a performer knows he must confess his sins to another that he may be healed (James 5:16), he may dutifully do so but very carefully and in controlled fashion, so that listeners may conclude that he is being open, honest, and real, whereas in fact he has only played a carefully controlled role. The real inner, raw, unprepared, unthought-out volcanic matter of inner turmoil is never let loose even to himself, much less to others. Most often, performance-oriented people will not even enter the role play of self-realization by confession. They are convinced that no one could love them if they ever knew what was inside them.

All this means that the healing balm of forgiveness is not allowed at the core of the inner man where memories are stored. Further, it means that the closer others become, the more diligently the performance-oriented person must work to keep up the front. Thus ancient guilts eat out the energy and strength of the performer. While he pours himself out for others, his own inner bank is being drained of resources until finally it is as though he skates over thin ice and plunges into the cold water of depression. Whether the resultant depression is sudden or slow in arrival, the cause is not whatever "final feather broke the camel's back." The cause lies in ancient guilts and loneliness never yet healed by the cross and blood of Christ.

A prayer minister was called upon to minister to a missionary lady sent home from the mission field overseas due to an unrelenting state of depression. The prayer minister ministered to her as we have outlined, until the lady was willing to talk about the possible causes of her depression. Though the lady was an evangelist, preaching the free gift of God's love to the heathen, she herself was so performance-oriented that at heart level she had never really believed God could love her if she didn't serve well or if she did some awful thing. At last it came out that at sixteen years of age she had had an affair and lost her virginity. Her performance-oriented character had prevented her from telling anyone. She had tried to confess it in secret to Jesus and had striven to believe she had been forgiven. But she had never been able to forgive herself and didn't see in her heart how anyone else could forgive her either, much less God.

"Oh," the prayer minister exclaimed, "there we have it. It's an old unforgiven guilt way down in your heart."

"What do you mean 'unforgiven'? I've been preaching salvation to the heathen for fifty years! I *know* God has forgiven me."

"Yes," she replied, "Of course the grown one knows you're forgiven. It's that sixteen-year-old girl inside you who has never felt it." If I remember the story correctly, the lady said something like, "That's preposterous," but the truth of the prayer minister's words reached too deep and touched that hurting heart until the grown one burst into tears and knew the truth of what she had said.

"But how can God forgive that little girl now? That was over fifty years ago."

"What if you could imagine you were just sixteen and it was the very day after you'd done it and you could walk right up to Jesus and tell Him all about it; would He be able to forgive you?"

"Oh, yes, yes. Of course He could."

"Let's do it."

So they prayed just that way, asking Jesus to walk up to that young girl and tell her He forgives her, just as He did to that other woman so long ago to whom He said, "Neither do I condemn you; go your way" (John 8:11).

The lady who had preached forgiveness to the heathen for fifty years had now received it herself, and her depression was gone, never to return. It had no more lodging place in her heart. And the performer knew at the deep level of her heart that she really was loved even when she hadn't done everything right.

Performance orientation could be said to lie in some degree behind every person in depression, even though it may not be the primal cause. The first cause, some blow or loss, guilt or rejection, is like the spark, but the performance orientation is the tinder. Or the wound is the seed, but performance orientation is the fertile ground where depression may quietly grow. It may not be that all depressed people are performance-oriented at the root, but in more than forty-five years' experience, Paula and I have never yet found a depressed person in whom performance orientation was not a major factor causing the depression. It is, of course, not true the other way around—not all performance-oriented people are headed for depression. But I tend to believe that each other cause might not have led to depression were not performance orientation a contributing factor.

Hidden, unresolved emotional factors of guilt, fear, resentment, and rejection

Ancient guilt is another cause of depression, such as was true in the missionary's story. Prayer ministers need to comprehend one thing most clearly: people, performance-oriented or not, may go through the proper steps of confession and still retain guilt. If they have confessed in private as the missionary did (which by the way is unscriptural, there being no command anywhere in the Bible to confess sins in private, but clear directives to confess to others, as in James 5:16ff), the question remains in the person's heart whether mankind could forgive if anyone knew. Most likely the inner being remains as unconvinced of forgiveness as the heart of the missionary was. The Lord truly forgives; sometimes we do not receive.

If a person has confessed to others, he may not have let the balm of priestly authority reach his own tortured heart. Sometimes the only way performance-oriented people have known parental touch was by punishment, and so punishment has subconsciously been connected with knowing oneself to be loved. Such people can unknowingly be punishing themselves by refusing forgiveness, thus grabbing a false sense that God does love them because look how He is punishing them! Hebrews 12 thus twists in their minds to confirm that God loves them because He seems to be punishing them as they punish themselves.

What Paula and I most often find in cases in which guilt has produced depression is that the other truly believes that God has forgiven, but he has never effectively been able to forgive himself. Needing love and needing to convince himself, he loves others. He could not forgive himself because, to his mind, had he loved, he never would have done such a thing, and of course he doesn't deserve to be forgiven. Paula and I have sometimes heard performance-oriented people say when asked to forgive others, "Well, I could forgive him if he just deserved it, but he did that on purpose!" Just so, such people judge and refuse to forgive themselves. Grace for them has to be deserved. Performers' hearts block out the fact that grace means "undeserved favor"—at the very moment their minds may believe firmly in unmerited grace! Even people who are not performance-oriented may do the same thing, blocking themselves out from forgiving themselves. We have all bought to some degree the idolatrous lie that we ought to have been gods and hate ourselves when our sins prove we aren't.

All this leads to another caveat. Prayer ministers *must not* believe too easily when people say they know they are forgiven. Fruits, not protestations of faith, reveal what is there. If the wound is still there, something hasn't happened, most likely forgiveness. Further questions, in different ways, may reveal what is actually lodged in the heart:

- ⤐ "How do you feel about that guy who did that to you?"

- ⤐ "Do you look back at that incident with deep peace, even gratitude that it happened, or with a shudder?"

- ⤐ "Do you like you?"

- ⤐ "How about liking that twenty-one-year-old you were when you did that?"

- ⤐ "Can you imaginatively take that younger person you were into your arms easily?"

- ⤐ "Would you just as soon forget that one and get back up here to be this present one?"

Somehow the person needs to be led to complete forgiveness of all involved, even to "forgive" God for letting it happen (2 Cor. 5:18–20), and most especially to forgive and accept himself.

Childhood wounds sometimes fester until youthful energy wanes or present stresses break down resistance, depression being the result. Again, present stresses may seem to be the cause, whereas they may only be the spark that lit the fuse to a bomb long ago set to detonate somewhere sometime.

Common wounds are deprivation of affection, the most common wounding in earliest childhood; early loss of loved ones as in parental death, divorce, or separation; being rejected and given away to desertion, orphanages, or adoption; the loss of a favorite grandparent, sibling, or even the family dog; and major illnesses in early childhood, especially the kind that necessitated long isolation. Or there can be too much responsibility too soon, as when parents are alcoholics or immature and an older child takes responsibility to care for the younger ones, often without adequate provision.

Other causes of depression

Prenatal and birth traumas can later produce depression. Earliest wounds are more likely to produce depression than later wounds. Childhood traumas after infancy can be dealt with consciously at the time or be remembered and wrestled through. But it is the earliest wounds that are often unknown to the conscious mind and incapable of being recalled. They are by far more powerfully effective in the unconscious. It is not true that what you do not know cannot hurt you. The reverse is more nearly true—what we do not know and cannot see within us *can* hurt us.

One could set it as a principle that whenever people think to protect others by not sharing troubles with them (at all, we mean; there is wisdom in choosing the right moments to share), they actually hurt their loved ones worse by leaving them to struggle in their spirits with feelings to which they can attach no names. It is often just this kind of unknown grief, guilt, fear, or rejection that so devastates the inner man that depression is the result. Truth sets us free. We make crooked the straight paths of God when we obscure, thinking to protect.

Loss of a job, retirement, too many changes too rapidly—like retiring and quickly moving to a new locality away from old friends and church fellowship—can result in depression. Women whose lives have centered in being mothers may slump into depression when children leave the home. Retirement may spell uselessness, especially to performance-oriented men. Business failure may load guilt on inner volcanic suppressions.

Death of a mate, or worse, divorce, may cast one into depression. Loss of a loved one means revolution in terms of long-practiced endearing actions and support. There is no mate to share gladness with, to laugh with at a comedy, to weep with over losses. Little rituals of comfort so long practiced, such as having a cup of coffee ready when he comes in the door, her fingers kneading sore shoulder muscles at night, or snuggling together in bed after a long hard day, now, by their absence, speak volumes of loneliness.

Depression seldom hits as severely those who have the gift of tears or the ability to rage. It is the stoic, the philosophic controlled ones who unwittingly add fuel to later fires of depression. Nice people become depressed over losses and griefs more often than people who can take things out on others. Aggressive people do not store up so many hurts that turn inward to attack the holder. Quiet, disciplined people determined not to hurt, not ever to bother or be a burden, are the people to watch after loss. It is these who can slip most often into depression, though aggressive people can, too.

Postpartum depression is common. What often happens, though not always, is that a woman may have been so wounded as a girl that in her hidden inner heart she did not want to live. She may have grown beyond whatever the wounding was and happily sought marriage and pregnancy, but secretly part of her did not want to bring forth life. The little one in the womb may have triggered into her hatred of herself in the womb. During the pregnancy, all of her energies were preempted by nature to produce that new life. Once the baby was delivered, the hidden desire to end life is exposed, not to love and produce life. Now the burden of that new dependent life becomes unaccountably just that, a burden rather than the clean joy she thought it would be. Sometimes physical chemistry is a causative factor in these cases, but we tend to honor the speculation that if there were not a prior predilection to sorrow and death, the woman's vitality would beneficially alter her chemistry, especially as the love the baby gives to her and the needs of nursing would draw her to life. Again, we have noted that it is most often performance-oriented women who suffer more than normal postpartum symptoms.

A physical or great emotional shock may throw someone into depression. Hysterectomies, the loss of a limb or an eye, or a disfiguring accident are often followed by depression.

Trauma or stress too long sustained, such as shell shock, may lead into depression. The head of a local TV station was brought to us, so far under depression he walked with a shuffling gait, led by the hand like a child, shoulders sagging, eyes vapid. The TV station had fallen on rough times— debts, hectic schedules, friction between personnel, and so forth—and he had tried dutifully to carry it all on his own heart and shoulders. Though it was the workload and emotional stress that acted as the catalyst, the cause lay in his childhood. He had been raised by a domineering, thoroughly performance-oriented, success-hunting mother, and his father was ineffective. He did not receive affection from either parent. In reaction, his heart unconsciously chose to believe he must earn approval. So long as the TV station seemed to be heading toward success and stability, he could withstand and even relish the pressure. Unconsciously he was being mama's good boy, succeeding despite all the odds and rewarding himself emotionally with feelings of magnanimity. He could accept the tycoon he had become. It told him he was loved (and mama and papa could love him, too). A few reverses were sustainable, but when failure seemed imminent, his own sense of worth was shattered. Looming failure sucked inner worth like a relentless vampire until all drive was gone and depression claimed its victim. It was necessary not only to lift him from depression but also to penetrate behind the business failures he saw as the cause to what in fact did eat away at his inner being.

Trips or heightened joys of any kind sustained too long may swing the pendulum to depression. The inner being, seeking balance, finds something to be sad about. Many saints have been amazed and dismayed to find the pit of depression claiming them just after weeks and weeks of glorious adventures, mystic heights, and great victories in the Lord. Everything seemed to be going great, and then seemingly out of nowhere there came feelings of depression. It is natural and healthy to swing to an opposite balance. But if some unhealed thing, from which perhaps we fled into serving the Lord so long and arduously, lies beneath the surface, we may land on the downside heavily enough to fall through into waiting glooms and find ourselves not able to swing up again. Counterbalancing emotions are OK. We need them. What is not good is when we can't bounce back up because the low hooked into some depressing thing in us that was waiting to happen.

The shortest way to speak of causes is to say that if some great wounding, fear, anger, hate, or guilt rampages unchecked within, any kind of shock or wound may propel us beyond it into the depths of depression.

Depressives *can* be helped. We need only know how and persist in prayer and counsel.

ANGER AND PREVENTING DEPRESSION

Two aspects need to be addressed before we leave the subject. One, we have not said much about anger. Some prayer ministers see anger as a major cause, suspecting that it lies behind most depressions. One friend walked into the room of a client who had so repeatedly fallen into depression as to need hospitalization and bluntly asked, "OK, what are you angry about this time?" It worked. The patient blurted it out and began to recover. If it is true that anger often lodges in the hearts of depressives, then we need to remember that performance orientation is the key. Anger expressed properly is healthy. Jesus looked around at them "with anger, grieved at their hardness of heart…" (Mark 3:5), and often rebuked the Pharisees and scribes in sharp words. Performance-oriented people suppress anger. So do we all at times. Most of the time we will find, however, that it is performance orientation that has locked anger inexpressibly into the heart until it festered and sickened the spirit of the holder.

Two, "What about catching the signs and preventing depression?" and "What can relatives and friends do who live with depressives?" People who have had more than one bout with depression can learn to recognize the signs. So can their relatives and friends. Several antidotes can check the slide.

1. Encourage the person to talk, to get it "off their chest."

2. Draw the person into sharing.

3. Change things. Break treadmill routines; have some fun; take a short holiday; get together with some friends who make the person feel good, who are not a responsibility, and with whom they don't have to put on a face or keep a guard up.

4. Get into a prayer meeting. (*Before* depression sets in, all the no-nos in the first part of this chapter may be good medicine.)

5. Take the person to a counselor or a prayer minister.

6. Best of all, give the person lots of warm physical affection and look for excuses to give positive affirmations and compliments.

7. If some family members are part of the problem, find a little space and time away from them for the potential depressive.

If the person has already slid into depression, family members need to go about family routines as though they are not terribly upset. Above all, avoid haranguing and scolding when the depressive fails to perform. Family members can unobtrusively pick up some of the chores the depressive is dropping. If the family carries on solidly, the guilt of the depressive is lessened. Normally such behavior would tell a person he is unwanted and not needed, but the depressive is likely to be more relieved than hurt.

In a hospital, about to undergo an operation, we are not at all helped by a nurse who exclaims, "Oh my, you look a wreck! Oh, you poor thing!" But if she proceeds about her business calmly and briskly, composed in her own self, we get a positive message and feel, "I must be OK. She doesn't seem too concerned. Everything's going to be OK, I guess." People who are depressed need that kind of "world-in-place" atmosphere about them. High tensions and clattering noises fray the nerves of nondepressed people; to depressives they are wearying and nerve shattering in the extreme, especially since as performers they have always taken emotional responsibility to hold things together, and now they can't.

Nature is good for people on the slide toward depression or already in the pits. I love that hymn that sings so truly:

> Into the woods my Master went,
> Clean forspent, forspent,
> Into the woods my Master came,
> Forspent with love and shame.

> But the olive trees were not blind to Him,
> The little gray leaves were kind to Him;
> The thorn tree had a mind to Him,
> When into the woods He came.

> Out of the woods my Master went,
> And He was well content.
> Out of the woods my Master came,
> Content with death and shame.

> When Death and Shame would woo Him last,
> From under the trees they drew Him last;
> 'Twas on a tree they slew Him last
> When out of the woods He came.[1]
> —PETER CHRISTIAN LUTKIN AND SIDNEY CLAPTON LANIER

Ever since God blessed Adam and Eve to till the garden, nature and mankind have been intended to care for one another. What soul is there so dead that his spirit finds little repose and refreshment in nature? Some are blessed by the sea. Nothing eased a friend of mine so much as being by or on the sea. Some are refreshed by woods, prairies, streams, or lakes. Forests sing to my tattered nerves a song of eternity and rest in God's goodness. Rippling grasses on the prairie or golden waves of ripening wheat soothe my over-busied soul and calm my spirit. The gentle prickling touch of grass on the feet. The searching warmth of dust between the toes. The kiss of tufts of breeze upon the cheeks. Lying flat and watching lacy shapes of white on blue form ships and dragons in the skies. All these things are tonic to weary souls and depressed spirits.

People who are nearing a depressive state need large doses of quiet nature before it's too late. Even nature on the rampage can have a therapeutic effect. Having been raised on the prairie, I absolutely love, cherish, relish, and get thrilled and turned on by a wildly crashing thunderstorm. I'm exhilarated and refreshed. When it's over, I feel like singing praises as I walk in the smell of new, wet earth and see the sparkle of drops falling from wet leaves. All the earth wears a mantle of freshness, and so does my spirit.

Some may have been frightened in a storm or depressed even more by nature's quietness. Know what is good for each, and apply it.

Finally, performance-oriented prayer ministers will try to remember the dos and don'ts above in precise order and will strive to apply them exactly—and become despondent in the process! But the secure will catch the principles of sensitivity and common sense, notch the cautions into the memory bank, and let the love and compassion of the Holy Spirit move through their eyes and voices and hands to lift the weary depressed to resurrection life again.

For all those who find themselves exclaiming, "Oh, my, I've blown it. How many depressed people have I already hurt?" let's forgive, love ourselves, and go on. Medical doctors with the best of intentions bled George Washington to death, but the field has matured, and so can we.

CHAPTER 5

"DEFILEMENTS," DEVILS, AND DEATH WISHES

Do not be deceived: "Bad company corrupts good morals."
Become sober-minded as you ought, and stop sinning; for some
have no knowledge of God. I speak this to your shame.
—1 CORINTHIANS 15:33–34

O ccasionally I have visited with someone, perhaps a total stranger, and felt for no exterior reason at all that I wanted to smash his face in! A few times, upon examining my own heart, I have found that that particular type of person has triggered long-forgotten animosities festering in my heart toward someone else. It was good to have those hidden feelings revealed so that friends could overcome them for me in prayer. I had been guilty of projectionism, which is what happens when an inner turmoil locates its enemy out there somewhere and projects its steam on some person who did not merit it at all. Thus I defiled him.

I knew in my spirit that the desire for violence, the desire to hit that guy, did not originate in me at all. Later, as I had opportunity to minister to him, I found that he percolated with violence. It wasn't that he wanted to inflict violence on anyone, but his spirit continually sent out signals to others to do violence to him! Such signals originate from a martyr attitude born of bitter-root judgments and expectancies to be struck and hurt by others. It was this attitude that emanated from him that defiled me and elicited those feelings and thoughts within me. When I say "defiled me,"

I use the phrase loosely. For no one can truly defile another. For as Jesus said, "What goes into a man's mouth does not make him 'unclean'...for out of the heart come evil thoughts" (Matt. 15:11, 19, NIV). Only the reaction that came from my heart could truly defile me. But I write this chapter so that you can recognize those times when others tempt you to react, and so "defile" you, so to speak, by handing you the means with which to defile yourself. Here's how it works: you sense and therefore feel what another is feeling. But, failing to discern that the feeling belongs to another, you interpret it as if it is your own feeling. Then you act upon it, and it becomes defilement.

Have we not all had occasions of being next to someone who radiated sexual uncleanness? Women tend to be more keenly aware of this than men. Many times wives have walked away from some chance meeting to fill their husband's ears with warnings about "that fellow," usually to the husband's bewilderment. "Hey, you just met that man! How can you know all that about him? Don't you think you're being a bit hasty and judgmental?" Later on he may discover that the fellow had seduced half the women in his office! She felt defiled in his presence. She knew, and fortunately she was able to discern it was someone else's lust, not her own, so real defilement did not occur. Wise husbands have learned to give some credence to such perceptions, at least to look for the outcropping of possible weeds in the garden.

Haven't we all met some people who instantly caused us to feel on guard? I remember hearing my friend who was a pastor raving about a teacher from another country who was teaching in his church. I was curious and strangely worried in my spirit. My friend sensed that and arranged for us to have breakfast with him and his traveling companion. I liked the teacher. My spirit could trust him. But what an evil presence radiated from his companion! My spirit sang out inside me almost audibly, "Enemy! Enemy!" I felt unclean inside myself in his presence, unsettled and wary. I knew him to be a wolf in sheep's clothing.

I warned my pastor friend, but he could not hear me. The teacher returned home. His companion stayed and ripped that congregation to shreds! According to him all art works and musical scores had to be thrown out of every home, unless they had the face or name of Jesus on them. They were of the devil. He pronounced curses over most of the congregation when they would not surrender to his wishes. Women in the congregation were told they would have uterine cancers if they disobeyed him or if they merely disagreed. The congregation finally rose up and threw him out, along with my pastor friend, unfortunately. But worse yet, nearly a third of the congregation, the babies in Christ, were "defiled" by his spirit and left with him to join him in delusion.

In this story we see the operation of the gift of perception of spirits on the basis of our spirit's ability to feel what is in the other, to sense and identify those things that can tempt one toward defilement. We may possess that gift purely from God, but it grows by experience.

> But solid food is for the mature, who because of practice have their senses trained to discern good and evil.
>
> —HEBREWS 5:14

The import of this story, however, is not to teach about the gift of discernment but the danger to those whose spirits are either not keen enough or not sufficiently mature to beware. That man in our story so infected and "defiled" the simple by his spirit that they found themselves thinking in ways and saying things they never would have allowed otherwise.

> Leave the presence of a fool,
> Or you will not discern words of knowledge.
> The wisdom of the prudent is to understand his way,
> But the folly of fools is deceit.
>
> —PROVERBS 14:7–8

> For a fool speaks nonsense,
> And his heart inclines toward wickedness,
> To practice ungodliness and to speak error against the LORD,
> To keep the hungry person unsatisfied
> And to withhold drink from the thirsty.
> As for a rogue, his weapons are evil;
> He devises wicked schemes
> To destroy the afflicted with slander,
> Even though the needy one speaks what is right.
>
> —ISAIAH 32:6–7

Incidentally, in about a year that man suddenly contracted intestinal cancer and was dead in six weeks! One thinks of Herod, who was eaten by worms (Acts 12:23), and the magician whom the Holy Spirit blinded through Paul on the island of Salamis (Acts 13:1–12).

The tragedy in my friend's church was one of defilement. As I had found myself thinking strange thoughts in the presence of the people in our first examples, so these people found themselves thinking in that wolf's ways. We are not speaking of hypnotic spells or of conscious thought-control techniques. That man himself was unaware that his spirit was being influenced by a demonic source, though he had learned to depend on his ability to influence people. Later we will return to expound about the devils behind the scenes. For now, we focus purely on what emanates from our own personal spirits. The immature Christians in that church lacked either perception or experience or were simply overwhelmed. They were unaware of what tempted them into defilement. They believed their thoughts were their own.

Early in our ministry, Paula and I served in a church in a small town that was the center of an agricultural area. The local banker held mortgages on nearly every business and farm in the community. He was also a member of our trustees board (in that denomination, trustees held the purse strings). Between meetings, individual trustees would come to me privately at night like Nicodemus to say of my ideas to start the church moving, "We know you are right, John. Come next meeting, you watch. We are going to be right with you." I am sure they meant it. They really intended to stand for the Lord and His servant. But what invariably happened was amazing to watch. The banker would enter the room, not saying a thing, and those trustees fairly fell over themselves to agree with his position! Money could rightly be said to be enough to explain the whole thing, but I knew something else was at work, because I felt it in my own being. I found my own thoughts tumbling and jumbling. Without a word being said, I felt the influence of his presence. It was strong. It tempted others. Of course it was not he alone. The god of mammon radiated through him. The men in the room sensed his feeling of confident self-assurance and misinterpreted it as their own feeling of confidence in him. I had to take hold of myself, center on Jesus, and meditate on His Word several minutes before my mind and heart would clear. Then I could see again where I stood and the rightness of it. My trustee friends were too new in Christ. They were not protected enough. They were carried away, "...tossed here and there by waves..." (Eph. 4:14). Could it be that St. Paul also meant by "waves" what teenagers at one time called "vibes"? Whether or not this is true, our trustees were constantly overcome by defilement.

Thank God it works the other way, too. Haven't we enjoyed visiting some people because we were refreshed by them? Don't some people somehow make us feel cleaner? I gave thanks to God for the little old "mothers in the Lord" He gave me in several congregations. When the "burden and heat of the day" (Matt. 20:12, KJV) would threaten to become too much, I would call on one or more of them, ostensibly to minister to them. The truth was I needed to visit with them a while to let their wholesome saintly presence wash through me. I could feel their chastised-by-life wholeness permeating their homes with peace. It hardly mattered if on the surface they seemed disturbed by some petty family problem and I could indeed minister to them, but it was their sweet spirits that cleansed me.

UNDERSTANDING DEFILEMENT

Defilement is a powerful force behind many of the sins of any people. But we do not write to cause people to be afraid to mingle. Far from it. We are overcomers, more than conquerors (Rom. 8:35–39). We teach to make aware. Wise ones learn spiritual hygiene. Often I have come home from ministry trailing clouds of little imps rather than Wordsworth's "clouds of glory." Paula and I have learned to pray this prayer, asking the Lord to cleanse us from all defilements:

> *Wash us clean, Lord, from whatever we may have picked up today. Lord, we release to You all the burdens and problems, and everything that entered or latched on to our spirits today. Cleanse us, Lord.*

It is amazing how a simple long hug from Paula chases wrong things away. It is as though through her spirit the Lord pours wholeness and such light that everything else simply flees from my spirit.

Sometimes in the night I am sure my spirit wars for the Lord. I think this is so for many who serve Him. Dreams are sometimes evidence of the warfare we have been engaged in during the night. It has been my experience to awaken brown and bugged, feeling like I want to shrug something off. Prayer helps and often fully cleanses, like taking a refreshing shower. Sometimes, however, I can't do it by myself, and prayer with Paula won't get it done either. If Paula puts her chest against mine (sans clothes) and just rests quietly, I feel the song of her spirit soaring through me. Pretty soon I'm all right again—and usually don't want to get out of bed quite yet! I hope I do sound a bit suggestive; I wish more couples would learn to refresh one another as God intended.

Paula and I are not different from anyone else. All people feel these defilements of which we have testified. The body of Christ needs to learn how to handle them by prayer and by the presence of loved ones.

A word of caution should be added. The Hebrew people were very much aware of defilements—too much aware. Old Testament law mentions many things that defiled and what to do about them—not at all repeated in the New Testament, which ought to tell us something! Many foods defiled (Lev. 11). Giving birth defiled (Lev. 12). Some diseases made people unclean (Lev. 13). Accidental or purposeful ejaculation defiled, and so did women's menstrual periods (Lev. 15). Immorality, idols, touching dead bodies—hundreds of things defiled. Jesus found Pharisees performing four hundred ablutions a day just to wash away defilements. The word *kosher* comes from those days of careful washings and preparations designed to avoid defilement. Simon the Pharisee was convinced Jesus was no prophet or He would have prohibited that woman of ill repute from defiling Him by touching His feet (Luke 7:36–50).

Jesus countered this by letting His disciples eat with unwashed hands and by teaching directly:

> "Not what enters into the mouth defiles the man, but what proceeds out of the mouth, this defiles the man." Then the disciples came and said to Him, "Do You know that the Pharisees were offended when they heard this statement?" But He answered and said, "Every plant which My heavenly Father did not plant shall be rooted up. Let them alone; they are blind guides of the blind. And if a blind man guides a blind man, both will fall into a pit." And Peter answered and said to Him, "Explain the parable to us." And He said, "Are you also still lacking in understanding also? Do you not understand that every-thing that goes into the mouth passes into the stomach, and is elim-inated? But the things that proceed out of the mouth come from the heart, and those defile the man. For out of the heart come evil thoughts, murders, adulteries, fornications, thefts, false witness, slan-ders. These are the things which defile the man."
>
> —MATTHEW 15:11–20

Once for all Jesus did away with exterior fears of defilement and consequent rituals to cleanse. No Christian need fear defilement from outside by *things*.

But as I said earlier, He retained warnings of inner defilements: "...out of the heart come evil thoughts, murders, adulteries, fornications, thefts, false witness, slanders. *These are the things which defile the man.*" Not what touches us from outside but what we *feel inside* and *do inside*, immorally or idolatrously, is what defiles.

Therefore, when we become aware that what is in the spirits of others can powerfully influence us, we need to counterbalance that with simple faith. We do not need to fear, only to pray away whatever we sense is invading our heart and mind through our spirit's involvement with others before our hearts have a chance to join them in their sin and thus become defiled. "Greater is He who is in you than he who is in the world" (1 John 4:4). Above all, Christians must not retreat from the world.

We must learn not to celebrate the strength of the flesh. When Paula and I first began to travel, we would enter a church, home, town, or area where we were to minister and soon discover many false currents. Sometimes there were streams of rancor and division because of what had been happening in the home, church, among the leadership, or waves of unbelief or scoffing from the audience. In the beginning and in our immaturity, we let that get to us. We would think, "There is no way we can minister here," or "This is going to be tough. I don't know whether we want to tackle this or not." We reaped according to the small measure of our faith. When we grew in faith to know in real terms that He *has* already won the victory, we realized that we were already victorious! In the beginning, we would pray up a storm and have a grand time chasing demons all over the place. It did clear the air, but it left us puffed up with ourselves in our soldierly power and quite distracted from the King of kings. We learned there is a better way to accomplish the same cleansing. We might, along the way, still say a short, "Clear the air, Lord," but that is relatively unimportant. We have learned that when we *know He has* already won the victory, *we carry that power with us.* He transmits it, and it flows through us. Now we ignore the devils and start praising Jesus. Pretty soon they can't tolerate that and depart, leaving Jesus with all the glory and them with none at all because nobody paid them any attention.

Nevertheless, let each soldier fight with whatever weapons he has faith to use, "...in accordance with the measure of faith" (Rom. 12:3, NIV). I am sure it was better to have battled as we did than to have abandoned the field altogether until we learned a better way. Sometimes today we still chase demons, but no longer because we are afraid they will get the better of us. We know the battle is the Lord's and the victory is His.

Sometimes I am tempted to be upset with brothers who begin every meeting by rebuking the devil and commanding him to leave; my spirit often sensed there was no need. The Lord reminds me then that my brother will grow beyond that as the Lord teaches him in His own time and way.

> And if on some point you think differently, that too God will make clear to you.
>
> —PHILIPPIANS 3:15, NIV

PROTECTION AND HEALING FROM DEFILEMENT

It is good to be aware of defilements for another reason, though, and this is to protect the unaware and the immature. St. Paul wrote most of his letters to protect the body from the defilements of the circumcision party. He wrote specifically to excise the corruption in Corinth through incest. (See 1 Corinthians 5.) Because we are members one of another, and when one suffers all suffer (1 Cor. 12:26), we know that immorality defiles all, and besides being a bad witness, could lead the weak into seduction. In 2 Thessalonians 3:6, he wrote to "keep aloof from every brother who leads an unruly life and not according to the tradition which you received from us." He did not want the weak contaminated by participation with uncleanness. One must remember, however, that abandonment of a brother is to happen only if all the other steps of Matthew 18 and Galatians 6:1 have been undertaken but the brother still refuses correction. We try first with everything in us to heal our brother before we abandon him to learn the hard way.

St. Peter wrote:

> For if after they have escaped the defilements of the world by the knowledge of the Lord and Savior Jesus Christ, they are again entangled in them and are overcome, the last state has become worse for them than the first. For it would be better for them not to have known the way of righteousness, than having known it, to turn away from the holy commandment delivered to them. It has happened to them

according to the true proverb, "A dog returns to its own vomit," and, "A sow, after washing, returns to wallowing in the mire."

—2 PETER 2:20–22

The word is that of an elder to protect the young in faith. We have that responsibility, even as in Ezekiel 33:1–6:

> And the word of the LORD came to me saying, "Son of man, speak to the sons of your people, and say to them, 'If I bring a sword upon a land, and the people of the land take one man from among them and make him their watchman; and he sees the sword coming upon the land, and he blows on the trumpet and warns the people, then he who hears the sound of the trumpet and does not take warning, and a sword comes and takes him away, his blood will be on his own head. He heard the sound of the trumpet but did not take warning; his blood will be on himself. But had he taken warning, he would have delivered his life. But if the watchman sees the sword coming and does not blow the trumpet, and the people are not warned, and a sword comes and takes a person from them, he is taken away in his iniquity; but his blood I will require from the watchman's hand.'"

We write, however, mainly about healing. Whether they come from people's spirits or demons, we are wounded by the influences that tempt us. When one recovers his way from defilement, whether he only felt it and took warning, dipped his toe, or took a fateful plunge, confession is the first step. We need to confess to the Lord our vulnerability. Listen to the wisdom of Isaiah when the glory of the Lord filled the temple: "Woe is me, for I am ruined!, Because I am a man of unclean lips, and *I live among a people of unclean lips*" (Isa. 6:5, emphasis added). Even if no iniquity can find a lodging place in us, we live in the midst of a "crooked and perverse generation" (Phil. 2:15). We still feel their corruption by being among them, and who knows if there is hidden sin in our hearts? It never hurts to confess, "I am unclean, Lord. Wash me." First John 1:8 says, "If we say that we have no sin, we are deceiving ourselves, and the truth is not in us."

Having confessed, we need to receive, to let forgiveness cleanse. St. John wrote, "If we walk in the light as He Himself is in the light, we have fellowship with one another, and the blood of Jesus His Son cleanses us from all sin" (1 John 1:7). Did the reader ever wonder, as we have, why St. John didn't simply say, "…as He Himself is in the light, and the blood of Jesus His Son cleanses us…"? Why mention "fellowship" in that context?

He said in verse 9, "If we confess our sins, He is faithful and righteous to forgive us our sins and to cleanse us from all unrighteousness." The context was forgiveness. Why did he place that seemingly irrelevant phrase about fellowship in that text? Because it is not merely the blood of Jesus that heals. The blood cleanses. But it is not the task of the blood alone to heal. It is fellowship that also heals and restores.

Remember when the woman touched the hem of Jesus's garment (Luke 8:40–48) and wanted to slink away unnoticed? She had been physically healed. But Jesus wouldn't let her escape. His questions made her come forward and confess her condition in a culture that regarded issues of blood as unclean! He wanted her to confess publicly why she was there! Her presence in the crowd had defiled everyone there. By biblical law she was not supposed to be there at all (Lev. 15:19–30). No wonder she wanted to keep her presence a secret. Why then did our gracious Lord make her embarrass herself like that, confessing in front of *everybody*? Because Jesus knew physical healing was not enough. He knew that whatever the embarrassment to her, she must be restored to the *fellowship* of her fellow citizens.* Only their acceptance and embrace could heal twelve years of suffering and ostracism! Let us hear the lesson, body of Christ. In ministry we must not stop with confession and application of the blood. That is redemption and restoration, but it is not yet healing. To be received with open arms, to be held and told words of love, is healing. We need arms and hands that touch and hold. When our mind hears wonderful, freeing words, our heart may still tremble and our spirit may still languish. Touch soothes the heart and restores the spirit. Tears of joy in fellowship tell us we are truly loved. That heals.

How much ought to be confessed, as in James 5:16, "to one another," and how much simply in private to Jesus alone is probably best told by the seriousness of involvement in sin, or by what it takes to make us whole again. Simple struggles in the heart can probably best be tossed off in flash prayers during the day. It is actions, especially those that have involved others, that need to be confessed in public. Most often, though, there is no need to say the names of others involved. Our confession should protect those who may not be ready for any degree of public disclosure.

---

* If He had not impelled her to come forward and confess before all, how would the community have known she was healed? Now, all knew Jesus had healed her physically, and acceptance in the fellowship of her community would heal her emotionally.

We can make nuisances of ourselves and wear out our friends if we think absolutely everything has to be talked out with someone. Martin Luther's confessor finally cried out in exasperation, "Martin, will you quit wearing me out with all these little peccadilloes? Go out and do some mighty sin and then come back here, but quit wearing me out with all this!"

Certainly, sexual sin must be confessed. So should violation of the law by theft, lying, and so on. These and similar things require oral confession. But our Lord can quietly cleanse simple sins of heart and thought as we go.

SEDUCTION AND WILLFUL DEFILEMENT

So far we have spoken only of inadvertent personal influences through the presence of others. Some people set out to seduce willfully, consciously. Whether into sex, theft, gambling, lying, or whatever, they not only want to persuade with words, but they also set out to influence spirit to spirit. They may be unaware of the power of their personal spirit, but they know they have influence, and consciously they try to use it. They want, as it were, to "weave a spell" over us. Countless times many of us have cleansed brothers' and sisters' hearts in church or by prayer ministry, only to see them overcome by seducers who purposely set out to defile them. St. Paul became so angry about this kind of thing while battling with the circumcision party that he cried out, "Would that those who are troubling you would even mutilate themselves" (Gal. 5:12). Haven't most of us who minister in any capacity experienced the same frustrations and angers? Temptation toward defilement is no rare thing. It is a part of every Christian's daily battle to walk God's way. We need to become more aware of defilement in order to snatch some from the fire (Jude 23).

St. Paul told us to admonish one another (Col. 3:16). Proverbs 27:6 says, "Faithful are the wounds of a friend, but deceitful are the kisses of an enemy." "Stripes that wound scour away evil, and strokes reach the innermost parts" (Prov. 20:30). Sometimes we must have courage to rebuke and "reprove them severely that they may be sound in the faith" (Titus 1:13). The trouble is, usually we become so agitated and tense about having to rebuke that by the time we muster up our courage to act, we blast a canary with a cannon! A word to the wise would have been sufficient, and we knew it, but we couldn't control ourselves enough to say only what was necessary. Or we can't summon enough fortitude, and we manage to fire only a BB against a bear! There is no other way to learn to rebuke rightly and wisely than to suffer the pain of trial and error. The body of Christ must learn. It really can't be taught from a "how-to" book. The Holy Spirit teaches by experience. We must simply plunge in and learn to do it.

It is seldom the one being influenced who needs a sharp rebuke. He requires warning and strength from us by love and acceptance. Maybe some talking *with*, not *at*, will help him see what he was already beginning to see anyway. *It is the tempter who needs the sharp rebuke!* I wish I had stepped in to sound off against that wolf in sheep's clothing in my friend's church. Perhaps my brother pastor would have been kept safe had I spoken not only to him but also to the wolf. Perhaps some would-be wolves would have been saved, too.

Whatever level of rebuke we undertake should be followed with healing hugs where possible. Lest we sound like apostles of embrace, I want to mention here that healing can take many other forms, such as sitting down to dinner together or playing a game of pinochle or golf. Once a brother pastor and I could not get along. So we went out to dinner together at the Clinkerdagger in Spokane. That restaurant has a balcony that hangs out over the Spokane River, providing a tremendous view of it cascading gloriously during spring runoff. We wanted to enjoy that scene while we were having dinner, but the waitress said, "I'm sorry, gentlemen, the only place I have left is the love seat." That is a two-seat bench table in front, affording the very best view of the river. Not thinking of anything else, we said, "Oh, good, we'll take it. That's just what we wanted!" She brought our order. When she returned to pour coffee, there we were, in prayer, holding hands! She was certain we were gay! When we saw the look on her face, we exploded in laughter. That conspiracy of humor, our private joke, we knew was the Lord's way of healing and knitting us together.

Demonic Influence and Defilement

Demons may be behind many influences that tempt us into defilement. We are not willing to say *all*. That not only gives Satan too much credit but also attributes to him an omniscience and ubiquitousness (knowing everything and being present everywhere) he does not have. Only our Lord has that.

When demons are a factor, it is usually easily discerned by those who are gifted by the Holy Spirit. The telling mark is the change in the people. When they misinterpret others' feelings as their own and act upon them, a demon can take advantage of this. So not only do they think and talk in ways foreign to themselves (which can happen solely by human defilement), but they also have a presence about them that is not their own. The timbre of their voice betrays something else acting in them. People influenced by people still seem somehow self-contained and in control of themselves, whereas people influenced or controlled by demons (not necessarily inhabited) enter a level of stridency or irrationality. One can almost see the demonic leaking out of the corners of their mouths. They sometimes come up with ideas and information you know they could not have thought of or known without help. It often happens that spiritually sensitive Christians discern the presence of something demonic by feelings of nausea or a sense of twistedness and oppression, which causes pain or pressure in the chest or head.

When demons are present in such instances, we commonly are not dealing with mere low-echelon spirits. It is "the world forces of this darkness...the spiritual forces of wickedness in the heavenly places" (Eph. 6:12) with whom we have to deal. Realization of this should cause us no fear. From the lowest imps of darkness to the devil himself, the least Christian has the victory easily, for "they overcame him because of the blood of the Lamb and because of the word of their testimony" (Rev. 12:11). Such movies as *The Exorcist* do us the disservice of teaching those of us who are weak that Satan has awesome power he in fact can no longer wield, except against those who do not know Jesus or Christians who give him that power by believing he has it.

Demons inhabit or influence people. *Principalities wield power*, usually *from outside people*, by turning the force of defiling currents upon them or setting up blockages. World rulers manipulate corporate mental strongholds of thought over people to control emotions and stifle freethinking. Such structures are typical ways of thinking within the mentality of mankind that are a part of the overarching fleshly tendencies we all share. Some common ones are racial prejudice, subjugation of women, greed, war and aggression, religious stereotypes, and false religious dogmas.

When people begin to practice ways of feeling and thinking that enter the field of a stronghold, opportunity is given to principalities to control them by enmeshing them in the web of such thought forms. Football players wear helmets to protect their heads from impact. To understand strongholds, one needs only to reverse the function of such a helmet. Instead of protecting our minds from harm, strongholds shield them from the light of God and prevent sane rationality. Instead of our minds being lined with padding to cushion them from blows, strongholds are themselves the blows from tentacles of defilement flowing through the corridors of the brain to chain and enslave the person to wrong thoughts and feelings.

Strongholds are devices by which principalities defile and control, under the tutelage of the world rulers of this present darkness. I hurt and ache when my brother can't wait to tell me the latest ethnic joke. I grieve not so much for the black people about whom these things are said, though of course such things wound any black brother and sister, but I grieve more for the imprisonment and defilement in the prejudiced brother's mind and heart. He has no idea of the extent of the invasion upon him. He possesses no awareness of the control that defilement has upon his life. Martin Luther King Jr. did wonders for African Americans in America, but he did probably greater service by far to the rest of us by leading the fight to break the bondages of defilement through the corporate mental stronghold of racial prejudice.

Do we not all yearn for our liberal brothers of the cloth who unwittingly spout doctrines of demons (1 Tim. 4:1)? They are defiled. Totally unaware of it, they have become mere puppets, spouting doctrines of foolishness, thinking these things are their own wise thoughts. The insidiousness of the defilement is that they think they alone possess the cleanness of truth, that those of orthodox faith are still trapped in yesteryear's defilements! Only the Savior, the Word, and the Holy Spirit set us free.

> Where the Spirit of the Lord is, there is liberty.
> —2 Corinthians 3:17

> For God hath not given us the spirit of fear; but of power, and of love, and of *a sound mind*.
> —2 Timothy 1:7, kjv, emphasis added

Many of our liberal brothers, mentally deprived and blinded, do not have life, thinking all the while that their mess of fleshly thoughts, which are actually wielded by the prince of the power of the air, are life. Only the Son is life.

You are from God, little children, and have overcome them; because greater is He who is in you than he who is in the world. They are from the world; *therefore they speak as from the world, and the world listens to them.*

It is mainly by corporate mental strongholds controlled through principalities that men are defiled, and their defilement defiles others in the world as they make the mistake of taking on these thoughts and feelings as their own.

Paula and I are not alone in having attended church conferences with high hopes, only to watch the conference gradually turn to rancor. After a while it took no great gift of discernment to see, as each speaker raised his voice more stentoriously in matters of discussion that didn't, in fact, amount to a hill of beans, that more than fallen humanity was expressing itself! Demonic powers defiled the assembly until they could raise their strident voices through the men who pridefully thought they were serving only the Lord's cause. The result was divisiveness, leaving men seeking their own tents to nurse petty grievances in isolation. Haven't most of us grieved to see such things? And haven't we all known that such futile dissensions over the law should be avoided (Titus 3:9), but all too often we couldn't stop ourselves when we too found ourselves drawn into the battle?

I (John) attended a denominational conference with a brother pastor (it could have been any denominational or nondenominational gathering). At the conference, one of the main speakers became more and more what he thought was anointed to call that group back to the good ways. These "good old ways" turned out to be fleshly traditions beyond which most of that body had matured. Mistaking zeal for anointing, he carried on more and more vehemently. Soon the entire audience was silently engaged in spiritual warfare. Some were rebuking the horde of defiling spirits that were coming over the audience. Others were loudly saying amen, caught up in his defilement and delusions, while their spirits wrestled with the disfavor they felt from all the others. The result was not edification and unity but rancor and division.

Positive "Defilement"

On the other hand, it works the other way. In a small town where Paula and I served for several years, there was a Roman Catholic priest with whom I became best buddies. It happened that he had a debilitating disease. His body became crippled, but his mind and spirit certainly did not. He soon had that place jumping. He could no longer drive, so sometimes I became his chauffeur. One time he wanted to go to a meeting of the entire priesthood of the Roman Catholic diocese of this particular state. The Roman Catholic bishop over this state was to be the main speaker. I enjoyed the dinner and then began to become strangely excited in my spirit as the meeting was to begin. I "knew" something was in the wind. Something great was brewing. Warfare was on, and the good guys were winning! I was too young then; I didn't have any part in the battle, but I could sense it was going on. Nothing out of the ordinary happened until the bishop stood up to speak. He said what was probably the ritual collect of the day, crossed himself, and began his talk by saying, "Brothers, I have news for you. On some points, Martin Luther was right!" The silence was deafening! Light was bursting everywhere!

Had the bishop spoken only in his flesh, he probably would have lost his congregation! But God had gone before. Angels and prayers of intercession had already claimed the victory. Jaws dropped open and eyes crossed for a moment, but hearts and minds did not close. They were *with* him. They were hearing, eagerly. He went on to teach all the fundamental facts of the gospel that Luther had rediscovered and said, "We were blind, brothers. We were blind." On the way out, I, probably the only Protestant pastor in that entire conclave, overheard group after cluster of priests muttering together, "Never thought I would ever hear a bishop of ours say things like that!" "How did he ever get up the courage?" But I felt no negative reactions. There may have been some negativity among some, but I am certain the majority were delighted with his word. Heaven had won a major victory. As John 15:3 says, "You are already clean because of the word which I have spoken to you." God's Word cleanses. But warfare in prayer opens ears to hear and eyes to see. Defilement blocks. Intercession prepares the way of the Lord in the desert. (See Isaiah 40.) (This is not at all intended as a criticism of the Catholic Church, which I love and among whom I often minister. I have seen Protestant strongholds of blockage broken open by the Lord. And that is the point: God is moving to break us out of defiling mental blockages. He loves unity.)

POLITICAL AND SOCIAL DEFILEMENT

Political demagogues spout streams of catch phrases designed to latch on to unthought-out demonic defilements over people. Hitler gained control of Germany that way, most likely unaware that he was himself a slave of dark powers. Lynch mobs in our southland were incited and controlled by the same kinds of inflammatory speeches, wielded from behind the scenes by principalities. In March 1984 our President Reagan was appalled to find congressmen and senators foolishly debating many irrelevant issues concerning his proposed amendment to allow prayer in public schools. He could not understand how men of logicality and the highest social and political standing in our nation could spout such irrelevant foolishnesses, and said so in a moment of commentary. Perhaps we *can* understand. World rulers wanted above all to block prayer. They concentrated energy to make foolish the wise. How? By wielding corporate mental strongholds of fear and control, by reaching into hidden latent childhood wounds and resentments against parents, teachers, pastors, and so on and connecting them to false places in the mind. Thus, they caused men of usual wisdom to be proud of their confused thoughts, and "professing to be wise, they became fools" (Rom. 1:22).

Here was a direct confrontation with powers of darkness concerning defilement in our time. Christians all over America were massed to pray as an intercessory army. We knew the battle was joined. Why did we not win? Because as Hosea 4:6 says, "My people are destroyed for lack of knowledge." God and His hosts will not invade and control; the Holy Spirit will not override anyone's free will. Powers of darkness will; it is their modus operandus. Who among us prayed as a warrior against the hosts of darkness over the nation's capital? I could wager that many did. But who directed the battle, sword of truth in hand, against the strongholds of thought control and the principalities who wielded it?

Teacher of this very thing that I am, one of the Lord's prophets who sees where the battle really is, who teaches others, knowing the battle was on, I forgot! Why? Defilement and demonic strategy. Paula and I found ourselves engaged in more pressing spiritual warfare here. I have no doubt that Satan purposefully distracted us and doubtless many others who could have seen and dislodged the demons' filthy hands. One almost could have heard Satan saying, "You and your troops run up there and keep all those intercessor types who really know how to do spiritual warfare occupied and distracted, lest they get onto our game there in Washington DC and put a stop to us." The moment I saw the newspaper announcing defeat, I knew what had happened. Satan had kept the knowledgeable warriors busy elsewhere while he won the victory there—temporarily.

Does this say he has power? No. Merely strategy. Delusion is his power, by defilement. In direct confrontation he flees.

> But resist him, firm in your faith.
>
> —1 Peter 5:9

> Submit therefore to God. Resist the devil and *he will flee from you.*
> —James 4:7, emphasis added

The devil wins whatever temporary victories are his by strategy, by bothering and distracting or lulling to apathy, above all by avoiding discovery. He knows he cannot win when Christians discover his presence and his tactics.

Sometimes he controls entire nations by defilement. Presently we are all watching how he manipulates Muslim extremists through religious fanaticism. Satan wields strongholds and fans emotional sparks by bonfires of hate and war, even as centuries earlier he caused Islamic warriors to sweep across Africa and into Europe, fired by zeal to convert or kill. That's defilement!

> How can a young man keep his way pure? By living according to your word....I have hidden your word in my heart that I might not sin against you.
> —Psalm 119:9, 11, NIV

One day I was puzzled at how so many Christians who know God's Word cover to cover can yet sin against Him again and again, and so easily it seems. So I asked the Lord to tell how this is so. He made me aware of the word *heart* and that His Word did not say His people laid it up in their *minds*, but they hid the Word in their *hearts*. So I asked Him, "How does the Word move from head to heart?" His reply was first just one word—*love*. He went on to teach me that only those whose awakened spirits *really love Him and who move out to love others in Him are those who truly laminate His Word to their hearts.* He said that until it is *lived in love*, His Word does not move from head to heart. He made it most clear to me that such love must be a direct meeting and cherishing of Him personally, "reclining on Jesus' breast" (John 13:23), or it does not bond Word and heart together.

How shall we resist becoming defiled by the world, the pride of life, and the lust of the eyes (1 John 2:16)? By letting Jesus love us. By soaking ourselves in His love, and then *pouring that love to others as a lifestyle twenty-four hours a day*! Those who selfishly want Him only for them-selves, only for the hope of heaven, will be defiled, again and again. But those who pour His love to others bond His Word to their hearts and sit, walk, and stand in Him.

We have insisted many times that we need the human embrace of fellowship in the body of Christ. We would never lessen or contradict that teaching. But it must be clearly understood that we cannot benefit fully from the body unless the Lord is the first love of our hearts. Some cannot find Him unless the body so loves as to enable their spirits to awaken and find. But if a child of God fastens on to the body of Christ and thinks that is enough, or for any reason will not let go and move on to Him, eventu-ally He Himself will sour the relation to all others. He is rightly a jealous God because He loves us. If we forget for a moment all the other insights we have shared so far and merely reflect, we will remember that it was at those times we let our love grow cold that we fell away or were tempted. It is that simple. However, for ability to enter warfare, in order to protect the weak, and to heal the wounded, we need to know all these other things.

DEATH WISHES

Now let us turn to speak of death wishes. We include death wishes in this chapter because it is the weight of defilement that one way or another lies behind every death wish.

Imagine the effect upon a pure and pristine spirit upon becoming part of this world's corruption! One way to envision the effect is to remember yourself taking your first ocean voyage or flying in a tiny airplane for the first time, caught in a thunderstorm, bouncing around wildly. Consider the nausea, the sickness. Remember the yearning to return to solid earth again. Recall how you cried out, "Oh, why did I come on this trip?" Remember how you hung over the rail or used the airsick bag and wished so fervently it were all over? How embarrassed you were. Even if you were not forced to flee to the restroom or use the airsick bag, remember how you did not want others to look too closely at you. You were sure they could see the bile splashing up behind your eyeballs! You were mortified. You kept telling yourself you would be OK after a while, if you would just hang on. If you can recall all that, you have only mildly described the feelings of your spirit in your first moments and days bouncing around in the womb in the midst of the defilement of the world!

In homes where children are longed for and loved, reception begins to heal first frights and nauseas, even in the womb. When traumas surround and invade the womb—fighting, bickering, loud noises, and hurtful emotions—the spirit of the child cannot overcome the nausea of the general defilement we all suffer by being here in this sickened world. The result is the cry, "Stop the bus! I want off!" We don't want to be here. Our mind may not know that, but that has become our spirit's determination. We have become determined to die because that is the only other option to having to live all the way through what has become to us an unbearable world.

Death wishes once settled into us manifest themselves in many ways. First, they may be the underlying cause behind abnormally dangerous and tenacious childhood diseases. The personal spirit does not sustain the body normally or easily throw off disease because it doesn't want to. It wants to act out our death wish. Our impulses run counter to themselves. Many parents have come to us for counsel and prayer, distraught and fearful because their child or children are either constantly ill or tremendously accident prone. We always want to know the family history: Did the child come as an afterthought, or was the conception desired and sought? How did the pregnancy proceed? Was it a difficult time physically for the mother? How did the parents relate to each other during the pregnancy? What economic, job-related, or other pressures were on the parents? Were there any great tragedies, deaths, or other traumatic happenings during that time? What kind of birth experience was it? Were other children jealous of the new baby, or did they welcome the child? Was there postpartum depression? Did any tragedies or traumas happen shortly after birth? And so on.

Most of the time we find readily identifiable causes behind death wishes in infants. These can be healed, as we have discussed in previous chapters.

We do not grow out of death wishes and leave them behind. If they are not dealt with, they remain, awaiting only the right triggers to send sickness and trouble pulsing through life.

Death wishes affect coordination and confidence. Some people go through life haltingly. Some look pinched, as though life has never been full of zest and gusto. Some people have haunted looks in their eyes, which say to my heart, "I'm in here somewhere; won't someone please come and lead me out to life?" Some have wistfulness in their eyes. Consciously they want to live, but they can't find the turn-on switch. Death wishes are one form of inner vow ("I choose not to live").

Paula has a body naturally built for athletics. But she too suffered an early spiritual confusion. Hers was not first a death wish. Rather, it was a message, as related earlier, that she had no right to live. What that caused was an athletic blockage. Instead of stepping into a tennis swing wholeheartedly, she held back so that her body was always out of position. Her swing would then be an awkward, lunging swat rather than an easy, coordinated stroke. Her body position always took power from her swing, so that she was never properly behind and flowing through any athletic movement. I used to watch in puzzlement as it seemed she wasn't able to throw herself into the game, only role-playing. In 1983 a dear friend ministered to the depths of her spirit, finding she had been deeply wounded in the womb. At once the mystery was resolved. She had felt she had no right to be here. That became a death wish—hidden, but by that even more powerfully able to affect her coordination. Her spirit had enjoyed no freedom to flow into fun and games. That robbed her body of its natural coordination. Now she is learning in playing tennis to step into a swing with her whole being. And she is enjoying aerobics classes. It is a joy to watch her becoming more "here," with her spirit flowing through her body in athletics.

Being an athlete and a prayer minister who is gifted with discernment, I watch the way people move. I observe how their mental intentions flow into athletic exertions. I study the way people walk, how they hold themselves, the "tells" in their hands and body positions. Once one takes hold of this key of early death wishes, it becomes amazing how easily one can learn to detect their operation in people's movements. Particularly one can see it in the overly controlled, pinched walk of mother-dominated people. One can see how they have never been free to let go and flow freely into life. There have been too many checks and rules. Movements are therefore curbed and cribbed. They have no abundant life. Every body movement and posture proclaims that fact.

Death wishes affect voice tones. I can hear in the way a man sings whether his spirit has been free to choose life. Some so lack authority they rob their diaphragm of power. Or they place the sound in wrong places on the palate and so sound ineffectual, breathy, breathless, or childish. Some sound hard and thin. In trained voices it is much more difficult to detect what is in the personal spirit. Their coaches have worked on those deficiencies. Untrained voices still manifest what conditions hamper or aid volume, pitch, and intensity. When one catches the keys, such perceptions lose mysticality and become easy common sense.

Death wishes are often behind "losers." We mean the kind of person who should have everything going for him, mentally, emotionally, and athletically, but who somehow frequently manages to snatch defeat from the jaws of victory. Such people proceed to the brink of success but no further. At the moment when it seems a breakthrough to success cannot possibly be thwarted, something happens. Either they do something foolish, or from some unlooked for, seemingly impossible direction, something blocks or destroys. Often the entire project crumbles. Wise men build securely on strong foundations; the foolish build on sand. (See Luke 6:46–49.) The difficulty is that these people do not consciously know what is the area of sand on which they have built.

Self-fulfilling loser tendencies

Not every propensity to lose has a death wish behind it. We can have self-fulfilling loser tendencies from parents' words like, "You'll never amount to anything," which our heart has believed and continues to act out, or from excessive performance orientation, or from many other quirks in our character. One man I ministered to who kept losing just when victory seemed imminent had a father who continually failed. The root in this son was that something in him had accepted a lie that he must never outperform his father! Therefore he unconsciously continually sabotaged himself.

On another day I visited with a young man whose parents had conceived him out of wedlock and were forced to marry because he was on the way. He had been born with his belly burst open around his umbilical cord. Questioning revealed that he had received the message that he was an unwanted burden and ought to die so the parents could be free to enjoy life. That death wish had manifested itself first in his physical condition at birth and then in an inability to take hold of his powers to accomplish.

Again and again he had nearly flunked out or quit projects when he possessed the mental ability to be at the top of his class. His death wish continually robbed his conscious mind of power to achieve.

Death wishes and sexual fulfillment

Death wishes most commonly affect sexual fulfillment. At taproot level, such people have never accepted being bodies. They view their bodies as necessary evils to be put up with so long as they still have to be here. They may learn to engage in sexual activity with their mate, whether for duty or whatever amount of enjoyment they have attained. But the glory is far from them. Their spirit is not free to cascade gloriously through every cell to ravish the other with love and joy. Usually people who have hidden death wishes tell us they would rather not be bothered sexually. Akin to slumbering spirits, they also cannot meet the other through their body.

Talents dwarfed by death wishes

As with slumbering spirits, those who have hidden death wishes also have dwarfed talents. The spirit may be awake but unfree to engage and venture life. I often am caused to see such people visually in prayer as frosted buds, unable to burst open the sepals and unfold to full bloom. In prayer the Holy Spirit often enables me to see the Lord causing the person to bloom gloriously. I watch and describe aloud to the person as their bud becomes a beautiful flower. Such people need a great deal of encouragement to continue to expand and choose life as they are set free.

Everyone who has a hidden death wish has anger at God in the depths of his spirit. His mind may be so unaware as to be affronted at the very idea that anyone could be angry with God. Behind this is the common delusion that the object of our anger must deserve it for us to be angry. Of course God doesn't deserve our anger, but that does not keep us from it. Proverbs 19:3 says, "The foolishness of man subverts his way, and his heart rages against the LORD." We may be angry with God for separating us from Him, for putting us in this messed-up earth, for letting us fall, for "not being there" when we needed Him in the womb. Of course He was there, but our angry hearts could not believe He was.

How to Detect a Death Wish at Work in Someone's Life

When we want to detect a possible death wish and/or we want to convince someone that he really is angry with God, Paula and I use the following series of questions. These questions are not to be answered by long thought but by the first feeling or thought that comes to mind. If a question cannot be answered without a long time to think, that itself is already a telling answer.

I usually explain that although traditionally the church has believed that we began at conception, for the purpose of this series of questions, let's imagine that we existed in the heavens. All questions are to be answered silently if the person so wishes. We will discuss them later.

1. Suppose we are sitting in a group in a heavenly place enjoying the angels and the saints. The Lord enters and says, "I would like three or four volunteers to go to Earth." Would you have been one of the volunteers?

2. If Jesus presented Himself before you, said your name, and asked, "Will you go to Earth for me?" would you have responded, "Oh, boy, yes, Sir, right away. Hallelujah!" or "OK (drat!)"?

3. If you had to come to Earth but were given your choice, would you choose the time and place in which you were born or some other century or country?

4. Would you choose to be born to your parents or some other?

5. Would you choose your father? Or some other father? Your mother?

6. Would you choose to be a boy or a girl?

7. Would you choose your face? Your body? Your mind? Your character and personality?

8. If you are a woman, are you beautiful? Pretty? Attractive? Desirable? Loveable? Would someone choose you? Should

they? If you are a man, are you handsome? Good looking? Attractive? Desirable? Loveable? Would someone choose you? Should they? Should you feel sorry for your spouse that he (or she) chose you?

9.   Do you like you?

10. If Jesus walked up to you in the present moment and said, "I'll give you your choice. You can either go all the way through life or straight up to heaven with Me right now," which way would you go?

As we ask these questions, the Lord tunes in our spirit to the other's spirit and causes us to sense by empathy what he really feels. Sometimes people are incapable of being fully honest. We may sense more accurately than they can express what they actually would have answered.

After completing the list, we say, "In whatever degree you would not have volunteered for life on Earth or would have agreed only reluctantly to come; in whatever degree you would not have chosen your time and place or either or both of your parents, or you would not have chosen the sex you are; in whatever degree you would not have chosen your face, your body, your mind or temperament; in whatever degree you do not think you are beautiful or handsome, loveable, or chooseable; in whatever degree you don't love you, to that degree you are angry with God. You are saying inside that He could have done a better job creating you. In whatever degree you would choose to go straight to heaven rather than live life here, you are telling God you don't like it here."

In prayer ministry, to help people understand, we may use an analogy, such as, "Suppose you prepare for your child a beautiful nursery full of toys and interesting things and put him in it, but five minutes later he comes running out and says, 'I don't like it in there.' How would you feel as a parent? Are you pleased? Are you honored? Are you dishonored?" We can then add, "Do you see that when we do not like the earth, which is our nursery, and we do not want to stay here, we dishonor the gift Father God gave us?"

Or, "Suppose you give your child a little red wagon. He isn't too happy with it and seldom plays with it. If he does, he leaves it upside down in the snow. How do you feel as a parent? Are you honored or dishonored? But suppose (something entirely fictitious) he loves it so much that he takes other children for rides in it, washes it, waxes it, and puts it in the garage. Now how do you feel as a parent?" Some have laughingly said, "Soaped," realizing how few children would be that responsible. All, however, get the point. Such behavior honors the giver. So we say, "The news we have for you is that you, in your body, your mind, your face, in every way you are, you are the little red wagon God has given you. If you do not love it and care for it, you dishonor God. You are angry with God for what He created you to be."

> Thou shalt love thy neighbour *as thyself.*
> —Mark 12:31, KJV, EMPHASIS ADDED

We cannot do one without the other.

Many might respond, "If all I got was a lovely nursery or a shiny new wagon, I could have accepted it. But for me it was more like a nursery that was trashed and a wagon that was broken." Many have been beaten, molested, or neglected by parents who should have loved them. I am not saying they should have chosen that! But however damaged the "nursery" might be, it and you are still God's creation. He created this earth. He did not create the damage. Is not what God created worth enduring whatever pain is inflicted upon it? Is light not greater than darkness? A person with a death wish is one who rejects not only the harm inflicted upon His creation but also creation itself.

"FORGIVING" GOD

One of the most strikingly overlooked aspects of our faith is our need to be reconciled to God. We seem to think that we should never be angry with God because He of course does not deserve it. More importantly we think that there is no way we could forgive God because He has not done anything wrong. We forget how many times we have mistakenly held things against others who never did what we thought they did, and yet we needed to forgive them. Forgiving them did not mean that they had done something requiring forgiveness, only that we needed to clear our own hearts. Just so in the matter of being reconciled to God. He is not to blame, but that did not keep us from pouting at Him, and it must not keep us from forgiving Him.

The early church had little confusion about "forgiving" God. St. Paul wrote incisively about it, as a command:

> Now all these things are from God, who reconciled us to Himself through Christ, and gave us the ministry of reconciliation, namely, that God was in Christ reconciling the world to Himself, not counting their trespasses against them, and He has committed to us the word of reconciliation. Therefore, we are ambassadors for Christ, as though God were entreating through us; we beg you on behalf of Christ, be reconciled to God.
>
> —2 CORINTHIANS 5:18–20

Note, St. Paul did not only say, as we might expect, "reconciled Himself to the world," as though all that was needed was that He should forgive us. It is true that He did need to forgive us; He accomplished that in Jesus Christ. Here, however, the context makes it clear St. Paul was speaking of both sides, God forgiving man and being reconciled to man, and man "forgiving" God and being reconciled to Him. Paul says, "We beg you on behalf of Christ, be reconciled to God."

If we could have voiced our cry in the vertiginous nausea of earth-sickness as we came out of heaven into this corrupted world, our cry in the womb would have been, "God, how could You? I didn't bargain for this! You didn't tell me it would be this hard! Where are You?" Or, "Lord, You sent me here with a job to do for You (Eph. 2:10), and then You put me in this messed-up family, and now I'm all mixed up! I can't even remember what I was supposed to do. Now how can I do the job? And how is that fair?" Or, "Where were You when I needed You? No conscientious earthly father would have let his child fall this far without doing something about it. Don't You care?" Never mind that He does care and has acted at horrendous cost to Himself. At the moment we are far from able to believe that.

We suggest the reader tackle reading both Job and many of the psalms with an eye open to the honesty of their cries before God. Try Psalm 88 for honesty of description; this is how far I have sunk, Lord, "I am set apart with the dead...whom you remember no more, who are cut off from your care" (v. 5, NIV). Read Psalm 44:9 for honest complaint, "Yet Thou hast rejected us and brought us to dishonor..." or Job, contending with God:

> But I would speak to the Almighty, and I desire to argue with God....Though He slay me, I will hope in Him. Nevertheless I will argue my ways before Him....Only two things do not do to me, then I will not hide from Thy face: remove Thy hand from me, and let not the dread of Thee terrify me. Then call, and I will answer; or let me speak, then reply to me. How many are my iniquities and sins? Make known to me my rebellion and my sin. Why dost Thou hide Thy face, and consider me Thine enemy?
>
> —JOB 13:3, 15, 20–24

Job's complaint is the cry of everyone, of our own spirits before God, if we only knew it. Every one of us has stored resentment against God. It is not very acceptable to think angry thoughts at God, so we won't admit we have them. But they are there.

It is this hidden storehouse that serves as access to demonic powers to defile us. It is for this reason we have placed defilement, devils, and death wishes in one chapter. Defilement from outside, from people, from things, or from devils, cannot lodge in us unless it finds interior fertile soil. Here is the soil of birth for all manner of evil in all of us, these hidden thoughts that, after all, God is unjust and uncaring—and we may say, "At least for me, whatever He may be for anyone else—or He would not have put me here in this situation of my life and left me in it! It isn't fair!"

Perhaps the most basic thing we can do in prayer ministry is lead people into prayers of "forgiving" God and being reconciled not only to Him but also to being who they are themselves. Every person needs to accept being what God has created him to be.

RECONCILING WITH SELF

Many years ago, Paula, our son Loren, and I conducted a seminar in Spokane especially for professional prayer ministers. Its purpose was to teach professionally trained people how to minister in Christ through forgiveness and death on the cross. Many clergymen, psychiatrists, and psychological prayer ministers attended this seminar. As was our custom, we divided the attendees into small groups so that immediately after each teaching, they could delve into each other with freeing ministry in prayer. They were to learn by putting into practice what had just been taught orally. We have done this with many groups and found it most effective. Usually people have leaped into honest confessions, prayers, and tears for one another with great healing results. To our chagrin, we found that these people could not and would not open up honestly to one another. Here were professionals whose daily occupation was to listen to counselees opening to them to confess lurid details frankly and honestly. It was their business to hear confessions. But these same prayer ministers could not open up and confess honestly to one another!

For several days I puzzled and grieved before the Lord. What was the matter? Then the Lord revealed the answer. It was not, as I had supposed, professional reserve and jealousy. This group had in it more than the usual number of people who absolutely could not accept themselves. Not liking what they found themselves to be as infants and children, they had struggled and hastened to grow up. They had worked hard to escape from being that child they had been. That struggle to mature had brought them to the place where they could help others. No way were they willing to look back! In some ways confession involves making oneself a child again, being vulnerable and open, trusting as a child trusts. They could not confess to one another (though they insisted that others do so to them every day) because they were adamantly unwilling to enter the risk of being childlike again, but God's Word says, "Whoever does not receive the kingdom of God like a child shall not enter it at all" (Luke 18:17).

We led the group through the above list of questions. Their answers were nearly unanimous. They did not like themselves. They would not have chosen to come to Earth. They saw that they were angry with God for creating them. They realized they had been unable to accept themselves.

Herein lies an important evangelical and theological point. We saw by this experience with those professional prayer ministers that many Christians have accepted Jesus as Lord and Savior precisely to escape being what they are, not to accept themselves as redeemed children of God.

It is OK to want to change. Jesus does come to transform us. But these people had missed the crucial first step. Jesus had come to them and accepted them just as they were, without change. The sweetest meaning of Jesus's being born in a filthy and smelly stable is that He comes into us at our worst, accepting us before we change in any way, "even when we were dead in our transgressions" (Eph. 2:5). These people had missed that. They were not about to accept that awful child they had once been. They had used Jesus and the cross to escape.

We asked these prayer ministers to imagine that runny-nosed, mess-in-the-diapers, screeching little kid they had been, standing tear-streaked in front of them, and to reach down and take that little one into loving arms. Not to clean him up first and then love him, but to hold and comfort him just as he was. We made sure they were not allowed to improve that little person in any way in order to love him. They were to love him and accept him as Jesus had, just as he was, without change. If he would never become any better, they would still love and cherish him.

We led them through a process of repentance. We asked them to pray this prayer:

> *Lord, we repent for rebelling against being born here on Earth where You put us. We repent for not liking and accepting what You created us to be. We repent for rejecting Earth and ourselves and all of Earth's experiences. We couldn't trust Your lordship and that You knew what You were doing. We confess our animosity toward You, Lord Jesus Christ, and Father God, for creating us and putting us here, and we let go of our bitterness. Reconcile us to Your fatherly goodness. We repent for rejecting ourselves. We accept our bodies. Reconcile us to ourselves. Reconcile us to our time and place, our position in this earth. Thank You, Jesus.*

That seminar turned from the worst to the greatest in one session! People broke through everywhere into genuine joy to be alive, to be here in the body, and to be children of God on Earth. It affected health, coordination, outlook on life, marital relations, sex, ability to worship, simple enjoyments like food and play, and so on. Some went home to look for old pictures of themselves as children with the intent to reinforce the prayers already said with more precise imagery and more effective acceptance of themselves.

We had found an important key. How many millions of people are there who have tried to grow up too fast because they wanted to escape being a snot-nosed kid? One can never make it that way. That "unacceptable" kid continually makes trouble in the heart. We do immature and foolish things because within us part of us has not grown up. Psychologists speak of this as fragmentation, or lack of integration, and as dated or fixed emotions. St. Paul spoke of it as "a different law in the members of my body, waging war against the law of my mind, and making me a prisoner of the law of sin which is in my members" (Rom. 7:23). We are at war with ourselves because part of our inner being throws tantrums at not having been accepted. First Corinthians 13:11 says, "When I was a child, I used to speak as a child, think as a child, reason as a child; when I became a man, I did away with childish things." We can never do away with childish things by stuffing them away to hide them, by pretending they aren't there, or by scrambling to cover them. We must accept ourselves with the same compassion and unconditional love the Lord has for us. Then we will be able to present ourselves nakedly, trusting Him, acknowledging our sin. It is only as we are "rooted and grounded in love," in His love which "surpasses knowledge," that we can grow into full maturity (Eph. 3:14–19).

So very many Christians want to use salvation to escape from being what they were, whereas Jesus would have us forgive ourselves and accept ourselves just as He has. That is not only redemption; it is inner integration. One little lady to whom I was ministering could not stop being immature and foolish until she saw her hatred for her own inner child and decided with me in prayer to receive her and love her. She had been bothered by inner voices that would not go away. For me, the temptation had been to cast away a foreign spirit. In this instance, that was not required. Once she accepted her own person, I asked, "Where are the voices?"

"Gone, Pastor. I am at peace." In this case, the voices had not been demonic; they had only been a way her inner child could throw tantrums for attention.

Behind all such inner turmoils are death wishes. When we cannot receive and love our child within, that easily becomes a death wish. Satan finds in that rejected little one fertile soil for his seeds of defilement. That battle is over when we join Jesus in loving and accepting ourselves just as we were, in every moment of our life.

It goes without saying that behind every suicide attempt, however manipulative, is nevertheless a death wish. The successful have only managed to act out what their inner spirit wanted all along—escape.

Once we detect the presence of a hidden death wish, we overcome it by prayer ministry. "Do you want to be whole? Do you choose life?" We ask the person to say it, decisively, even as Jesus so often asked those who came to Him to declare what they wanted. We ask Jesus to minister to the child within, wooing him to life. We take up authority to break whatever inner vows not to live may have been formed. We pray for integration of spirit, heart, mind, and body, that all inner parts may accept and work harmoniously with each other. We pray for bodily coordination, that the spirit may flow freely into action unimpeded through all parts of the body. We ask the person to exercise an ongoing discipline of daily choosing life.

It is amazing what such simple ministry accomplishes. Our files are full of letters from persons testifying to new freedom to enjoy the abundant life Jesus came to give. We are confident the body of Christ can easily learn to discern defilements, to see how principalities wield defiling corporate mental strongholds, and to see how these things create and then work through death wishes. We can set one another free!

CHAPTER 6

IDENTIFICATIONS AND SHRIKISM

For lack of wood the fire goes out, and where there is no whisperer, contention quiets down. Like charcoal to hot embers and wood to fire, so is a contentious man to kindle strife. The words of a whisperer are like dainty morsels, and they go down into the innermost parts of the body. Like an earthen vessel overlaid with silver dross are burning lips and a wicked heart. He who hates disguises it with his lips, but he lays up deceit in his heart. When he speaks graciously, do not believe him, for there are seven abominations in his heart. Though his hatred covers itself with guile, his wickedness will be revealed before the assembly. He who digs a pit will fall into it, and he who rolls a stone, it will come back on him. A lying tongue hates those it crushes, and a flattering mouth works ruin.

—PROVERBS 26:20–28

A woman came to us, bringing her husband. Her problem, she said, was that she could not stop ruling the roost. Her husband would never rise up to stop her. She dominated him completely but was tired of it. She said she could never rest in him, and she wanted to. Could we find the cause and set him free to be a man?

It did not take long to discover that he had been raised by a controlling mother and older sisters. He was accustomed to being dominated. It was the way he had learned to identify love. Now, if his wife bossed him around, he knew she cared for him. The role was familiar and comfortable, though demeaning. That was the price one paid for peace and love.

Her father, as one would suspect, was a weak man, dominated by her mother. Neither parent could show affection. Both were controlled by performance orientation. But the father was a gentle and kindly man, whose feelings were constantly lacerated by her mother's vicious tongue. From the age of six until she left home at eighteen, her most vivid memory of her father was that from time to time he would come to her and begin to tell her of the awful things her mother had said to him. He would break down and cry and put his head on her shoulder and she would comfort him. This was the only physical experience of love she knew. It became her identification of love, that of being a strong woman to comfort a weak man.

As she matured she became such a beautiful woman that she won a major beauty contest in one of our eastern states. At forty-plus she still retained such striking beauty, she could have won a Miss America competition. In her twenties she went to work for a leading sports figure. In that position she met many of America's top athletes. Her beauty won her many dates with men of great physical stature and strong character. Somehow she could never become romantically interested in any of them, though they pursued her ardently. Then she met the man who became her husband. He was about the same height as she, was not athletic, not broad-shouldered, but was gentle and kind. It happened that recently he had been jilted by his fiancée whom he had loved dearly. His heart was broken. On the first date, as he began to share his hurt, he cried, and laid his head on her shoulder.

Who could miss seeing what happened? She identified love! He needed her. Now she could know herself as a loving woman comforting a weak man. None of the strong men had been able to trigger into that identification. She had no built-in ways of relating to strong men who didn't "need" her. This familiar role she could identify, accept, and walk in with a sense of worth and belonging. So she married him.

Need relationships are never stable or permanent. Participants realize eventually that they want more than to be needed, or the weak one develops enough gumption to want to change. The strong one then has to learn to relinquish that role or be upset and displaced. Warfare ensues. Old roles must die. New bases for relating must be found. Some marriages survive, especially those in which Jesus is Lord. Most relationships based on need fracture as individuals mature because they cannot accept the changes that have occurred. The mate may not be able to give up the old identifica-tions and consequent roles, nor can he or she appreciate the new.

My (John's) task as a prayer minister was to make this wife aware of her need for her husband to be weak. I explained to her how she had learned to identify herself as a loving person by ministering to a weak man and asked her whether she could face the fact that she really did not want him to be strong, though she thought she did. She protested vigorously that she was tired of the whole thing, that she wanted nothing so much as for him to be strong for her, but I could see that her heart was far from what her mind believed. In no way, by teaching and counsel, could I cause her to see what she was actually in her heart determined to maintain.

So I did what prayer ministers have learned to do in such situations: I started a fight! We know how to ask a few questions, well aware that the answers will provoke a battle. In the ensuing argument, what is truly the inner content of the heart will often surface. The prayer minister can see behind masks then to what actually transpires between the couple. Sure enough, this pair was soon at it hammer and tongs. Before long his sensitive heart broke and he wept. Instantly her entire mood and behavior changed. She had what her heart wanted. She became the comforting strong one, taking his head on her shoulder, crooning sweet things to him.

"There," I cried. "Do you see it? Do you see what you just did? You weren't satisfied until you reestablished the kind of relationship in which you could identify yourself as loving. You needed him to be the weak one who cries so you could be the strong one to comfort him. Do you see that though a part of your mind and heart wants him to be strong for you, the ruling part of you is determined not to allow that?"

"Oh, yes, John. I see it. I see it. Oh, what am I going to do?" she said.

There followed much counsel and prayer for the transformation of the inner man. She needed to see her family's generational pattern of domi-neering women and weak men. She needed to confess her hatred of both her father and mother and be forgiven. Most of all, she needed to haul that false identification of love to death on the cross. He needed to see the same things in his family patterns: his own hatred of his father for being weak and of his mother for domineering, likewise his sisters, and his own false identification of love and the false comfort of abdicating leadership.

Paula and I want to point out two things of spirit and resultant char-acter structure: the power of identifications and shrikism.

PACKAGES OF LOVE

As our spirit encounters life, it seeks nurture. As babies instinctively search for a nipple and learn to suckle, so our spirit seeks touches of love. God has designed us so that our spirits find love and thus power to live through warm physical affection. He Himself flows through us in His Spirit when we give and receive affection. The primal drive of our spirit is to find and live in the way for which it was created.

When we do not receive expressions of affection, which are food and nurture to our spirit, we latch onto whatever substitute we can find. We then identify love not by affection and openhearted interplay of "I—thou" interchange spirit to spirit, but by whatever form love seems to take. It is as though we latch onto the package rather than the contents. If we can't have the true contents, the package becomes all-important. Since the form love comes in replaces love itself, and never satisfies, we must secure more and more. It's like buying a candy bar, only to throw away the candy and eat the wrapper! It never satisfies.

For this reason, plus what we all inherit in Adamic sin, love in all of us becomes something warped and twisted. All "love" that has not died on the cross and been born anew is use, manipulation, exploitation, demand, and control! The world honors love and ideally accepts all forms of love as good. Father love, mother love, mate love, filial love, neighborly love, and so on—all are accepted as beneficial. But none are pure. All unregenerate love is carnal and sick.

There is only one letter's difference between mother love and *smother* love. That *s* dies only with surrender to Christ on the cross. Our Adamic inhuman character causes us to pervert love to its opposites. *True love lays down its life for others, but unregenerate love lays down the lives of others for itself.* A father who thinks that because he loves he is encouraging his son to play football or his daughter the violin may in fact be squelching the life of his son or daughter, whose talents may lie elsewhere. A mother who interferes with her daughter's marriage because "I just love her too much to see her suffer" may in fact destroy her daughter's life for her own image of motherhood, under the false name of "love."

As each girl grows, her life with her father and other primary males builds into her images of what a man who loves her should do and be. Those subliminal images define to her what love and hate are. That set of images (especially as it is composed of forms love came in—the candy wrapper—rather than affection itself) and her drive to have those images fulfilled spell captivity rather than freedom for her mate. The same for a boy with his mother. He too owns a set of prerequisites his wife must fulfill. *True love sets the other free to become all he or she can become. Unregenerate love imprisons the other so that he cannot become who he is.* For example, a girl may have learned that her father would make all her decisions and bail her out of all problems. In effect, that way of loving may have smothered her life. She may have resented it, but it is the only package by which she has learned to identify love from a man. She may marry a wise and free man who instinctively senses when her demands would reduce her to being a child curled up on her daddy's lap. He insists she make her own decisions and stand to the consequences. She may interpret that which is true love as unlove and rejection. Unless he is very strong in himself, her "packages" can prevent him from expressing his own wisdom and thus act out the roles she unconsciously sets for him. We sense what the other wants. When there is no freedom not to be that for fear of seeming to reject, "love" imprisons.

One wife who came to us reported that her father was a hardworking farmer. He arose early and labored in the fields until sunset. He was a kind and loving man, but after his evening meal he would tumble exhaustedly into bed, so she hardly ever saw him. The one time he was truly present for her was when she would become ill. He would postpone his chores, stay home, and fix delicious chicken soup for her. He would sit by her bed, put his warm strong hand on her forehead, speak reassuringly to her, and linger until he was satisfied that she was all right. That was how she grew to identify love, according to the only package in which it came. She learned to wallow in such attention, milking every headache and fever for all it was worth.

Naturally, she married a workaholic like her father, kind and gentle but gone most of the time. The first time she developed a migraine, she went to bed and waited for the chicken soup, but it never came. She remonstrated and called out for help, but her young husband only said, "You're a big girl now; take some aspirin. You'll get over it." Then he left for work.

She was devastated! "This man doesn't love me!" Of course he did, and her mind accepted that within a few months, but it took her heart years to learn to recognize and receive as real love what he had to give in his own way. She had to consciously bring to death in prayer the power of what that childhood "package" had trained her heart to identify as love. She had to walk in a discipline of choosing to believe that she was loved, until the

Lord developed within her new eyes with which to see and interpret her husband's unique expressions of caring for her.

Countless images in our hearts form the package of love—for me, the way Mom cooked a meal, took care of me when I was ill, ironed clothes, stored them in the right dresser drawers, played the piano, got us ready for school, packed lunches, saw to it that our hair was combed, even the "spit baths" in the car several blocks from our destination and the "unnecessary" worrying over cuts and bruises, bothersome as they were, spelled love. All these things and countless others formed the package Paula had to fit or I believed she didn't love me—except for the spit baths!

Paula's father was strong, present when he was home, loving, witty, and caring. By the time her mind was formed, he was wise by experience. When she married me, I was still a wild-eyed, immature mystic searching everywhere except the right places for truth. No way could that boy fill the man-sized image she identified as love.

We had boxes the other had to fit. Until our packages died on the cross, we pushed and pulled, demanded and were disappointed. Every few months we would hassle our way through the fogs and confusions until what lay bare was that each of us felt the other didn't really love or at least wasn't expressing it. Then we would have to confess to being hurt by that. Each of us thought we were trying harder to love than the other one, and to be told we hadn't been perceived as trying at all was the cruelest cut of all! It was the packages. We could not perceive as love what the other one did do because that hadn't been a part of our package. More powerfully, we *could* perceive as *unlove* what the other one *didn't do*, which he or she didn't do for the same reason, not part of the learned package in which love came in our families.

It should be said that in families where copious amounts of physical affection have been daily fare, it is usually the case that so much security has been generated in personal spirits that offspring do not latch onto the "packages" so intensely. They are more able to read love in what the other does. Alternatively, in families where little affectionate touch was experienced, there is likely to be little flexibility. Given the relative predictability of human nature, the maxim is, to the degree of lack of affection, to that degree there is usually rigidity in identifying love. However, it should also be stated that when a person who has experienced much affectionate touch in early years marries a mate who is reserved and unable to demonstrate caring with warm hugs and freely expressed admiration and affirmation, that contrast over a period of years may undermine security and put a crippling strain on flexibility. This occurs unless the person is walking in very close relationship with the Lord, whose grace sustains and maintains. Also, in some, affectionate touch can have become a package in itself: "People hug the ones they love. My husband never holds me unless he wants sex; therefore I feel used, not loved." But the maxim still stands. Where the spirit has been so nurtured in the early years by affectionate touch, there is that initial base of security and flexibility that will enable more easily forgiveness, compassion, and the forbearing of the other in love until the Lord can melt the heart and empower change in one or both.

Images and demands are present in every person, whether secure or insecure. For that reason, many couples have come to us and said, "We don't understand. We have a mystery. Before we married we felt free with each other. We could discuss anything. We never fought." (Slight untruth here; memory can play tricks.) "It was fun to be together. Then we got married. We were at each other's throats from the honeymoon on. We battled about everything. We couldn't be ourselves anymore. Every word had to be guarded. It wasn't fun to be with each other anymore. It was like living in prison. Then we were divorced. It felt so good to be free. After a while we began to date each other again and found out we still liked each other. So we started to think about remarrying. Man, we were into the hassles all over again! How come? Aren't we meant for each other? Are we supposed to be friends but not married?"

The answer? Identifications. Pictures. Packages. So long as they were not married, they had some emotional distance. They could still be their own persons. The closer they drew to each other, the more their unseen inner needs took over to have their images of love fulfilled. They would then measure and judge each other's performance and feel trapped and cheated. Unregenerate love has no way other than separation to overcome the vast world of unconscious demands that individuals impose upon each other.

In this sense, the cruelest thing many churched have inadvertently done is to teach the Christian ideal of marriage without teaching Christ. Our movies, novels, neighborly examples—every way our own good marriages cannot be hid but are as a city set on a hill—all have painted vivid pictures for the non-Christian world as to what their married life ought to be like. That image has become their death knell, because it becomes part of their world of demand. They cannot live up to such images without Christ, and so the demand and the attempt to respond do nothing more than imprison. We are not saying we should not be examples, as though failing would make it easier on unbelievers! Our example should be part of what convicts and creates hunger for Christ. We *are* saying that we Christians need to comprehend the dynamics. We ought to be aware, standing by, ready to evangelize and pick up the pieces. In other words, it is better that men and women hear the gospel and begin to die to their demand worlds inside the healing milieu of the Lord and His Church. But if people have *not* surrendered to Christ, they *will* learn the hard way, and our example will be part of what makes it tougher. We need then to evangelize by healing and restoring hearts and marriages.

Unfortunately, many Christians have thought themselves totally changed by conversion, which in fact only began the process. So they too have not only continued with their inherited unconscious demand worlds, but also they have added to them everything they presently are learning in Sunday school and church! They draw the prison lines even tighter! Christ said of lawyers what sometimes also applies to us Christians: "Woe to you lawyers as well! For you weigh men down with burdens hard to bear, while you yourselves will not even touch the burdens with one of your fingers" (Luke 11:46). It takes a lot of dying with Jesus before our "ought" and "should" worlds quit attempting to compel our mates to be what we want them to be rather than what they are meant to be by God's gift. Strangely, when we finally die to self, we discover to our delight that what the other actually is blesses our hearts far more than what we thought we wanted.

There is no other way out of our morass of unconscious demands on each other than death to them through prayer and discipline. Jesus is the answer, not in a once-for-all conversion, but in a conversion that continues anew every day as we discover more of what needs to die.

Let us posit one distinction as vividly as we can. When we become convicted by the Holy Spirit that we are sinners and we receive Jesus, the natural proclivity is to think that all the evil in us died on that cross. That is fine. It did. But two facts must be faced. Experientially, not all of that evil has yet found the death it has died positionally. Paula and I have said that repeatedly in all of our books and tapes. But now let us be clear concerning the second fact. Not only the bad in us must die; so must also the good. What God has put in our nature is good. What is wrong with the kindness we naturally have, or our natural generosity, and all the God-given natural talents that have been ours from day one? What is wrong with them? Nothing, except they are all veined with impurities of sin. We may have taken it for granted that those good things died and were reborn at conversion and that all the impure motives died out of us then. But experientially not so.

When I received Jesus, let's say that I recognized ten talents or God-given abilities within me. Suppose that in two areas I recognized I had become so rotten I needed a Savior. "Praise be to God; Jesus died for my sin. I'm born anew. I'm washed clean. Now I'll take the eight pure qualities, add the two redeemed, and thank You, Jesus, I'm on my way, whole again." The Lord allowed that for a while. Then, because He loves me, He sadly said, "John, there aren't any eight pure ones. It's all shot through with sin."

The incisive message of this chapter is first that all those pictures and ways of loving in which we were raised are infected with sin and need to die. Those good things that became part of us as we grew up—loyalty, fondness, gentleness, gratitude, courtesy, whatever else—all are corrupted by sin and must find their death on the cross. For example, family loyalty seems good. It is good. But suppose a pastor properly chastises our brother and sister. Uncrucified loyalty is still carnal, belonging to the old world. If we listen to it, we attack the pastor self-righteously, thinking family loyalty has made our case just and right. Mothers may justify screaming at their children because, "After all, I guess I just care too much," whereas true mother love in Christ would have respected the child and called him to account without railing. What really operated was parental pride masked as love. A husband's jealousy may cause him to attack someone who befriends his wife, thinking it is love and righteous possessiveness that impels him. In truth it was undealt-with angers and fears dating back to the time when his parents separated. *We have no pure motives.* There is nothing purely good that dwells within us. (See Romans 7:18.) All our righteousness is as filthy rags.

For this reason Jesus said:

> If anyone comes to Me, and does not hate his own father and mother and wife and children and brothers and sisters, yes, and even his own life, he cannot be My disciple.
>
> —LUKE 14:26

IDENTIFICATIONS AND SHRIKISM

The word *hate*, like *love*, is used in many ways. I love the Lord, I love
Paula, and I love a hot dog—all differently. No way could Jesus have meant
to license us to hate anyone in a wrong way. He means that we are to
hate that continuing carnal influence through our families and ourselves
that would press the old wineskin's ways upon the new. All the ways we
learned to do all the good things of family have to be hated and put to
death on the cross so that the new way of Jesus can be ours. This teaching
can be found in fuller form in our book *Restoring the Christian Family*, in
chapter 18, "Renunciation, or Cutting Free," or on our tape "Cutting Free."
Let it suffice in this context to grasp that it is all those good things in us
(which also comprise the package we have identified as love) that must
die on the cross, and the sooner the better. We do this simply by praying
for that crucifixion to happen as we see our packages one by one, day by
day. Jesus then accomplishes that death in us, the easy way if possible, the
hard way if necessary. And He gives everything back to us, resurrected
and redeemed.

One man who came often to our home to visit had been raised by an
extremely critical mother. She was incapable of giving affection, and she
lashed him with her tongue continually. That became his identification of
love, to be scolded and harangued. If he came alone to our home, within
a few minutes he would be saying, "I'd better call home and let my wife
know where I am, or boy, I'm going to get it." When they came to visit
together, we would notice that he would say little barbed things calcu-
lated to provoke her, until finally she would explode and lash out at him.
That satisfied his need for assurance of love. He would throw up his arms
as though to ward off blows. The comically tragic thing was that he stands
six foot seven and she is only five foot two! She was no threat at all! His
way of knowing he was loved was to provoke her to attack. Then the little
boy inside the grown man could ward off blows and feel loved again.

We share this story to demonstrate the difference between learning the
easy way or the hard way. This man could not hear our attempts to show
him the true agenda in their battles. If he could have, they could have
prayed them to the cross and laughed together at themselves. Since he
could not, what could have been jovial became deadly serious. The only
way our loving Lord could set them free was to sicken them into disgust
and loathing for the game. Their battles became worse and worse, until
there was nothing left in him that unconsciously wanted to be hassled.
He could no longer identify harangues as love, only hate. Their marriage

survived, but only after reaching the pits of disgust by which they truly wanted to die to self.

Sometimes identifications of love are built so strongly by fantasy and projected so powerfully as demand that they totally block out recognition and acceptance of love that is very genuinely and warmly given. For instance, a girl grows up with a father who is hypercritical, demanding, insensitive, and self-centered. She comes to the belief that men will not notice her, care about how she feels, affirm her, or provide for her but will use her to serve their selfish ends. At the same time she builds a picture of what she desperately thinks she needs from a man and dreams that someday she will marry a husband who will stay at home with her, listen attentively to all she has to say, bring her flowers and candy, take her to exotic and exciting places, tell her she is beautiful, and do all the romantic things for her that she has heard about in movies and books. She marries a man who, in spite of his own childhood woundings, tries to do what he thinks will bless and please his wife.

Her birthday approaches. She begins to build pictures of what a perfect celebration she will have. She imagines the man of her life coming home from work early to take her to dinner and a late show. Dinner will be in a fine restaurant with candlelight and soft music and no one to rush them or break in on their privacy. They will hold hands during the show and go for a moonlight drive around the lakeshore afterward. He will tell her how lovely she is, and she will smile and sigh and feel goosepimply all over. "The Day" arrives, and she gives him hints: "You could *surprise* me with..." All day long she rehearses the wonderful evening they will have. About five o'clock he calls to say he will be delayed; he is sorry, but it can't be avoided (he is being truthful about this), and he will arrive as soon as possible. Two hours later he comes breathlessly in the door with a beautifully wrapped gift and a box of chocolates in his hand (she is crazy about chocolate), an awkward apology on his lips (he was never good at saying "I'm sorry"), and they hurry to the restaurant. Service is slow and irritation mounts as it becomes apparent that they won't be able to get to the show on time. Attempts at conversation degenerate rapidly to accusation and defensive response and finally to brooding silence. Her dream is shattered, and she sinks under a black cloud of "he never thinks of me," leaving his gift and the chocolates unopened and forgotten. "What's the use?" he thinks. "I can't win."

SHRIKISM

The second factor we want to discuss is shrikism. A shrike is a bird that impales its victim on a thorn and then tears it apart muscle by muscle. In human terms, a shrike is a person who so gathers all the righteousness to himself or herself that everyone else must act out wickedness. Then in the very act of seeming to try to help, the shrike actually destroys the other bit by bit. Worse, the shrike actually thinks he or she is truly trying to be loving and helpful.

In the story with which we began the chapter, the wife had become a shrike. She needed to destroy her husband so that he would be weak and she could be the strong one. As a result, her very ministrations to him, the comforting and crooning, actually demeaned and debased him. Her attempts to love were in effect a shrike's demolition of his manhood—"muscle by muscle."

One of the most powerful forces at work in creating and maintaining shrikism is the fleshly way we counterbalance one another in all relationships. For instance, if one mate is overly talkative, the other may become silent. It is not that the mate has nothing to say. Being half of the other, the need to counterbalance tempts him or her to retire. If one is very extroverted and aggressive, usually the other balances by becoming quiet and introverted. If one won't discipline the children, the other tends to overdiscipline. The counterbalancing is not conscious. It is a deeply unconscious pattern that happens simply because of our oneness in marriage.

In the beginning of our marriage, I was the superspook mystic, always having dreams, seeing visions, and having far-out experiences. Paula was as mystically gifted as I but dared not express it. She became the down-to-earth, practical one. The wilder I became, the more sensible and controlled she became; conversely the more determined to be a rock of common sense she became, the more "head-in-the-skyish" I became. We were driving each other off balance.

Behind that driving was shrikism in each of us. Paula had grown up with brothers with whom she competed in sibling rivalry. They were good in sports, fun loving, and mischievously adventurous, so she excelled with high marks at school and in trying to be more dependable and wiser than they. Subtly it was built into her to ace a man out in the very act of ministering to his mistakes. She would be the solid righteous one in whom the family could take comfort. That would have been fine except that her role required someone to play the opposite. Her heart could not purely want me to be wise and stable. She unconsciously needed me to stumble about and make mistakes.

I fit that pattern excellently. I had grown up with a critical mother. Taught to be obedient and dutiful, not only to the gentle but also to the overbearing (1 Pet. 2:18), I determined to do the right thing no matter whether abused or complimented. I became the martyr who would perform, take the abuse, and go right on serving anyway. It was good to be willing to serve no matter what, but my role needed a persecutor. My judgment was that the woman is the vicious one who attacks the nobly suffering man. So my game was to venture out on the frontiers of faith, a pioneer searching where no one else dared to go, already suffering "the slings and arrows of outrageous fortune," taking up "arms against a sea of troubles,"[1] only to find myself not only seeming to be unsupported by Paula, but in my eyes also attacked and criticized. The criticism, which I could not help but recognize as good for me, also proved again my long-suffering "righteousness."

The essence of shrikism is that it establishes personal righteousness at the expense of others. Not all performance-oriented people are shrikes, but all shrikes are performance-oriented. Having bought the lie that they must perform well to be loved, but insecure about their performance, they are driven unconsciously to contrast themselves with others; others must look bad in order for the shrike to look good. The shrike fears rejection more than anything else, yet in his striving to outperform everyone, he gathers righteousness to himself. Without knowing it, he does the very things that make him almost impossible to live with. His end is rejection.

Wanting love, the woman in our first story ministered to her husband, unaware that, in her need to be the strong one helping a weak husband, she was disemboweling him, until in the end he could only hate her. He became vulnerable to any woman who could make him feel strong and capable. Sure enough, he had an affair, and his gorgeous Christian wife could not understand how he could have chosen *that* creature over her! Fortunately they sought counsel in time, and their marriage was saved.

There was a man, we will call him Dick, who was an extremely competent engineer but who nonetheless lost one job after another. He had been raised with two brothers. Tremendous demands were put on the children to perform chores around the house, but there was almost no parental affection. Dick was soon bigger, stronger, and faster than his brothers; at least he could outwork them. The scraps of parental praise he received for outperforming the other two became his identification of love. It was also the making of a shrike, for feelings of self-worth and being loved required someone else to perform less well than he. Soon after Dick would go to work in an office, his superior intelligence would enable him to master a job others had taken months to learn. Being a generous, loving person, he would set out to help his fellow employees, unaware that he was putting them down. People felt demeaned and accused. Soon he would be the center of dissension in the office. Eventually the boss came to him and said, "Dick, you're a great worker, you're intelligent and well trained, and I'll give you a high recommendation, but somehow you don't fit in this office. I'm going to have to let you go."

Dick went through three positions in the first several years we knew him. I attended a banquet with him at which his current boss was the speaker. Three times Dick interrupted his boss's speech to correct him with "helpful" suggestions! He seemed to be totally unaware that his "help" undermined his boss and his own position. I visited Dick's home. He continually berated his wife as she prepared supper, fussing around her in the kitchen—"helping." He had no idea what he was doing to his wife's sense of worth. His ability to feel loved and OK depended on his being able to outperform his wife in the kitchen. Dick was also a trained pianist. His children were taking lessons. I watched him sit down beside his daughter, "lovingly" wanting to help. Within a few minutes his daughter slunk away in tears while Dick sat there playing a magnificent solo.

Shrikes often have loving outer natures. They go out of their way to help others and can't understand why others reject them. They usually become noble martyrs who keep trying to help anyway.

Shrikes take their place among the noble saints of the church. They usually work more diligently than anyone else. But they can be detected by the fact that people around them who are usually competent and confident become fumble-fingered or forget to show up. People in prox-imity to shrikes perform less well than they normally do in proximity to anyone else. In this case, the cause is defilement, as discussed in the previous chapter.

All of us are afflicted with shrikism. It is latent in every person insofar as all of us have some degree of performance orientation and have competed in a form of sibling rivalry at home or in school. We all live from an inner wellspring of well-being. If ours is drained and we fail to fill it with Jesus, then we either puff ourselves up or knock a hole in someone else's reservoir. That person needs our help. So we help him and thus make ourselves feel big and great again. That is shrikism, making oneself feel OK at the expense of others.

Presently there is an epidemic of shrikism in the Church, especially among women, though men also can become shrikes. Many have been raised in homes lacking in affection. Competing with brothers and sisters for scraps of parental attention, they learned to win the game for love at home by being more righteous than their brothers and sisters. Unaware that this has remained an active pattern, they may have come to the Lord first in the family. As they became more pious and devoted, tending also in their immaturity, like me, to become more and more mystical and religiously experience-centered, usually their husbands unconsciously counterbalance by becoming more and more earthy and then worldly. That hooks into the earlier game of sibling rivalry. These wives, being new children in the family of God, then pray fervently for their husbands to be converted, unaware how their hearts were sabotaging their prayers. They are again involved in sibling rivalry, their new righteousness dependent upon contrast with "that awful man." The more pious and holy they become, the more sinfully their husbands react. Shrikism then becomes the active operational force. The wife is not that good. The husband is not that bad. She is not that pious and prayerful, and he is not that worldly and callous. Their counterbalancing of one another is driving them to positions that are polar opposites.

Her church friends, or "Job's comforters," do not help. They praise that saintly woman who continues by the grace of God to live with that heathen sinner. His friends cannot understand how he can stand to live with that "crazy superspook" and her hypocritical religious fanatical friends. Many prayers are said by the wife and her friends, who can't understand why God will not save that wretched creature. The dynamic of counterbalancing and shrikism stands in the way of his heart. He wants the Lord, but accepting the Lord has become tantamount to surrendering to her and her ways rather than to God. Quite apart from the blockages of pride, a man senses in his spirit something wrong about that. Besides, he is afraid he will become like her and her friends. Her example is not at all evangelistic to him.

Sometimes it happens the other way around, with the same results. We have ministered lately to several men who lost their wives when they came to the Lord and heard their call to ministry. The same counterbalancing dynamic and the same kind of shrikism took effect.

SQUELCHING SHRIKISM

Such polarism need not result. Spiritual people need to climb down off the pedestal. Let them be earthy and real, human and vulnerable at home. What is often aggravating is that the mate of a new Christian feels, often rightly so, that the Lord has become a rival. Mate love has been transferred to the Lord, where it does not belong, and the unconverted mate feels aced out by a love no one can compete against and win! New Christians tend to broadcast, "I have a new and vastly satisfying love; I don't need you anymore." Let the Christian drink humbly from both the affection and the wisdom of the non-Christian mate. The non-Christian is sanctified through the believing one (1 Cor. 7:14). By faith a believer can draw God's wisdom powerfully from an unbelieving mate.

Mary, whose story is told in chapter 3, "Spiritual Imprisonment," soon soared to great and glorious heights in the Lord, while her husband still desisted even from attending church. But we were grateful to the Lord that no such polarism or shrikism developed. Without breaking confidentiality, Mary continually asked her husband's advice for help for people to whom she ministered. Never have I heard wiser counsel than what the Lord gave her through her husband! She asked him the questions of faith or about the Bible that stumped her. She honored his headship in every way. She did not believe that if he would only accept Christ as Lord, then could he act as her head. She activated him in that position he already held (Eph. 5:22–23). She gave herself to him more warmly and womanly the more she knew the Lord. One day she said chuckling, "My husband keeps sitting there thumbing through his Bible, muttering to himself that he *has* to learn to understand this thing!" It was not long before he was such a solid churchman that several men in his company began to attend base chapel saying, "If my colonel says there is something to this, then there must be."

True faith separates us from continuing carnal influence from our families, but it never separates us from them personally. If distance is resulting seemingly from the faith of one and the lack of faith in the other, it is nothing but delusion to believe that our Lord Jesus is causing that separation. Not He but flesh, most likely counterbalancing dynamics and shrikism, is causing harm to the family. Let Christians repent of elitism, specialness, "spookism," and every other "ism" one can think of, and return humbly to the arms of the mate God gave them.

We do not have to fear being overcome by what the mate is. We are more than overcomers. No one is all evil or all good. By faith we can follow St. Paul's prescription in Philippians 4:8:

> Finally, brethren, whatever is true, whatever is honorable, whatever is right, whatever is pure, whatever is lovely, whatever is of good repute, if there is any excellence and if anything worthy of praise, let your mind dwell on these things.

We can by faith draw from our mate the best rather than the worst.

DETECTING SHRIKISM IN OURSELVES

The following are the sharpest questions we have found to determine whether shrikism is at work through ourselves:

1. Do people around you act out their best selves or their worst?

2. Is your mate becoming a better or worse person by living with you?

3. Are you drawing wisdom and goodness from your spouse or less than what he/she is capable of?

4. Could you really rejoice if your mate came to the Lord? Or would part of you have to try harder to become a better Christian than your spouse can be?

The Bible says in Philippians 2:3 that we should "do nothing from selfishness or empty conceit, but with humility of mind let each of you regard one another as more important than himself."

Janet Wilcox, an in-house prayer minister who once lived with us, was fond of saying, "Humility is nothing more or less than the direct result of seeing things as they are." The final check for shrikism is therefore:

5. Which do you see first and most easily: the other fellow's faults or yours?

6. In an argument, do you seek to bless and protect the other's heart while finding truth together, or do you seek to prove him wrong and you right?

A CONFIRMED SHRIKE

Mercifully, there is a difference between the general shrikism to which we are all occasionally subject and being a confirmed shrike. A confirmed shrike is one in whom the drive to establish oneself is so all-consuming that shrikism is the basic stance of life. These people live in and for a picture of themselves. They work at it twenty-four hours a day, though they may be totally unaware of it.

Dick had become a confirmed shrike. Everywhere he went his behavior was the same, with the same results. His wife eventually grew tired of being treated as an inept child in her own home and left him. When she finally individuated enough to be her own person, her repressed angers erupted like a volcano. No matter how friends pleaded, she pressed with vitriolic intensity for divorce. She had had it. He would never change. Later, since we become what we judge (Rom. 2:1) and in her eyes Dick could do nothing right, she shriked on him from a distance through his children, while she played the role of the righteous divorcee.

The following is a list of symptoms by which to detect the presence of a shrike. Though we speak here in the context of church life, the same applies in offices, clubs, athletic teams, and so on, wherever society is.

Shrikes always have a reason, an excuse, or an alibi to justify what they do. The fault is never theirs. If true accusation is inescapable and they must admit they did a wrong thing, someone else has put them into an untenable position. They *had* to do it. Unconsciously, to them, blame is tantamount to not being loved; they cannot conceive that someone could love them despite their faults, so they must never have any faults. A shrike cannot comprehend that most people already see his faults and love him anyway.

Shrikes falsely discern what others do and impute to them wrong motives. One divorced woman we knew was greatly ministered to by her church. They gave her groceries, helped her with her yard, brought cut wood for her stove, assisted her in finding a job, prayed for her, carried her in their hearts, and withstood her assaults. To hear her tell it, that church is filled with hard-hearted and self-centered people who never do anything for anyone else unless it is to make themselves feel good or to enhance their own reputation. She could not perceive any of their efforts truly as love for her and imputed her own false motives to their good works, which leads us to the next symptom.

Shrikes often impute their own unconscious motives to others and bitterly charge them. The divorcee of whom we have just spoken (we'll call her Alice) was always running about doing things for others, but she was tragically unaware that her motives for serving others were mixed, often rooted in her own unhealed insecurities. She continually projected what was in her own heart onto others and attacked it as if it were in them.

Shrikes carry tales. They are usually the gossipmongers of the church. St. Paul wrote to Timothy: "They also learn to be idle, as they go around from house to house; and not merely idle, but also gossips and busybodies, talking about things not proper to mention" (1 Tim. 5:13). Their ability to feel good depends upon contrast to the failings of others, so they make sure everyone knows about everyone else's faults. Commonly, however, such gossiping is masked, even from themselves, as "concern." "Let's pray about so-and-so. They have been doing this and that." By defilement, solid people who normally would not gossip at all often surprise the pastor by being carried away by shrikes. Shrikes do not believe they are gossips; they hotly deny it. One shrike told the same story to the pastor and every elder in the church, always with the identical refrain, "I haven't told anyone else. And I'm only telling you so you can pray." When confronted by the group, each one revealing how she had told them the same thing, she could not believe it and would not admit it. She insisted that they had gossiped to each other and were putting this on her. She had done no such thing. She was a good person, and they all knew it. The very idea!

Shrikes do attempt to do works for the Lord, but inasmuch as they are so out of the flow of the Spirit, it devolves to mere "dead works." (See Hebrews 6:1.) Their many works become more of a bother than a help; thus in this sense they are "idle."

Shrikes cannot arrive at a knowledge of the truth. The simple truth they are incapable of hearing is that they are loved unconditionally. Their extreme performance orientation and pitiful attempts to establish their righteousness so they will feel loved and secure are the very things that block them from comprehending or receiving that Jesus can love and accept them without all that labor. Shrikism is thus one of the "various impulses" St. Paul wrote about when he said that there "are those who enter into households and captivate weak women *weighed down with sins,* led on by *various impulses,* always learning and *never able to come to the knowledge of the truth*" (2 Tim. 3:6, emphasis added).

Though St. Paul mentioned women, we have seen the same thing in men. In one of our small groups, a man repeatedly raised carping questions. Most thought he merely loved to argue. He would jump into a quarrel at the drop of a hat. What we discovered actually lay behind his constantly irrelevant questioning and bickering was the heart of a shrike. He would prove his superior biblical knowledge at the expense of everyone else so that he could be the true one setting everyone else straight. After a while all of us perceived what was going on, and our hearts bled for him. Shrikism is a wicked trap, a construct of Satan to keep souls away from true fellowship with the Father, Son, and from one another.

Shrikes rewrite history. One woman was raised by a father who could not give affection. He demanded performance. She saw him fly into a rage and beat mercilessly on her beloved older brother. She could not admit anger at her father. That would be sinful, and she must be a perfect lady in order to be loved. By the grace of God she married a gentle, kindly man not at all like her father. That very fact threatened to expose her real feelings toward her father. From then on, her husband could do nothing right, while in her mind her father became more and more saintly. She had also competed with her brothers, who could work in the fields alongside her father whereas she could not. Therefore in front of her children she had to appear to work much longer, more dedicatedly, more nobly, and more self-sacrificingly than her husband did. Over the years, incipient shrikism became more and more confirmed.

By the time I could begin prayer ministry for them, I had known the family for many years. I knew the actual facts of their life together. Each time I tried to help her face the truth, the next time I saw her she had gone back over the incidents we had discussed and reworked them all, thoroughly convinced that the fabrications she now told me were in fact the true history. "These new stories...you could not have known about because I never told anyone before, wanting to protect his reputation." The new "revelations" always made it appear that she had nobly protected that evil man from discovery. Eventually, her versions of their life together came to bear almost no resemblance to fact. She remained convinced that her story was the only true one and that, poor martyr she was, no one knew all that she had suffered. When someone remarked to her that though she had divorced him, he had never wanted it and always had loved her, her reply was, "Why, of course, he never had any grounds. I was a perfect wife to him." She believed this despite the fact that all of her children and grandchildren honored and loved him and had little to do with her since she ripped them as viciously as she did him. Such people are to be pitied and fought for in prayer.

Shrikes enlist armies. They find cronies in the church who will believe they are as good as they are trying to appear to be. They keep these friends supplied with "evidence," concoctions of half-truths twisted to put the pastor (or whoever needs to be shot down) in the worst light.

> But these men revile the things which they do not understand.... These are grumblers, finding fault, following after their own lusts; they speak arrogantly, flattering people for the sake of gaining an advantage.
> —JUDE 10, 16

"If only all those people knew what is really going on! We've just got to hold this church together. I'm sure glad you're standing true and straight. Someday it will all come out, and you'll see I was right all along. That awful man! But we've just got to love him. Let's pray for him." They really believe they are champions of the faith, not realizing their own need for others to be wrong so they can be right has twisted their perceptions of reality.

> ...in which are some things hard to understand, which the untaught and *unstable distort*, as they do also the rest of the Scriptures, to their own destruction.
> —2 PETER 3:16, EMPHASIS ADDED

St. Peter was speaking of unstable people in general, but his words aptly describe how shrikes misunderstand events in the life of the church and twist them to their own destruction, since whoever reviles the Lord's anointed is in trouble with the Lord.

Shrikes perceive attempts to help them as attack. One day in my office a husband was attempting to reach his wife's heart. She had made sure everyone in the church knew what an awful man he was. Time and the

Lord had vindicated him, and she had left that "bunch of backsliders" to find a "true" church. Now we were attempting to save their marriage. Sitting beside her, full of love and zeal to reach her, he gently took hold of her arm as he pleaded with her to hear him and me. But she flounced away and exclaimed, "Did you see what that awful man just did? He hit me!" She was firmly convinced in her mind that his touch was violently intended. In her spirit she knew she was lying, of course, but her heart was so completely engaged in the effort to establish herself as righteous and him as wicked that the slightest pretext would do.

Shrikes are always controlling. They don't have the security and trust to let things happen as they will. They cannot be at rest and trust that others will like them. They either must be the center of attention or so manipulate that they are in control of what is happening. A man who was semiretired was hired by a church to design and build a new entrance and front to the church building. The change also was intended to expand seating capacity and beautify the rear of the sanctuary. He was doing a magnificent job and loving it. Another man, a trustee, manipulated other trustees, whispered in the ear of the pastor, and finally made things so difficult that the first man gave up in disgust and left the church. The trustee then finished the work, unaware that what really impelled him was not concern for the work but sibling rivalry and the need to be in control. This man continually disrupted the life of the congregation.

Shrikes cannot rest. They are chronically exhausted, if not physically, then emotionally. The reason is that they must forever work for love. The more diligently they work, the "behinder" they become, for their labors turn people away, so they redouble efforts. The losing game goes on and on.

Shrikes resist inner healing. After all, nothing is wrong with them. It's those other people. If they do allow themselves to be ministered to, it is only so far as they remain in control, revealing nothing that might lead to real inner depths of sin. They are role-playing the righteousness of humbly being ministered to. One shrike used to tell me about the dumb mistakes she had made. But her confessions were intended to show how her good and loving heart caused her to continue to do kind things (stupidly) for undeserving people.

Shrikes usually have slumbering spirits. Not all do, and certainly not all who have slumbering spirits are shrikes. Insofar as they do have slumbering spirits, they read what is going on in worship services and meetings from within their own mentality instead of by the true mind of the Holy Spirit. Thus they are apt to perceive distorted versions and repeat those to outsiders.

There are many other symptoms, but whoever picks up the basic keys of fear, performance orientation, striving, and sibling rivalry, and then connects them to the need to establish one's own righteousness at the expense of others, will soon compile his own list. What is important is that the Church learn to recognize and minister to the many shrikes in its midst.

SETTING FREE A CONFIRMED SHRIKE

Setting a confirmed shrike free is the most difficult work we have encountered. The success we have experienced has come about only by the long hard route of patience, persistence, and forbearance undergirded by prayer, but we continue to search for a simpler way. The problem occurs not only in the fact that such people find it extremely difficult to admit fault. It is that shrikism has become the basic stance and drive of their entire life! Even if the shrike sees it and loathes it, it is so ingrained in every way he thinks, feels, and acts that dislodging it may take years of painful self-discovery and crucifixion. Added to that is the fear and confusion: "If I die to the only way I know, then how shall I live? In what new mold can my impulses flow?" To have an inner bitter-root judgment or expectancy is to suffer from one sick area of the total being. One can root that out and go on. It's the same for inner vows or prenatal wounds and sins. Shrikes are not merely sickened in one area while remaining somewhat whole in others, but they suffer an ailment of the personal spirit that has built their entire soul structure and way of meeting life as a wrong answer to the threat of isolation and fear, loneliness and rejection.

Replacing shrikism calls for radical and total death on the cross. That death cannot be accomplished unless the personal spirit finally catches what the mind received in the first conversion experience—that Jesus loves us *unconditionally*! The heart has long been inclined toward earning love. It is a total revolution to upset that lifetime of learning. The shrike's spirit may catch glimpses of being loved, but the strongman of the self can quickly rebuild familiar tracks to run in. In short, our self has a life of its own and fights not to die. Shrikism becomes the fortress and stronghold of the nature of the self.

Shrikism as a general tendency in all of us is fairly easy to heal. We deal with the root causes in the same way that we pray for any other condition inside of us. Confession, repentance, forgiveness, absolution, death on the cross, and resurrection to new life are the simple route to wholeness. Once we have recognized the problem and the basic ministry has been accomplished, the discipline of walking in the new way can be a delight. We laugh at ourselves as we say, "Oh, there I was, shriking again." "Hey, you're shriking on me again." Or, "Oh, dear, I was, wasn't I? Forgive me."

But it's different with confirmed shrikes. These need long-suffering friends who will indeed stick closer than a brother (Prov. 18:24). These must be people who are able to express affection when the shrike least deserves it. They must be generous, openhearted people who are not turned away, upset, or defeated by slights and insults. Again and again we have ministered to those who wanted desperately to change. Ministry was well received and initially effective, yet the fabric of healing was ripped apart by loved ones in the home who had learned by hurt over a period of years to close themselves off behind defensive walls, to hide and throw retaliative barbs.

Often a wife's newly born intentions have crashed against the steel walls of negative expectation and judgment of a husband who feels that he has "had it" and that she will never change. His attitude sets her up for a fall into old familiar patterns, reinstating the program she has just rejected.

Loved ones in the family of the shrike must be open to ministry to enable them to deal with the sin in their own hearts that caused them to reap such a relationship and the defensive attitudes developed in themselves that refuse the shrike room to change. Through prayer the family must be given enough strength of spirit, a sovereign gift of trust, and courage to open again to the one who has repeatedly wounded them so that they can give unconditional love and affection, which are essential to healing.

Those who minister to shrikes must be people who have the ability to gently but firmly confront and rebuke again and again. Shrikes must be told when they are shriking, in no uncertain terms. They have to be taken off the pedestal of righteousness again and again, *coupled with such acceptance and affection* that the inmost spirit finally accepts the idea that it doesn't need that display of righteousness to be loved and will not be rejected when wrong.

But be advised that using the label "shrike" may only nudge him back onto his pedestal, for he mounts it to avoid perceived shame. Use the term *shrike* privately, only to give yourself a handle to identify a set of behaviors. Do not even use the term when discussing the shrike with others, for those whom he has wounded might gladly paste him with such a monstrous title and so prevent his healing. It is better to identify his actions and confront them as such.

Paula and I were not confirmed shrikes, but we had plenty of it in us. We learned to confront each other consistently when we were at it. It often seemed not to work in the moment. Paula or I would steam off in a huff, certain the other had misread us. But the Holy Spirit had us, and sooner or later we would have to admit the truth and "fess up." As we learned not to locate the "enemy" in the other person, but to discipline ourselves to choose compassionately to unite with the other person against their bondage, words of confrontation became more and more effective. As we learned to affirm the other before the confrontation—"I love you, appreciate you, but this is what you are doing"—we discovered that our attempts to help one another were more readily received. As we developed a personal relationship with the Lord so that our own sense of worth and well-being was dependent first of all upon Him, we were not bound to take either the attacks or the bumbling attempts of the other to "help" as personally threatening. The Lord Himself could more and more enable us to discern the concern in a criticism, the truth in a lie, the hurt of the other in a quick sharp answer rather than first the intent to hurt. Praying together became a way of lifting problems to common ground at the foot of the cross and releasing our imperfect perceptions of truth to Him who is the truth. We found that unwillingness to pray together concerning a misunderstanding or disagreement or anger was a sure sign of our individual unwillingness to give up the game of proving the other wrong and nursing our own offendedness.

For confirmed shrikes, we must not assume that because we have prayed several times about the deepest things in the personal heart and spirit, they ought therefore to have been healed. We must pray over the same areas again and again until the heart and spirit, in which they originate, are finally and totally healed.

CHAPTER 7

OCCULT INVOLVEMENT

When you enter the land which the LORD your God gives you, you shall not learn to imitate the detestable things of those nations. There shall not be found among you anyone who makes his son or his daughter pass through the fire, one who uses divination, one who practices witchcraft, or one who interprets omens, or a sorcerer, or one who casts a spell, or a medium, or a spiritist, or one who calls up the dead. For whoever does these things is detestable to the LORD; and because of these detestable things the LORD your God will drive them out before you. You shall be blameless before the LORD your God. For those nations which you shall dispossess, listen to those who practice witchcraft and to diviners, but as for you, the LORD your God has not allowed you to do so.

—DEUTERONOMY 18:9–14

In the next two chapters, it is not our purpose to catalog and fully describe all the various forms of occult involvement and other spiritual sins. Many authors have already done that. Any competent sales associate in any Christian bookstore can refer the reader to several good books on the subject. Our purpose is to teach the body of Christ how to heal whatever wounds have been inflicted upon the personal spirit. Therefore we will chronicle and describe some of the more important occult sins so that sufficient understanding serves as a base for comprehending what should be healed and how to do it.

All occult involvement wounds our personal spirit. We need not only deliverance and forgiveness but also healing. As prayer ministers, we are called to see what are the conditions in the history of the person that made him vulnerable to temptation and attack. We need to heal not only the effects of sin but also the causes. People who have been involved with occult activity may retain the same deep wounds that originally caused their fall and more great bruises in the spirit as a result of their occult sins. The Church needs to learn how to persevere until the work in the other is complete and the person is not only free but also whole.

DIMENSIONS OF THE OCCULT

Occult involvement is unequivocally forbidden by the Lord. The word *occult* means "something hidden" or "the act of hiding something." In astronomy, when the sun's rays hide a star, that is termed an "occult occurrence." In that context the word *occult* bears no negative connotations. It is merely a descriptive scientific word. In religious circles, however, it means, "of the nature of or pertaining to those sciences involving the use of the supernatural (as magic, alchemy, astrology, theosophy, and the like)."[1]

Magic in this context does not mean those tricks done by quickness of hand and eye that are often accomplished by modern-day performing "magicians." Such tricks are properly called "legerdemain." To practice magic means to "influence the course of events by compelling the agency of spiritual beings, or by bringing into operation some occult controlling principle of nature."[2]

Magic thus has two dimensions. In the first, magic means the operation of principles by our own paranormal energy to accomplish our own purposes. In this dimension, the user of magic operates alone, employing only his own power to influence and harness nature to his purposes. He may himself be operated unwittingly by demonic principalities, but for the purpose of our distinction, he is unaware of it or at least not consciously inviting any agencies or powers other than his own. In the second dimension, the wielder of magic consciously invokes the aid of other beings. This kind of magic is thus also necromancy, spiritism, sorcery, and sometimes mediumism.

- Necromancy is the art of consulting with the dead (often with the help of objects) to obtain knowledge of the future or to cause things to happen.

- Spiritism is a term used by many coterminously with spiritualism, which is an entire religious philosophy centered around the practice of attempting to confer with alleged spirits of departed persons.

- Mediumism refers to the practice of a medium in contacting such spirits, sometimes in allowing the use of his own body, specifically his vocal cords, for alleged departed spirits to speak through.

Sorcery will be defined later in this chapter.

Concerning spiritualism, the Lord is both concise and stern:

> As for the person who turns to mediums and to spiritists, to play the harlot after them, *I will also set My face against that person and will cut him off from among his people.*
> —LEVITICUS 20:6, EMPHASIS ADDED

The Word is far sterner concerning the mediums themselves:

> Now a man or a woman who is a medium or a spiritist shall surely be put to death. They shall be stoned with stones, their bloodguiltiness is upon them.
> —LEVITICUS 20:27

The command is given also in Leviticus 19:31:

> Do not turn to mediums or spiritists; do not seek them out to be defiled by them. I am the LORD your God.

SEEKING PERFECTION AND POWER WITHOUT GOD

Alchemy, the second word listed above from my dictionary, does *not* refer to the popular notion of men with pointed hats seeking the four implausibles:

1. To turn baser metals into gold

2. To find the universal solvent (an acid which supposedly could dissolve anything)

3. The elixir of youth (a potion thought to bestow eternal youth on whoever drank it. Some historians believe that Ponce de Leon was searching for such an elixir when he became one of the discoverers of Florida.)

4. A machine of perpetual motion

Alchemy is an ancient science, far antedating the rise of the Hebrew nation. Under persecution from Christians and others, alchemists masked their actual purposes behind the four searches listed above, causing the public to esteem them foolish seekers after the impossible. Their true purpose, however, was nothing neither more nor less than the quest for perfection of the soul!

Perfection in this context does not mean maturation into Christlike moral and ethical virtues, such as are listed in Colossians 3:12–17. Rather it means a discipline and purging of the soul's faculties until one can discover and harness the power of one's own personal spirit to accomplish miracles, without the intervention of God. The quest is for power to release the power locked within our personal spirit. Latently, every person does possess such power. For example by analogy, science has learned how to destroy everything within a twenty-five mile radius by unleashing power through splitting or fusing tiny atoms. If such infinitesimally small things as atoms can be caused to release such awesome power, consider what may be locked within one solitary person's spirit!

When sin entered Adam's heart, the Lord had to shut down and hide the power He had built into him, lest one man alone be more devastating than many H-bombs!

> For the creation was subjected to futility, not of its own will, but because of Him who subjected it, in hope that the creation itself also will be set free from its slavery to corruption into the freedom of the glory of the children of God.
>
> —ROMANS 8:20–21

It is as though God turned the rheostat down from bright to dimmest dim in both nature and mankind lest the power He placed there be used by corrupt minds and hearts. Ever since the Fall, Satan has worked to release the power of mankind before time, thus leading to all the occult strivings that God has forbidden. At His Second Coming, Jesus will restore mankind to fullness of glory, of which we presently see the first fruits.

> But if the ministry of death, in letters engraved on stones, came with glory, so that the sons of Israel could not look intently at the face of Moses because of the glory of his face, fading as it was, how shall the ministry of the Spirit fail to be even more with glory? For if the ministry of condemnation has glory, much more does the ministry of righteousness abound in glory.
>
> —2 CORINTHIANS 3:7–9

But until sin has been destroyed from the heart of mankind, God will not restore men to power. Satan, knowing what damage would result, seeks to restore the psychic powers of men, even as he promised Jesus power. (See Matthew 4:8 and Luke 4:6.)

Dunce caps, which were pointed conical hats some of us as children had to wear many years ago as part of our punishment while sitting in a corner on a stool in grade school days, originated from the pointed conical hats alchemists wore during the Middle Ages. Alchemists appeared to be fools; thus, whoever had to wear the dunce cap was ridiculed for being a fool. But neither were alchemists fools in that sense, nor did conical mean comical. They were in dead earnest. Theirs was the first sin reenacted: the attempt by study and practice to become like God, wielding His kind of power.

The story of Aladdin's lamp, a bedtime story beloved by many generations, is actually an alchemist story. Aladdin searched through three successively deeper caverns. Alchemists speak of arcane, esoteric (interior, hidden) searches through three successive inner caves of the being—the mind, the heart, and the spirit. In the deepest, Aladdin found a magical lamp. At the depths within a man's spirit, alchemists thought to find wondrous knowledge. When Aladdin rubbed the lamp, a genie would appear and do wondrous things, whatever Aladdin requested. Rubbing produces heat by coefficients of friction. Alchemists wrote of the "argent," which meant the golden heat of fire by which the spirit within would be excited and enabled to do wondrous things in response to the will of the alchemist.

In the introduction to *Hermetic Philosophy and Alchemy*, Walter Leslie Wilmhurst wrote this of alchemy:

> If we speak of it as an Art, it is because it is usually so called in the literature of the subject, but it is rather an exact science—and a divine science at that, holy Alkimy as its professors have called it— one involving deep knowledge of the *mental, psychical and spiritual* elements in man and of the way in which they may be practically *controlled and manipulated.*[3]

Again, on page 26:

> Simply stated, Hermetism, or its synonym Alchemy, was in its primary intention and office *the philosophic and exact science of the regeneration of the human soul from its present sense-immersed state into the perfection and nobility of that divine condition in which it was originally created.*[4]

Humanism—the attempt of mankind, without God, to become everything man was created to be—is nothing new. Alchemists of countless generations have made our modern humanists look pale.

> [Alchemy] views man, i.e., the soul or true ego of man, as in process of restoration from the terrible calamity of his "fall," in the course of which process development under the operation of the forces and laws of nature has partially redeemed him from chaos and disorder and brought him to a point from which, *by the right application of his intelligence and will,* he can cooperate in *effecting his complete regeneration.*[5]

Alchemy is thus gnostic, embracing the heresy that one can be saved by right knowledge. Alchemy is therefore also Pelagian, perpetuating the heresy that one can save oneself without accepting Jesus Christ as Lord and Savior.

THE WHITE STONE

Alchemists were fond of speaking of the *lapis lazuli*, or white stone (actually a rich azure or sky blue). When discipline and training had progressed sufficiently and when purification warranted, the subject would be placed in a hypnotic trance, in which in some mysterious way his soul was to be congealed into the white stone, or "Philosopher's Stone." His spirit and soul, guided by the mesmerizer, were to travel through regions and "ethers" to become one with all. All knowledge of all mankind was thus to be "on tap." Alchemists sought by science and discipline to become the white stone by which they could have all knowledge and wisdom.

Mankind and Satan have always copied what God does. By alchemy these men were trying to *achieve without God* what our *Lord promised to give* through the Holy Spirit.

> But the Helper, the Holy Spirit, whom the Father will send in My name, *He will teach you all things,* and bring to your remembrance all that I said to you.
>
> —JOHN 14:26, EMPHASIS ADDED

St. Peter wrote to "those who reside as aliens, scattered through Pontus, Galatia, Cappadocia, Asia, and Bithynia" (1 Pet. 1:1). Throughout that entire region were many alchemists. On the island of Cyprus, St. Paul encountered Elymas, who as a magician was most likely also an alchemist, and called down blindness upon him when he would not stop making "crooked the straight paths of the Lord" (Acts 13:10). To new Christians in those days, alchemy may have seemed a welcome lure, a shortcut to power to insecure "aliens."

But we are to seek a far better kind of stone. Jesus is the one chief and true cornerstone, the only perfected soul or white stone. Note: alchemists would arduously build themselves into perfected stones by science and hypnotism. St. Peter called for Christians to *be built* "as living stones" and "as a spiritual house" (1 Pet. 2:5). Alchemists would build themselves as *individuals.* Christians are to be built *as a spiritual house,* a chosen *race,* a royal *priesthood,* a holy *nation,* a *people* for God's own possession (not to possess themselves for themselves).

> Therefore, putting aside all malice and all guile and hypocrisy and envy and all slander, like newborn babes, long for the pure milk of the word, that by it you may grow in respect to salvation, if you have tasted the kindness of the Lord. And coming to Him as to a *living stone,* rejected by men, but choice and precious in the sight of God, you also, as *living stones,* are being built up as a spiritual house for a holy priesthood, to offer up spiritual sacrifices acceptable to God

through Jesus Christ. For this is contained in Scripture: "Behold I lay in Zion a choice *stone*, a precious *corner stone*, and he who believes in Him shall not be disappointed."

This precious value, then, is for you who believe. But for those who disbelieve, "the *stone* which the builders rejected, this became the very *corner stone*," and, "a *stone* of stumbling and a rock of offense"; for they stumble because they are disobedient to the word, and to this doom they were also appointed. But you are a chosen race, a royal priesthood, a holy nation, a people for God's own possession, that you may proclaim the excellencies of Him who has called you out of darkness into His marvelous light; for you once were not a people, but now you are the people of God; you had not received mercy, but now you have received mercy. Beloved, I urge you as aliens and strangers to abstain from fleshly lusts, which wage war against the soul.

—1 PETER 2:1–11, EMPHASIS ADDED

Furthermore the Lord has promised:

He who has an ear, let him hear what the Spirit says to the churches. To him who overcomes, to him I will give some of the hidden manna, and *I will give him a white stone*, and a new name written on the stone which no one knows but he who receives it.

—REVELATION 2:17, EMPHASIS ADDED

In Hebrew culture a white stone was given to a man who had been forgiven great sins. The wearing of the stone was a sign of his having been forgiven.[6] A former occultist who embraces Christianity might see a *rhema* word in the following: "To him who overcomes I will *give a perfected soul*; no one has to study alchemy to *achieve* it." We are all in process of being transformed into His likeness, which will finally be accomplished in "the twinkling of an eye" (1 Cor. 15:52) as a gift, not something accomplished by alchemic science or its modern counterpart, humanism.

By peering into his white stone or perfected soul, an alchemist thought himself able to know things at a distance or in the future. These are of course gifts given only at God's discretion through the gifts of knowledge and prophecy, two of the nine gifts of the Holy Spirit. Today carnival fortune-tellers mimic alchemy by pretending to gaze into their "crystal ball." The crystal ball is none other than a cheap imitation of the philosopher's lapis lazuli, or white stone.

The philosopher or alchemist, of course, never achieved his desired end. He found nothing but counterfeits, which Simon knew when he saw the true wonders the apostles performed and cried after them that he might be given this power, too. (See Acts 8:9–24.) But alchemists or wizards did find enough results to astound the common people, as Simon "formerly was practicing magic in the city, and astonishing the people of Samaria, claiming to be someone great" (v. 9). By what they did accomplish, they deluded themselves that they were on the right track.

The magicians of Egypt were most likely adepts of alchemy, but whether they were or not, they duplicated the first signs of Moses and Aaron! Their rods also became serpents, though Aaron's rod-turned-snake swallowed theirs (Exod. 7:12). Aaron stretched out his hand and "lifted up the staff and struck the water that was in the Nile, in the sight of Pharaoh and in the sight of his servants, and all the water that was in the Nile was turned to blood. And the fish that were in the Nile died, and the Nile became foul, so that the Egyptians could not drink water from the Nile. And the blood was through all the land of Egypt. *But the magicians of Egypt did the same with their secret arts*" (vv. 20–22, emphasis added). Again in Exodus 8:6–7, "Aaron stretched out his hand over the waters of Egypt, and the frogs came up and covered the land of Egypt. *And the magicians did the same with their secret arts*, making frogs come up on the land of Egypt" (emphasis added). When Aaron caused gnats to plague Egypt, "the *magicians tried with their secret arts* to bring forth gnats, *but they could not*" (v. 18, emphasis added).

It was in Greece that philosophy flourished (and within it the science of alchemy). With the Greek love of philosophy in mind, perhaps we can see more in the familiar passage of 1 Corinthians 1:17–25 (emphasis added):

> For Christ did not send me to baptize, but to preach the gospel, *not in cleverness of speech, that the cross of Christ should not be made void.* For the word of the cross is to those who are perishing foolishness, but to us who are being saved it is the power of God. For it is written, "I *will destroy the wisdom of the wise,* and the cleverness of the clever I will set aside." Where is the wise man? Where is the scribe? Where is the debater of this age? Has not God made foolish the wisdom of the world? For since in the wisdom of God the world through its wisdom did not come to know God, God was well-pleased through the foolishness of the message preached to save those who believe. For indeed Jews ask for signs, and *Greeks search for wisdom*; but we

preach Christ crucified, to Jews a stumbling block, and to Gentiles foolishness, but to those who are the called, both Jews and Greeks, Christ the power of God and the wisdom of God. Because the foolishness of God is wiser than men, and the weakness of God is stronger than men.

In chapter 2 St. Paul continued:

And my message and my preaching were not in persuasive words of wisdom, but in demonstration of the Spirit and of power, *that your faith should not rest on the wisdom of men, but on the power of God.* Yet we do speak wisdom among those who are mature; *a wisdom, however, not of this age, nor of the rulers of this age, who are passing away;* but we speak God's wisdom in a mystery, the hidden wisdom, which God predestined before the ages to our glory; the wisdom *which none of the rulers of this age has understood;* for if they had understood it, they would not have crucified the Lord of glory; but just as it is written, "Things which eye has not seen and ear has not heard, and which have not entered the heart of man, all that God has prepared for those who love Him."

—1 CORINTHIANS 2:4–9, EMPHASIS ADDED

When we understand what alchemy taught and strove to accomplish, we comprehend more fully why St. Paul said so clearly, "The wisdom which none of the rulers of this age has understood" and "Your faith should not rest on the wisdom of men but on the power of God." Only Christ, not men's wisdom, can restore us and perfect us.

We err if we regard magic or alchemy as mere foolishness. God has made it foolish, as St. Paul said, but God would not have forbidden it so sternly were it only harmless mistaken imagination! Probably most who become involved are mere dilettante dabblers, encountering little else than their own imaginations. But there is a reality, terribly real. It is for the damning sinfulness of that reality that God destroyed the inhabitants of Canaan before Israel and repeatedly scolded, warned, and disciplined Israel.

SORCERY

So far we have discussed magic and wizardry or alchemy. Some wizards are solely alchemic wizards. Some, however, add sorcery to their sins. Not all sorcerers are also alchemists, just as not all alchemists are also sorcerers. Sorcery is a particular form of magic or witchcraft. Sorcery is that second kind of magic that contacts and uses other spirits and powers in order to manipulate nature or cause things to happen. There is no such thing as white magic. Satan uses such things as the 1970s TV program *Bewitched* with "Samantha" to beguile us by cute nose twitches that some magic is innocent and fun. *All* magic is sin. However, in so-called white magic the operator at least thinks he is doing good. His intentions may be benign; however, they are shot through with sin. Not so with sorcery. Sorcery is black magic. Its intent is consciously, deliberately evil, for selfish purposes only. Black magic is never for others but *against* them, for the sole gain of the sorcerer.

Satanic cults use sorcery against the Church. They "pray" in chants and rhythms to cause unaccountable mechanical breakdowns, temper flare-ups, gossiping, adultery, and so on. It may seem something too far out to believe that men and women in the twenty-first century can engage in such evil, seemingly superstitious activities, much less be effective in it, but Paula and I have been in direct prayer warfare against demons sent by witches' covens. We know by experience the kinds of things that can happen.

During one such battle, Paula was pregnant with Andrea. An unseen powerful force pushed her so strongly that she almost tumbled down the stairs. It was not imagination. It was an actual attempt to harm her.

Another time, our eldest son, Loren, was working for a friend of the family, who at the time was building a house on a cliff, plus a boat dock and garage below beside the river. Loren was doing some of the carpentry work. One morning in prayer I felt an urgent impression from the Lord. I asked Him what it was, and I was given a vision of Loren swinging down from a high place, using long yellow lines, with great danger all around. Before Loren left for work, I called to him and asked, "Loren, are you going to be working up high today or down below?"

"Down below today, Dad. I'll be working on the boat dock."

"Well, just be careful today, will you?" and I told him about the vision.

That day, the wife and the children came out to inspect their new house. The wife squatted by the edge of the cliff to examine something about the foundation. A powerful, invisible hand hit her in the back with such force it tumbled her over the edge of the cliff! The children took a long yellow extension cord and lowered it down to Loren, who had clambered up that steep, shale-covered cliff side to reach her. Loren was a weight lifter at the time. Having tied the electric cord about his waist, he took the wife in his arms, trying desperately not to move or jostle her spine, for fear it was broken. He stepped down that steep incline balancing precariously with her in his arms. Thank God he was always blessed with the agility and balance of a cat. With the children steadying him by pulling on the cord, he made it safely all the way down and put the wife in the back of the station wagon, which he had "happened" to park at the bottom instead of on top as usual.

At the hospital it was determined that the wife had fractured three vertebrae, but not one had slipped out of place! Any one of the three could have sliced her spinal cord! Her right heel bone was sheared off. But the heel and back were soon healed, so that within three weeks she was swinging happily along on crutches without a cast!

Her accident had been no accident at all. This woman had been a student of ballet. Her balance was excellent. There was nothing imaginary about the blow that toppled her. At the time, her family and ours had been involved in spiritual warfare together against demonic assignments sent by covens.

Another incident occurred when seven of us had been invited to conduct a teaching mission on the island of Vancouver. I would teach, and they would lead prayer groups. No sooner had we arrived at St. Mary's Priory, Victoria, than a committee came to say, "Thank God you're here. There is a coven of witches headed by a man on an island nearby who have been hating a boy to death. He is dying of a mysterious blood disease, and the doctors don't know what it is or what causes it." Before we could say anything, word came that the boy had died. We decided to go to battle in prayer and put a stop to the activity of that coven. That began the war.

People in the village on the island reported that some had seen apparitions of this man flying over the village! Many were terrified of him and the coven. Few dared to cross him.

After we returned home, we continued in spiritual warfare. In a few days I began to feel drained. In a month or so, prophetic people were telling me that I needed more protection around me. Friends in an audience where I spoke sat with tears streaming down their faces. Afterward I asked, "Was what I said so bad it made you cry?"

"No, John, we could see in the spirit that you are being hit, again and again, moment by moment, day after day." Truly, I felt like a punching bag, black and blue all over, though nothing physical showed.

I went to speak at a Christian camp. There, a friend who is gifted as a Christian massage therapist saw the hurt and ache in my body. She said, "Maybe it would help if you let me give you a rubdown." Then, making sure I had someone else present with me, we spread a blanket on the grass and she began to massage my back. Again and again she came to the same spot midway down my spinal column on the right side. She seemed puzzled. Finally I asked, "What is it? You seem disturbed about something."

She replied, "I don't know, John. I've never encountered anything like this. There's something evil here."

We sent the other person to find a woman we knew at the camp who possessed a keen gift of discernment. When she arrived, the massage therapist said, "Marilyn, there is something in John's back. I don't know what it is. I want you to take it away." We told Marilyn nothing more than that and gave her no indication where on my back whatever it was might be.

Marilyn prayed in the spirit for a few minutes, then grabbed forcefully exactly on that spot in my back and jerked something out and away from me, screaming in fear of it! We asked her what it was. When she had regained her composure, she said, "It was a spear, an evil thing of Satan, sticking right there in John's back!" Lest that seem impossible, implausible, or fanciful, listen to the scripture:

> In addition to all, taking up the shield of faith with which you will be able to extinguish *all the flaming missiles* of the evil one.
> —EPHESIANS 6:16, EMPHASIS ADDED

Perhaps one reason the Lord let that happen was so that we could know beyond doubt that the Scripture sometimes means what it says exactly as it says it, not merely poetically. Those darts are real. No one can tell me otherwise. I had felt the sickness of it in me, I felt it when Marilyn pulled it out of me, and I knew the relief and the health that flooded into me again. Spiritual warfare is real, and apparently I had not taken warfare seriously enough to put up my shield!

Subsequently I heard from someone on that island that the man and his coven had suffered a terrible car wreck. He wasn't being seen flying over that village anymore! His power had been broken.

SATANISTS AND SATANIC CULTS

When covens exist they seek actively to attack the churches that seem to have life in them. For a while, a group of Satanists decided to make the Rathdrum Prairie adjacent to Coeur D'Alene their headquarters. Horrible, weird things began to happen. Animals were found gutted or with sexual or other parts excised. One of our friends, a nutritionist who traveled regularly throughout the region to supervise nutrition programs in schools and hospitals, was advised unofficially by an official in the sheriff's department to carry a gun in her glove compartment and that she should not step out of her car for any reason while she was in that area. He advised her not to travel alone, but if she had to, never to stop her car. He warned her that if a chain of people appeared before her across the road, she was not even to slow down. If she hit someone, she was not to stop or to report it! She was to have her car repaired and say nothing. Another acquaintance of ours, in that same time period, encountered such a human chain across a country road in front of a tree that had been felled. Having been similarly advised, she gunned her car, turned off the road, and bounced across a field as fast as she could go to a neighbor's house.

Many prayer ministers and counselors have counseled persons afflicted by satanic cults. I ministered to a lady who had been conceived and dedicated in the womb to be a child of Satan. Her parents and other Satanists continuously used her in unspeakably degrading sexual rituals. Dung was used for the bread of communion. St. Paul wrote:

> Do not participate in the unfruitful deeds of darkness, but instead even expose them; for it is disgraceful even to speak of the things which are done by them in secret.
> —EPHESIANS 5:11–12

St. Paul's teaching is woefully appropriate today! Decency forbids me to relate further details of the incredibly debasing activity that surrounded this child and to which they subjected her. Amazingly, something within her resisted throughout. Appeals to the government finally delivered her from such abuse, and the Lord subsequently saved her. Now she wanted inner healing for all those years that still plagued her memories through nightmares and terrors.

Many have ministered to former Satanists who have all related similar debaucheries involved with the most debasing forms of sorcery. We share this much so that the body of Christ may once and for all take its head out of the sand! It is blind foolishness to think that because most modern men have learned not to believe "foolish superstitions," such horrible satanic rites do not exist today or that they are only ineffectual fantasies and foolishness. Believing that Satanists and their black sorceries do not exist will not make them go away! These evils are rampant and on the increase as our world turns more and more from the truth of God's Word.

> And just as they did not see fit to acknowledge God any longer, God gave them over to a depraved mind, to do those things which are not proper, being filled with all unrighteousness, wickedness, greed, evil; full of envy, murder, strife, deceit, malice; they are gossips, slanderers, haters of God, insolent, arrogant, boastful, inventors of evil, disobedient to parents, without understanding, untrustworthy, unloving, unmerciful; and, although they know the ordinance of God, that those who practice such things are worthy of death, they not only do the same, but also give hearty approval to those who practice them.
> —ROMANS 1:28–32

The body of Christ must learn how to set free and heal those our Lord would snatch from Satan's sorcery. We must know how to minister victoriously against the reality that ensnared them. And we must know how to set free and heal the wounds of those whom the Satanists have afflicted.

When we were young in faith and first into spiritual warfare, Paula and I used to be jumped on in the night in our sleep. This experience is common to many Christians. A demonic thing would enter our room and jump on me, paralyzing me instantly. I could not move a muscle. I could hardly breathe. Knowing that Jesus who is in me is stronger than he who is in the world, I would begin to pray silently, repeating, "Jesus is my Lord. Jesus, You are Lord." In a minute or two, I could say Jesus's name aloud and begin to throw that entity off. Sometimes in the process, my struggles would arouse Paula, who would join in prayer until we were freed and the house was clean again. A few minutes later we would be sound asleep again, and the same or another demonic thing would jump on Paula. She would go through the same struggle, awakening me, and we would pray again. Now, years later, we are never so attacked, perhaps because the devil knows our faith is too strong. We know firsthand what St. John meant when he wrote:

I am writing to you, fathers, because you know Him who has been from the beginning. I am writing to you, young men, *because you have overcome the evil one.* I have written to you, children, because you know the Father. I have written to you, fathers, because you know Him who has been from the beginning. I have written to you, young men, because you are strong, *and the word of God abides in you, and you have overcome the evil one.*

—1 JOHN 2:13–14, EMPHASIS ADDED

Several years later, one of our United Church of Christ missionaries on sabbatical from Africa related several stories of natives being killed by what they called "the black wraith." He described the same experience we had suffered. We had been protected by faith. Strangely, we had never been really afraid, only annoyed. We knew by faith the devil could not kill us. We had been able to fall asleep immediately afterward, sure of our Lord's protection. Those natives had died because of fear. Their fear had empowered the demons and the witch doctors behind them with more power than they should have held. The missionary from Africa and others from Haiti (in other denominations) reported also about the power of witch doctors to afflict people with pain, troubles, and accidents from a long distance.

One of our friends, a pastor, had a daughter who was recruited by a team for summer missionary work. Before she left, the pastor spoke of it when Paula and I were visiting him. My heart sank. I knew there was danger for her and that she should not go. But how could I communicate that? I knew that she would encounter witchcraft and be unprepared to handle it. The pastor hardly believed in such things. Of course, it ought not to be assumed that anyone traveling to Haiti would be in danger. This was a specific warning for her. She did cross such forces of evil and came home with a rare disease no medical doctors seemed able to cure. I am sure the family could not believe me when I tried to tell them what was really causing it. Later, a deliverance minister perceived a demonic thing afflicting her, cast it away, and she is well again.

Is it enough? Those who have had similar experiences will already know that what we say is true. Sorcerers can wield demonic powers to afflict; demons can physically attack people. But when we pray, our all-powerful God protects.

ASTROLOGY

Astrology is also listed in my *Oxford Dictionary* as one of the occult practices. Many Christians have thought that astrology is not one of the evils the Lord prohibited. But the Word of God is clear. Isaiah scolded Israel for turning to sorcerers and astrologers:

> Stand fast now in your spells and in your many sorceries with which you have labored from your youth; perhaps you will be able to profit, perhaps you may cause trembling. You are wearied with your many counsels; let now the *astrologers, those who prophesy by the stars,* those who predict by the new moons, stand up and save you from what will come upon you. Behold, they have become like stubble, fire burns them; they cannot deliver themselves from the power of the flame; there will be no coal to warm by, nor a fire to sit before! So have those become to you with whom you have labored, who have trafficked with you from your youth; each has wandered in his own way. There is none to save you.
>
> —ISAIAH 47:12–15, EMPHASIS ADDED

Astrology participates in the sin of divination. Divination is the practice of peering into the future or the unknown. It is Satan's copy of the gifts of knowledge and prophecy. Sometimes in God's wisdom He does not want us to know things, much as a wise earthly father conceals from his children information about sex until he knows they are mature enough to deal with it.

> It is the glory of God to conceal a matter, but the glory of kings is to search out a matter.
>
> —PROVERBS 25:2

When the Lord does want us to know, He may choose one of many ways to involve us "kings" in the glory of searching out whatever it is, according to His knowledge of our maturity.

> I have many more things to say to you, but you cannot bear them now.
>
> —JOHN 16:12

He knows when to hide knowledge and when and how best to reveal it.

Divination breaks His providence. Divination happens when we fail to trust God. We want a handle on life. We want to know what is coming so as to be prepared for it. To use our minds and computers to project what is mathematically probable and to be prepared is not yet divination. That is not yet an improper taking "thought for the morrow" (Matt. 6:34, KJV). That is to use the God-given natural wisdom God expects us to maintain.

Divination occurs when we want more than that. When we attempt to find security in assurances by knowledge gained illicitly, it is divination. The key behind the sin of disobedience in divination is fear and lack of trust. We install something else as god to us when we can no longer trust blindly the hand of God.

> Who is blind but My servant, or so deaf as My messenger whom I send? Who is so blind as he that is at peace with Me, or so blind as the servant of the LORD?
>
> —ISAIAH 42:19

The Lord's servant is willing to see nothing and hear nothing, trusting in the Lord.

Fortune-tellers, palm readers, tea leaf readers, and so on are all diviners, forbidden by the Word of the Lord.

> There shall not be found among you…one who uses divination, one who practices witchcraft, or one who interprets omens.
>
> —DEUTERONOMY 18:10

GUIDANCE FROM THE LORD OR DIVINATION?

There is a fine line between seeking the Lord's guidance and unconsciously attempting to turn that into divination. Again and again the kings of Israel sought out the Lord's prophets, saying, "Inquire of the Lord for us." Sometimes their hearts were right, and sometimes they were so full of fear they were attempting to involve His prophets in divination.

Common everyday listening can be turned by a wrong heart to divination. Paula and I visited a farmer friend in Arkansas. As we drove in, we asked him what was wrong; his bean crops looked very unhealthy. He explained that by his experience and natural wisdom he had planned to plant wheat that year. But he had been trying to do everything by listening to God, and he was sure he had heard God tell him to plant beans. It turned out that the kind of weather that occurred during that growing season would have been good for wheat but was terrible for beans. Now he was going deeply into debt.

On the surface it seems like trying to listen to God about all things is good. But God does not want to reduce us to slaves or robots. He has given us good minds, and He expects us to use them. Moreover, questioning soon revealed that our friend had been fearful of failure. He would use "listening to God" to be overly certain. That became the sin of divination. Had God wanted to steer him away from one crop to another, the Lord would have taken the initiative to speak and would have confirmed by at least two witnesses. But our friend's fearful heart sought to turn God into his diviner. The Lord let him listen to a wrong voice as both discipline and teaching. That was a tough way to learn, but it was certainly written on our friend's heart to listen when God wants to speak but not to push God to be his diviner. The same mistake and consequent dire results have happened to many in the body of Christ.

THE FINE LINE BETWEEN SOME RELIGIOUS MOVEMENTS AND MAGIC

In the same way, there is a fine line between prayer and magic. When we discover the laws of God's universe and hear the promises of God, we can claim those promises and activate those principles by prayer with such a wrong heart that we have actually merged into magic rather than prayer. Magic would take hold of God's Word and so claim His promises as to try to manipulate or force God to do what we want. True prayer is petition, humbly respecting the free will of a Father who may in wisdom say no. Authority in prayer to accomplish something can and ought to be expressed, but only after careful listening to God so that it is the Holy Spirit who acts in and with us as we express what is also the Father's will. But when we grasp His promises and insist that He do what we want because He promised—"And Lord, Your Word is true, so we know You have to"— we are actually trying to manipulate God. Our prayer has become magic! We are operating in His principles to obtain what we want!

For instance, we can improperly use seed faith so that it becomes a kind of magic. When a servant of the Lord sends a nickel, for example, enclosed in his letter asking for help, he is working the principle on you, whether or not he is aware. The force of that principle to cause you to give him a gift in return is magic. The key of discernment is courtesy. The way of the Lord respects the free will of all men. Such a gift as a nickel or a penny, sent in that context, works to overcome our free will by the force of the principles of law. It disrespects our right to make up our minds freely whether or not to give to that ministry.

I used to listen to a well-known teacher of healing and would occasionally hear the Lord saying in my spirit, "This teacher is teaching magic." The teacher was urgently insisting that if we apply faith, God *must* heal. Please, dear body of Christ, never try to get a handle on God! God doesn't *have* to do anything! To try to make Him do anything is magic; magic is the operation of principles or laws of God to accomplish our own selfish ends. Even healing in this context is our own selfish end. It might not be God's will to heal in that moment, though later He might. We cannot force Him to act on our timetable. To operate a car is not magic. In that, we are only cooperating with the laws of nature as an engine propels by the laws of combustion. Our own energy is not added to it. We are not interfering. Magic interferes by the will of the magician, forcing a thing to happen by occult or hidden principles.

In this regard, some teachers of the recent faith movement unwittingly have led many who are sincere Christians into the operation of magic. We plead with the body of Christ to repent, to pray for all who have stumbled into this kind of magic, and above all, not to condemn people or fracture the unity of the body by rejection. We all pioneer in frontiers of faith, stumbling by trial and error into maturity. Let us love one another, be reconciled, and be healed.

THEOSOPHY

Theosophy is a claim to have esoteric knowledge of the interplay of natural elements and the world of the spirit (not in this instance meaning only our own personal spirit, but the spiritual world that pervades all things). Theosophists commonly see their view of life as deeper and more profound than recognized religious doctrines. They view Orthodox dogmas as mere exoteric outworkings or expressions of the deeper truths only they, the enlightened ones, are privy to. Again the sin is gnostic. They believe they are being saved by their esoteric knowledge. These "masters" or "illuminati" then feel it incumbent upon them to teach "lesser lights" the way. But they are impelled by principalities of delusion. They teach doctrines of men.

> You hypocrites, rightly did Isaiah prophesy of you, saying, "This people honors Me with their lips, but their heart is far away from Me. But in vain do they worship Me, teaching as doctrines the precepts of men."
>
> —MATTHEW 15:7–9

Worse, unwittingly they teach doctrines of demons.

> But the Spirit explicitly says that in later times some will fall away from the faith, paying attention to deceitful spirits and doctrines of demons.
>
> —1 TIMOTHY 4:1

Theosophists, like alchemists, also are Pelagian (perfecting oneself by human effort without God) and humanistic, though they would prefer to call themselves theistic (believers in God), being normally quite religious. Rosicrucianism, the works of Madame Blavatsky, and others are examples of theosophy. Theosophy attempts to discover truth by experience. Unfortunately, these are not the God-given experiences we Christians are benefited by under the tutelage of the Holy Spirit, checked by the Word and by brothers and sisters in the faith. They seek experiential apprehension of false doctrines in secret "mandami" and psychic experiences. Rosicrucians enlisted students in a discipline of theosophistry, and each month lessons, or "mandami," were mailed to adherents with supposed revelations of great mysteries. Having studied philosophy in university, I soon recognized that these were nothing more than eclectic selections from philosophic treatises coupled with psychic practices that would supposedly increase students' power. Little else than practices employed by yogis, the mandami and practices were a hoax that claimed to lead "initiates" into deeper "mysteries."

The aims of theosophy are not much different from those of alchemists. They differ only in method, not enduring the alchemist's rigorous self-disciplines and inner searches to produce the white stone. Theosophists also seek integration and wholeness to be restored to the pristine perfection of Adam. However, we know that "no one comes to the Father, but through [Jesus]" (John 14:6). Man and Satan have continually sought any way other than death on the cross to be born anew and restored to the kingdom. Perhaps we should say that Satan has continually sought any ploy, any device, any teaching, anything that will lure men away from the

tough way of the cross to the wide and smooth road of destruction. He
always appeals to man's desire to become who he is supposed to become.
This is the very same temptation set before Eve's wondering person and
nascent eyes! The temptation is always for a person to achieve perfection
in himself, sometimes with the help of others but essentially on his own
without God.

The root, therefore, of every occult sin is pride! One primary reason for
the cross is to humble us. God's plan is to divest us thoroughly of pride
through continuous application of the cross. "Where then is boasting? It is
excluded. By what kind of law? Of works? No, but by a law of faith" (Rom.
3:27). The essence of all occultism is to become something in oneself,
to have and wield a power that elevates oneself, even as Simon wanted
people to think of him as someone great. Regarding that sinful proclivity,
St. Paul wrote:

> For if anyone thinks he is something when he is nothing, he deceives
> himself.
> —GALATIANS 6:3

> And if any man think that he knoweth anything, he knoweth nothing
> yet as he ought to know.
> —1 CORINTHIANS 8:2, KJV

> Let no man deceive himself. If any man among you thinks that he is
> wise in this age, let him become foolish that he may become wise. For
> the wisdom of this world is foolishness before God.
> —1 CORINTHIANS 3:18–19

HYPNOTISM

Among the occult practices listed in Deuteronomy 18:10–11, there remains
only mediumism (to be discussed in the next chapter) and "one who casts
a spell." Friedrich Anton Mesmer, born May 23, 1733, and died March 5,
1815, was the modern rediscoverer of hypnotism. Friedrich believed in
"magnetism," supposedly derived from astrological forces. He attempted
to use magnetic forces for healing. It was through hypnotism primarily
that he thought he could apply such "magnetism." After him, what we
now know as hypnotism was called "mesmerism." Today his name has
become part of our daily vocabulary. When we become enthralled with a

performance or a person, we say we were "mesmerized." In biblical days hypnotism was spoken of as "casting a spell," and a hypnotist was called a "charmer."

Hypnotism is strictly forbidden. Christians should need no reason; obedience should be enough. Hypnotism is prohibited for a number of reasons:

1. We are not to surrender our will to any other than the Lord Jesus Christ.

2. Such surrender opens inner supernatural doors that should be open to no one but our Lord.

3. None other than Jesus can be trusted to rule our will.

It is not true that hypnotism cannot cause one to act against one's will and is therefore supposedly safe. If a hypnotist can discover and lay hold of an inner hatred, resentment, anger, or fearsome usable latent-but-powerful inner drive, he can use that to cause a person to do all manner of ill, evil, or embarrassing things he never would have thought himself capable of doing in his right mind.

At a seminar, I was teaching on some other subject when a question necessitated an answer concerning hypnotism. I explained how the Word of God forbids it and that the use of it in parlor games is entirely foolish and reprehensible. I said that no Christian prayer minister, secular counselor, or psychiatrist should use it. If he wanted to discover something in a client, let him ask questions or let the Holy Spirit reveal it by gifts of knowledge and discernment. I explained that hypnotism could reveal what the Lord is not ready yet to heal, whereas the Holy Spirit will reveal each thing only as the other is prepared for healing. Concerning its use for orthodontic operations for people who cannot stand to undergo anesthesia, I said that I felt for those in such predicaments, but that the Word of God forbids its use.

Immediately after, I sat down to lunch directly across the table from an oral surgeon who was then the president of the national association that teaches doctors how to use clinical hypnosis! He told me he agreed fully in every way that such warnings were valid and necessary. Only, he did use hypnotism for patients who could not be anesthetized. Ten years later, that man came to me and sadly said, "John, the Lord has shown me

the hard way. Never again will I use hypnotism for any purpose whatsoever!" Crowds surrounded us and carried me away, and I never found
opportunity to ask what had happened. What had he experienced that
filled him with such sadness and determination?

At another conference, when the subject came up, a psychiatrist testified that he also had used hypnotism in the past and never would again.
Again, there was not sufficient time to discover fully why, but we should
not need to know. Obedience to God's Word should be enough. Praise
God that He is revealing His Word to professionally trained servants.

At a school of pastoral care, a Christian psychologist was asked about
hypnotism. He also testified against it and reported that a counselor had
hypnotized a counselee. He gave her a posthypnotic suggestion that she
would never smoke again. It worked. She stopped smoking. Two weeks
later she jumped out the second-floor window! The counselor concluded
he had removed her steam valve without healing her inner pressures.
The Christian psychologist observed that it was not merely unwise use of
hypnotism that made it wrong but the use of hypnotism at all.

There are many other forms of occult involvement, but perhaps all
could be subsumed under the headings we have discussed. Our purpose is
not to chronicle or expose all the various forms of occultism to the light of
God's Word. It is rather to teach the body of Christ about occult involvement so as to enable healing.

HEALING THE WOUNDS OF OCCULTISM

All involvement with occultism wounds. God did not build us for it. Our
system is wrenched, whether we operate it or have it used on us, knowingly
or unknowingly. Involvement in occultism is like forcing a lovely soprano
voice to sing bass. That harms the vocal cords. Our bodies and spirits do
not naturally flow in occult ways. Shakespeare knew this, concerning all
sin. In his play *Macbeth*, Lady Macbeth said it most clearly:

> Come, you spirits,
> That tend to mortal thoughts, *unsex me here,*
> And fill me from the crown to the toe, top-full
> Of direst cruelty; *make thick my blood,*
> *Stop up the access, and passage to remorse,*
> *That no compunctious visitings of nature*

> *Shake my fell purpose,* nor keep peace between
> The effect of it! *Come to my woman's breasts,*
> And *take my milk for gall,* you murdering ministers,
> Wherever in your sightless substances,
> *You wait on nature's mischief!* Come thick night,
> And pall thee in the dunnest smoke of Hell,
> That my knee knife *see not the wound it makes,*
> *Nor heaven peep through* the blanket of the dark,
> *To cry, "Hold, hold!"*[7]

Sin, especially occultism, destroys the wholesome flow of the spirit in action in the body. Again Macbeth says:

> Methought I heard a voice cry, "Sleep no more!
> *Macbeth does murder sleep,"* the innocent sleep,
> *Sleep that knits up the ravelled sleave of care,*
> The death of each day's life, *sore labour's bath,*
> *Balm of hurt minds,* great nature's second course,
> *Chief nourisher* in life's feast…[8]

Remember that the play begins with three witches who *tempt* Macbeth by false prophecies of glory. The unfolding drama of *Macbeth* is a revelation and teaching of the twisting effects upon God-given conscience and courses of thought by sorcery. We suggest that any who would counsel and heal the effects of occultism would profit by studying the play *Macbeth* with an eye to seeing how occultism perverts nature and mankind from their natural courses. We have provided below what these effects are.

Disturbed sleep

A common first result of occultism is disturbed sleep. Insomnia, fretful sleep, and nightmares are caused by many things, but one of the causes Elijah House prayer ministers routinely look for is past or present occult involvement or whether the person is under occult attack. Questions soon reveal whether the person has ever been involved. Many people assume falsely that occultism could not be the cause of their difficulties because they never practiced anything occult regularly. They may have forgotten the one time as a child when as a lark they went with some friends to see "Aunt Fanny," who took hold of their hands and enthralled them by knowing things that had happened to them and by telling them about what would happen in their future. Or they may have forgotten how they used to have fun playing with the Ouija board. They may have forgotten that even today they play that devil-created game called Dungeons and Dragons, which directly involves the players in occult practices. They have forgotten the few times they tried to hypnotize one another or played at holding a séance. However innocuous it may seem, sin is sin, and it sets in motion forces that must later be dealt with in one way or another.

God is not repulsed or upset by children's playful dabblings. He understands. But the laws of the universe are neither compassionate nor indulgent. However gleefully we may step off the roof of a tall building, the results are disastrous. It only takes one time. God is compassionate. (See Psalm 103.) He was not incensed at our childish misadventures. But just as gravity cannot be denied, neither can God revoke His laws because foolish children do not understand. How foolish it would seem to us if a child thought he could swim unaided by scuba equipment in an underwater cave for five minutes. We would *expect* him to drown. No one would try to blame God. Whoever understands the law concerning occultism is not surprised or offended when dire results crop up years after the event. Only now are we beginning to see the awful effects upon Vietnam veterans who came into contact with Agent Orange years ago. Results from one instance of occult activity in childhood may afflict someone horribly in adulthood. Prayer ministers need to see that we are dealing with legal cause and effect. Dabblers in the occult do not generally immediately reap what they have sown, but it is inevitable that one day they will.

Disturbed sleep due to occultism can be healed through these four steps:

1. Forgiveness for whatever degree of involvement the person experienced

2. Closure

Occult dabblings, however insignificant, open doors to occult forces. Playful explorations give access to powers that otherwise would have no means of afflicting the individual. Prayer ministers should pray that the Lord may shut all psychic doors.

3. Hiding the person in Christ

You have died and your life is hidden with Christ in God.
—COLOSSIANS 3:3

A Christian normally is obscured from Satan, guarded by the angels of God. Demonic powers cannot see where to afflict him or how to prevent his plans, but occultism exposes a person to view. In Tolkien's fantasy *The Lord of the Rings*, whenever Frodo put on the *magic* ring he carried, he became invisible to everyone—except to the powers of darkness! He had entered by magic into their world, and now they could see him more clearly than if he were only his natural self. Just so, by occultism we enter Satan's world and his minions see us. We heal such exposure simply by praying the person be rehidden.

Sometimes I will say, "Lord, as the angels reached out and gathered Lot in and blinded those men in Sodom so that they groped for the handle all night and could not find it, so I draw this person into the body of Christ and ask the angels to blind all the powers of darkness. They can no longer see my brother (or sister). From now on he is hidden from them. I obscure all the pathways over which they have tracked him. 'Let their way be dark and slippery, with the angel of the LORD pursuing them'" (Ps. 35:6).

4. Praying for physical healing

We ask the Lord to pour His healing balm throughout their body and spirit, healing and removing any devices the devil may have implanted by draining one's energies through sleeplessness.

Annoying inner voices

A second effect of occultism is that the person may be pestered by hearing annoying inner voices. Sometimes that has natural psychological causes, but sometimes the voices may be from demons invited by occultic involvement or one's own psychological manifestations made worse by meddling with demons. Questioning and discernment are needed to determine which is the cause for the person hearing voices. If one is not sure, it does not hurt to pray away occult influence, just in case. If occult influence was not the cause, at least one rules that out by having taken care of the possibility. The same four steps that were mentioned above to heal disturbed sleep are taken in prayer to heal the person from hearing inner voices. We add a fifth as well. We rebuke the spirits and voices, cast them away, and command them in Jesus's name to be silent. Occasionally such prayer catapults us into a full-blown exorcism, of which we will speak more fully in the next chapter.

Recurring accidents or tragic happenings

A third common effect of occultism is recurrent accidents or tragic happenings. Sometimes after we have checked out and prayed away bitter-root judgments and expectancies by which the person is continually mysteriously defeated or reaps tragedy (see chapter 8 in *Transforming the Inner Man*), the person still retains an uncanny ability to snatch harm out of the arms of safety. The Holy Spirit may then reveal that because of occult involvement sometime in his or her life, the powers of darkness know how and when to cause just the right wrong action that tumbles his or her house of cards.

We have all suffered damaging coincidences, such as someone's choosing to phone us just as we were stepping out the door for an important interview, causing us to miss our appointment! We have mistakenly committed ourselves to courses of action that turned out to be wrong for us, only to learn moments too late that bit of information that could have saved us all that pain and trouble, only then to discover that a strange set of circumstances kept that knowledge from arriving on time. Or if something doesn't happen in time, all our plans will come to naught, such as a company forgetting to pay a debt so we cannot do some special thing or a person neglecting to recommend us for this or that. However, Christians are constantly being surprised at the Lord's providence and timing. Just when things are going wrong, the right set of coincidences happen to turn everything to roses.

For people who are hindered by occultic involvement, it happens the other way around. If there is any loophole, if anything can foul up the works, and just as circumstances begin to improve, trouble will happen like clockwork! They never seem to luck out. They become fond of saying, "You know, if it weren't for bad luck, I wouldn't have any luck at all."

We stop Satan's game by the same steps outlined above, only we add to the prayer a direct command that his inroads into the person's life be stopped. We command him to take his hands off that person's life. Perhaps it should be added that the most common cause of such accidents and hurtful happenings is a curse. By this we mean that some power of darkness or person involved in sorcery may have placed a curse on this person's life. We simply break the curse by the authority and the name of Jesus. Second, the person unconsciously cursed his or her own father or mother in his bitterness and judgments against them. Jesus reminded His followers that "Moses said, 'Honor your father and your mother'; and, 'He who speaks evil of father or mother, let him be put to death'" (Mark 7:10). The death we die is to our abundant life. Cursing our father or mother, in that sense, puts a curse on our life. Nothing will go fully right from then on. We insert this here because we know that if a prayer minister discovers and casts away occult destructions but does not uncover and bring to forgiveness whatever lay between a person and his parents, the troubles most likely will not stop. Unforgiveness would retain the curse on the person's life, continuing to give Satan access.

Affliction and physical illness

A fourth result from occult involvement may be affliction and physical illnesses. A person may feel bothered and tormented, or he may be subject to recurrent rashes or illnesses for which medical doctors can't find the right cure. Again, there may be many psychosomatic or purely medical causes, but on the other hand it may be unwise to overlook the possibility of occult influence. One woman in our prayer group many years ago had been complaining of inability to arrive at full healing and health. There was always something nagging. Through the Spirit of God, I saw occultism in the family history and prayed for it to be stopped. Just a few days after our prayer, she handed me a letter full of rejoicing that our prayer in the group had set her free.

Sometimes physical afflictions happen not because of past involvement but through effects of present spiritual warfare. A Christian teacher ran afoul of a batch of witches' covens in a foreign country. It was as though she had stirred up a hornet's nest. The conflict was affecting her through headaches, weariness, blocked moments in her teachings, fits of despondency, and feelings of futility. She called me for help. Under anointing, knowing everything else had been tried, I told her, "Try getting out into nature. Walk in the woods. Roll on the grass." She tried it, and it worked, especially rolling on the grass. It was as though all those negative effects drained out of her into the earth. She wrote back that some people thought she was one crazy lady, but she sure felt better!

I might interject here that my Osage Indian ancestors used to say that one reason the white man loses track of who he is and does wrong things is that he lives too far away from the earth. His houses and streets isolate him from the good earth. Indians purposefully sat on the earth and slept on the earth whenever possible for the reason that they knew it was good for them. Nature camps have been established for city children because of sociological studies that observe the effects of a lack of a wholesome natural environment. We recommend as one antidote for occult influence, besides all the ways we pray for healing, large doses of time outside in the good earth. When the numbers of people needing prayer ministry have piled in on me one after the other, and I feel defiled, I may take ten minutes between appointments to walk out into the garden and let my fingers work in the soil. It drains away that feeling of defilement that by then I can no longer successfully pray away.

Memory lapses and blocked thought patterns

A fifth symptom of occult attack is lapses of memory, blocked thought patterns, inability to remember where one has put things or what one is doing, and loss of one's stream of thought while speaking. Having suffered effects of hypoglycemia at one time and acute stress at others, I know firsthand that these symptoms can be the result of physical and psychological causes. Nevertheless, discernment may also reveal occult causes. Neither cause need rule out the other. Perhaps one would be able to overcome the physical causes were occultism not tipping the scales or be able to withstand occult attack were not one already so exhausted or stressed. However, sometimes effects can be there by occult interference when no physical reason exists.

Many years ago when Agnes Sanford and I traveled together as a team, it was for that reason. Opposing spirits had been blocking her thoughts and constricting her throat, severely restricting her ability to speak. I seldom spoke, usually only in the mornings. I was not there for that purpose. We would pray together during the day. At the meetings, I would read the Scriptures and say a prayer. Agnes would teach, and afterward I would close with prayer. During her talk I sat in the audience close by where I could watch her, interceding the entire time. So long as I remembered to attend to my duties instead of being caught up in what she was saying, power flowed through her without interruption. She had also been plagued by tension headaches, partly from the stress of so much speaking and the burden of intercession, but also from occult opposition. I was there to protect her so that she might be free to concentrate on the ministry. Many speakers have learned to enlist prayer warriors at home, and some have intercessors as part of their traveling team as a wall of protection, as in Psalm 8:2: "From the mouth of infants and nursing babes

Thou hast established strength, because of Thine adversaries, to make the enemy and the revengeful cease."[9]

Family turmoil and tragedies

A sixth effect of occult involvement is constant family turmoil and tragedies. Satan often attacks the Lord's servants through afflictions upon their families. Church members should learn to pray regularly for their pastor's family. Traveling teachers, prophets, and evangelists need groups who dedicate themselves to prayer on their behalf, especially to watch over their families, since their frequent absences from home leave their families vulnerable and subject to bouts of resentment toward them.

If occultism has been engaged in at any time in life, family doors have been opened that ought to have remained shut. Hear again the Lord's Word concerning those who have been to séances: "I will... *cut him off from among his people*" (Lev. 20:6, emphasis added). The law of sowing and reaping flows into operation. When a man turns to the occult, in effect he cuts himself and all those in his charge off from the Lord. That is the seed he has sown, and therefore that is what he must reap. Powers of darkness take advantage of that to add the ravages of turmoil and tragedy to the discipline of the law. Guilt that fails to find its way to the cross then becomes a handle demonic powers can pump.

We stop such interference by the same applications of forgiveness, healing, and hiding the family in Christ, but let us remember the lessons of our first chapter. There is need for much healing of wounded spirits, lest we go through the proper motions but fail to hug and heal as my father did after he spanked us. Torn and tattered feelings and relationships need to be mended. It will not do to rebuke Satan's hosts away, only to leave the door open through unhealed wounds and remembrances.

Endless financial drain

A seventh common symptom might be summed up under previous effects but deserves mention on its own. Sometimes it seems as though there is an unending drain on family finances. Just about the time the mother and father hope to lift their heads above water for a while, sudden unlooked-for expenses plunge them under again. Every light at the end of the tunnel is somehow snuffed out or proves to be a false hope. The key thing is that expenses occur in the most outlandish, unfair, mysterious ways! Life does not flow evenly. Budgets are so disrupted as to be impossible to adhere to. It is as though there is a curse on the wealth of the family. If the family is not tithing, of course there is, and that needs to be corrected first.

> Will a man rob God? Yet you are robbing Me! But you say, "How have we robbed Thee?" In tithes and offerings. *You are cursed with a curse,* for you are robbing Me, the whole nation of you! Bring the whole tithe into the storehouse, so that there may be food in My house, and test Me now in this," says the LORD of hosts, "if I will not open for you the windows of heaven, and pour out for you a blessing until it overflows. Then *I will rebuke the devourer for you,* so that it may not destroy the fruits of the ground; nor will your vine in the field cast its grapes," says the LORD of hosts. "And all the nations will call you blessed, for you shall be a delightful land," says the LORD of hosts.
> —MALACHI 3:8–12, EMPHASIS ADDED

Sometimes, however, the family may be tithing faithfully and hurting all the more because now it seems that God's promises fail to be true. "I'm doing my part! Why isn't God coming through? This isn't fair. I know He has a reason, but how come when things go wrong He always has an excuse and I never have one?" So the latter effect of occult involvement is more important than financial loss; there is nothing the devil would rather do than break our trust in the faithfulness of God.

Sometimes in prayer by vision I have seen a great lake of blessing God has stored up that He wants to pour down, but the curse has turned the funnel of reception upside down. The waters of blessing splatter off the sides like an umbrella and only a trickle comes through the small opening. In faith, we take the devil's hands off the supply line, and see the funnel properly situated, reaching out to catch the floods of goodness and channel them to His child and His family.

Healing is needed not only for the family for all the strains of financial loss but also between them and God. They need to be enabled to say words of forgiveness to God, as St. Paul urged, "On behalf of Christ, be reconciled to God" (2 Cor. 5:20). The same reconciliation with God could also be applied for all the other hurts we have discussed, but here it is specifically required in that a specific promise of God *seems* to have been broken, that of His faithfulness to provide and protect.

Generational trouble and harm

An eighth result of occult involvement is not merely to be expected, it is an absolute requirement that, by law, it *will* happen. Because of generational sin, the descent of trouble and harm will come to generation after generation. (See Deuteronomy 5:9.) We briefly mention this here, but it is discussed more fully in chapter 9, "Generational Sin," in *Transforming the Inner Man*.

There are many other results of occult involvement, but the eight that are listed above are the most common. The body of Christ needs to become aware of these to know the power and authority of our God.

> God takes His stand in His own congregation; He judges in the midst of the rulers. How long will you judge unjustly, and show partiality to the wicked? Vindicate the weak and fatherless; do justice to the afflicted and destitute. Rescue the weak and needy; deliver them out of the hand of the wicked.
>
> —PSALM 82:1–4

The least Christian wields the fullness of power and shares the joy of the battle. In the following scripture, the kings and nations upon whom we shall execute the vengeance of God are human, but the same principle can be applied to the demonic powers. "For our struggle is not against flesh and blood" (Eph. 6:12).

The calling is urgent:

> Let the godly ones exult in glory; let them sing for joy on their beds. Let the high praises of God be in their mouth, and a two-edged sword in their hand, to execute vengeance on the nations, and punishment on the peoples; to bind their kings with chains, and their nobles with fetters of iron; to execute on them the judgment written; this is an honor for *all* His godly ones. Praise the LORD!
>
> —PSALM 149:5–9, EMPHASIS ADDED

CHAPTER 8

SPIRITUALISM AND DELIVERANCE

As for the person who turns to mediums and to spiritists, to play the harlot after them, I will also set My face against that person and will cut him off from among his people....Now a man or a woman who is a medium or a spiritist shall surely be put to death. They shall be stoned with stones, their bloodguiltiness is upon them.

—LEVITICUS 20:6, 27

Spiritualism, or spiritism, holds great appeal for those who have insufficient faith or who lack biblical knowledge. The lonely who have lost a loved one, who cannot simply believe they will share eternity together after this short life, see spiritualism as a means to have some contact with that loved one and reassurance from him. They may have little or no conscious awareness that God forbids it. It seems good to them to ease an aching heart by such contacts. There may be other reasons to turn to spiritualism. There may be a great need to find a lost bank box key or last will and testament. "If we could only contact Uncle Will, he could tell us. What's wrong with that?" Some have great fear of death, or more accurately, fear of vanishing into nothingness after death. Not having fullness of faith in our resurrected Lord, in their hearts, though their lips may confess faith, they feel that they need experiences that seem to grant assurance that something real does exist beyond the grave. Séances seem to provide the evidence they want. But God provides better ways to answer such needs, and nothing in any instance can make spiritualism right.

Spiritualism is the practice of attempting to contact and communicate with those who have departed this life. The one through whom contact and communication are made is called a medium.

As we see by the above scriptures, spiritualism is strictly forbidden by the Word of the Lord. Our Lord does not explain why it is forbidden, except to say, "You shall have no other gods before Me" (Exod. 20:3), which implies that we human beings cannot contact a departed spirit without entering into some form of idolatry. But God does not have to explain Himself. It is enough that He forbids it.

However, we can easily see at least some of His reasons. The first is the idolatry mentioned above. We may give allegiance and obedience to spirits that ought to be given to God only. For example, we have known people so hooked on spiritualism that they would not make any decision without first consulting the spirits. That relegates to spirits (probably demons masquerading as Uncle Bill or Aunt Betsy) what ought to be given only to God.

> Commit your way to the LORD, trust also in Him, and He will do it.
> —PSALM 37:5

> Commit your works to the LORD, and your plans will be established.
> —PROVERBS 16:3

A second reason is defilement. Most scholars of the Word maintain that upon death, a person's spirit is immediately taken into chambers in heaven. They say spiritists can never contact a departed soul. These scholars say people only contact that satanic "angel" (or "familiar spirit") who watched over the person all of his life who can therefore perfectly counterfeit his ways and voice and proclaim things that seemingly only the departed person could have known. Such scholars therefore maintain that whoever attempts to contact a relative only becomes contaminated by demonic spirits. I lean toward that explanation. As we will explain later, a minority of scholars wonder whether that explanation covers all the facts. They say there may be cases in which persons do actually contact the spirit of a departed person. In either case, defilement is the result. By such contact, one opens doors of his spirit that ought to remain closed.

On Earth before death, as we have expounded earlier, living persons can lure us into defilement by their presence or by what emanates from their spirits across space apart from us. But people do have bodies. Their spirits must abide within their own bodies. This is not so with departed spirits; these do not have bodies. The minority believes that this means that they can attach themselves to a living person or enter and inhabit and perhaps eventually possess him or her altogether. I have indeed had to cast away from living people spirits. Some would say those were only familiar spirits. They may be right, but humility ought to check our tendency to dogmatize. Thus a person who attends séances not only is defiled but may also become demonized.

Often, those who try to contact spirits only fool themselves, and mediums are sometimes only charlatans attempting to beguile their clients for money or some other advantage. Children frequently play foolish parlor games, attempting to hold séances. Because nothing real seems to happen, some have thought there is no reality at all to spiritualism and have simply scoffed.

However, spiritualism is forbidden for more reasons than idolatry, defilement, exposure to demonic contamination, and so on. All of those things can happen even if attempts to make contact with departed spirits are unsuccessful. God so sternly countermands it because of the possibility of people becoming involved in relationships with ghosts or demons who can lead them astray. Our Lord would not have become greatly concerned about mere imaginative foolishness. Many only fool themselves. Nothing happens but the sin of trying. Nevertheless, even misfired attempts open forbidden doors and sow to later reapings of judgment. Even childish games like the Ouija board cause great harm. Sometimes, however, mediums and séance participants do invoke and make actual contact. It is the stark reality of such things that arouses our Lord's anger.

Contacted spirits, whether in fact a departed person or a demonic counterfeit, are not to be believed. Demons want to begin by telling a person on Earth, through the vocal cords of the medium, some simple, easily verifiable facts, such as where a lost item treasured by the family can be found. They do this to establish belief and trust. Once so established, they can thus lead the person gullibly into delusions and baser and baser deceptions and doctrines. Continued contacts increase footholds in the person's spirit and soul until finally he is fully snared and on his way to hell.

There are many "spiritualist churches" who name Jesus as Lord and continue to believe they are fully Christian while treading the broad path to torture in eternity. Satan blinds their eyes (2 Cor. 4:4) to scriptures like Leviticus 20:6 and 27, careful to encourage them to pray to God and to continue in their "church." He knows that if once the veneer of being good Christians is stripped away, his deception will be exposed for what it is. Therefore Satan wants them to continue with all the trappings of Christianity while his own "trappings" remain operative in their lives, their true nature unsuspected.

As mentioned earlier, most scholars maintain that since the departed go to heaven or to hell, mediums can only contact counterfeit spirits whose intimate knowledge allows them to fool those who contact them. In the main, I think those scholars are correct. But some would say that perhaps one ought not to be too dogmatic about pronouncements that mediums and those who attend séances *only* contact counterfeits. They base their questions on the story of Saul and the witch of Endor. When Saul became agitated before the great battle he was to fight the next day against the Philistines, and no prophet would speak God's Word to him, he arose and rode all through the night behind enemy lines to find the witch of Endor. He knew that to turn to mediums was forbidden, but he was desperate and frightened. He himself had "cut off those who are mediums and spiritists from the land" (1 Sam. 28:9). But being mentally disturbed, Saul decided to contact a medium anyway. Saul asked the witch to call up Samuel. Nowhere and in no way does Scripture indicate anything imaginary or that Samuel did not in fact speak with Saul. Rather, the account is straightforwardly factual:

> When the woman saw Samuel, she cried out with a loud voice; and the woman spoke to Saul, saying, "Why have you deceived me? For you are Saul." And the king said to her, "Do not be afraid; but what do you see?" And the woman said to Saul, "I see a divine being coming up out of the earth." And he said to her, "What is his form?" And she said, "An old man is coming up, and he is wrapped with a robe." And Saul knew that it was Samuel, and he bowed with his face to the ground and did homage. Then Samuel said to Saul, "Why have you disturbed me by bringing me up?" And Saul answered, "I am greatly distressed; for the Philistines are waging war against me, and God has departed from me and answers me no more, either through prophets or by dreams; therefore I have called you, that you may make known

to me what I should do." And Samuel said, "Why then do you ask me, since the LORD has departed from you and has become your adversary? And the LORD has done accordingly as He spoke through me; for the LORD has torn the kingdom out of your hand and given it to your neighbor, to David. As you did not obey the LORD and did not execute His fierce wrath on Amalek, so the LORD has done this thing to you this day. Moreover the LORD will also give over Israel along with you into the hands of the Philistines, therefore tomorrow you and your sons will be with me. Indeed the LORD will give over the army of Israel into the hands of the Philistines!"

—1 SAMUEL 28:12–19

Whether or not Saul would have been defeated and killed anyway the next day had he not visited the medium, Samuel made the pronouncement of his death because whoever consults a medium will be cut off!

The majority of biblical scholars contend that this was a one-time exception. They propose that in this case God chose to allow Samuel to appear to fulfill God's own purposes. They say that the alternative would be to assume that a witch had the power to force a prophet to do something to which he would never give consent—participation in a séance. But even if it is possible to bring up the authentic spirit of a departed person, it would not make any visits permissible. They are sin, forbidden by God, and that should be enough for any believer.

It is an interesting footnote that the witch of Endor prevailed upon Saul to eat a meal before he left. Not only was it the custom to urge hospitality and to give a meal whenever possible, but also the woman was terrified that Saul, who had been putting to death all mediums, would recollect himself and do so to her. When he ate her food, he ate her salt. It was one of the strongest customs of the day that a person could not harm another whose salt he had eaten. So by offering such kindness, she thought to save herself from the king. Apparently it worked. Whether or not Saul would otherwise have harmed her, he did not. In just such ways, however, by being warm and kindly people, those who are involved in the sin of spiritualism sometimes think to save themselves. "Look at all the good, kind things we do. Certainly God could not reject us. We aren't wicked." But in the final judgment neither the witch of Endor nor any other well-meaning, loving but misguided spiritualist will be able to escape the judgment of God. Sin is sin, no matter how nice our character or kindly our intentions.

One time, while making routine hospital calls, I (John) came into a room in which I soon discovered that the lady to whom I was ministering was a long-practicing spiritualist. She was on her deathbed, and I began to witness to her of the saving grace of the Lord Jesus Christ. Yes, she said she would receive Him as Lord and Savior, but she wondered, had she not always known Him in her spiritualist church? Yes, I supposed she knew *of* Him. Now I would have her *receive* Him, be forgiven, and be born anew. She would do that too, she said, and she received Him in prayer as her Lord and Savior. Then I said, "Now that you have received Jesus as Lord and Savior, you will have to renounce your workers and let them go." Some spiritualists entitle the spirits they think they contact on the other side as their "workers." Some workers are regarded as good and others as evil and not to be trusted.

Before this exchange occurred and as I entered the room, her eyes had widened and she had exclaimed, "Oh, you are surrounded by the very best workers!" I knew instantly she was a spiritualist, and so I had responded, "Yes, that is the Lord Jesus Christ and all His company." That had begun our conversation.

Now the lady demurred, "Oh, no, I need my workers."

"No, Bessie, you don't need anyone but Jesus."

"No, no, I need them!"

At that moment the glory of the Lord came upon us. The Lord Himself was approaching her. But she was writhing in pain and drew back in abject fear of Him. I saw what the Lord was doing, and so I spoke again. "Do you see? It's those spirits that are afraid of Him. You have nothing to fear. You belong to Him. He loves you. Just let those workers go, and it will be all right."

"Oh, no, I couldn't."

Again the glory of the Lord came, more intensely. Again the lady blanched in terror. "Let those workers go. Jesus loves you. It will be OK."

"No, no, I can't."

"Yes, you can."

So we went around and around, several times. Finally, apparently the grace of God touched her with His empowering love, and she said, "OK, I'll let them go." With that I commanded every spirit—whether ghost or demon—to leave her, except the Holy Spirit, and forgave her the sin of spiritualism. She relaxed, and the glory of the Lord came again—and stayed! The lady was no longer afraid. Her fear had not been hers but the terror of the demons within her. She was at peace. When I left, I looked back to see a joyously serene expression on her face. Her family reported that she passed away soon after, calmly and peacefully.

WHEN SPIRITS MAKE CONTACT WITH US

As I have said, spiritism involves intentional contact with spirits; Scripture clearly forbids this. But what about times when spirits contact us through no intention of our own? Scripturally, this issue is not so black and white. Our Lord Jesus as the Word is with God and is the very Creator God (John 1:1–14; Col. 1:15ff; Heb. 1:1–3) who gave the Law to Moses. Yet we see Him on the Mount of Transfiguration conversing with both Moses and Elijah. (See Matthew 17:1–8.) Elijah had not died but was translated to heaven. Moses had died. Since our Lord never sinned (2 Cor. 5:21) and was found here speaking with a departed person, apparently not all contacts from heaven to Earth are forbidden! But the reverse occurs in spiritualism, men trying to contact the residents of heaven. That we must never do. We mention this in no way to attempt to excuse spiritualism. We seek rather to ease the hearts of some who have been troubled by experiences in which the departed have seemed to come to them uninvited. Even the fact that our Lord embraced such an experience is, to me, a part of the grayness. The lines are not always clear. However, it should be noted that in the case of the Transfiguration, God Himself sent Moses and Elijah from the other side. This can never be said of what happens at séances. If God chooses to send a spirit, then that is His prerogative. But it is *never* ours!

I share here (quite reluctantly, and only in obedience to the Lord) a few stories from our family history, knowing that most every family holds in memory similar happenings. I share them to make several points. It must be understood that these are not testimonies. We are not proud of them and do not see them as giving any glory to the Lord. We do not share them to encourage others to try to have such experiences or to think of them as admirable. Rather it is to say that as Spirit-filled Christians we need to disallow and so far as possible avoid such encounters, not because they are unmistakably bad or forbidden, but simply because we do not know. They are in the gray areas, and we need to be careful to keep our garments unspotted from the flesh (Jude 23). We share these things also to say that we need to talk with the wise about what we experience.

My mother purchased a used recliner chair, and having brought it home, she was cleaning it before use. While reaching deep between the cushion and sidewall, she suddenly heard what she understood to be her mother's voice (several years after her death) saying, "Reach deeper, Zelma." She did and found an extremely valuable diamond ring, which the jeweler later sized to fit her. She wears it to this day, sure that it was a gift from her mother.

My mother did not attempt to contact anyone. This happened *to* her. But by what agency? Did God allow it, so that it really was Grandmother's spirit who spoke? Or was it a demon, attempting to convince my mother so as to weaken true faith and lead her astray? Some would be adamantly convinced either way. Surely there are gray areas that no one fully understands.

For Spirit-filled Christians, I am more concerned about the gray areas than about spiritualism itself. Spiritualism is a known evil. We can easily recognize it and avoid it, determined to obey God's Word. But the gray areas spark immense curiosity. Scriptural guidelines are not so clear. We have seen some move step by seemingly innocent step into greater and greater off-balancedness, if not into outright deception and sin. Many have by mystical occurrences unwittingly been caught in idolatry, looking for consolation and guidance from sources other than the Holy Spirit. It is for these reasons that I expose our family stories. I know from years of prayer ministry that almost every family can share similar stories. I am not counseling fear and withdrawal but rather caution and propriety. Let us be determined to keep our way pure according to His Word (Ps. 119:9). Then if something like the above happens to us, we can simply release it to the Lord, ask forgiveness if in any way we have been open to what we ought not to be, praise God for His grace, and go on in Him, wise enough not to share stories where the immature might be tempted into false adventure. We must, however, be secure enough to speak of such experiences with the wise, that we may gain wisdom from all we experience.

In my office as a prophet and as a pastor I often knew beforehand about a death coming within my congregation. That was easy to understand as part of the gift of knowledge.

> Surely the Lord GOD does nothing unless He reveals His secret counsel to His servants the prophets.
>
> —AMOS 3:7

That knowledge called me to intercede. Often I was in prayer for the person when the call came to tell me of his death. That was my function as a pastor and a prophet. But sometimes things would happen that were not so easy to understand. One time when trying to determine what to say in a funeral sermon, I entered quite a wrestle because I knew so many things both good and bad about the person, which the community also knew. I was alone in my office, praying about it while my left hand lay extended on my desk. At last I decided the Lord would have me focus only on His grace, and, since I could not ignore all things about my friend's life because the congregation expected me to say something, I would speak only briefly, with compassion. My eyes were still closed, head bent in prayer. A hand clasped my left hand and squeezed, unmistakably meaning the same as when we give a gentle squeeze to express affirmation. I recognized the presence of my friend, the departed person. What in fact did happen? Was it indeed the spirit of my friend, affirming my choice? Was it the Lord, assuring me? Or was it something trying to delude and lead me astray? I did not seek to contact anyone or to experience anything. It happened, unbidden, *to* me. I am sure many pastors have puzzled about similar experiences. Here again is a gray area. What shall we make of it or do about it? We need to be free to talk about such things with brothers and sisters in the faith. Isolation, especially due to fear, does great harm. Sharing can bring resolution.

I share this story to testify to what I have done. I have prayed that the Lord preserve me from all false experiences, that the Lord bring to death all fleshly mysticism and close in me anything that ought not to be open. On the other hand, I have prayed that if the Lord wants me to be vulnerable to such things, He protect me and "lead me not into temptation." I know from years of ministering to many pastors that many are "pestered" by experiences they cannot quite put away in definite boxes, and they hesitate to share them anywhere, for fear of what people might think or do.

One time I was visiting my mother, who at that time was emotionally upset and in danger of making some wrong decisions, among them, to divorce my father. Though people travel thousands of miles to counsel with me and I am internationally known for my expertise as a prayer minister, I, of course, could not get to first base with my own mother. (See Matthew 13:57.) Exasperated and grieving, I walked away into another room. No windows or doors were open. No water was running anywhere in the house. Suddenly I felt the presence above me of my Grandmother

Potter, who I knew was weeping for my mother. A drop of water fell onto my brow and ran into my eye, so real and so copious I had to take off my glasses and dry out both them and my eye! There was no moisture on the ceiling, and no physically explainable reason for it! What happened? Was it in fact a tear? Why? Why would the Lord allow such a thing to happen to one who has spoken against spiritism and spiritualism and is determined to walk circumspectly before the Lord? I know I risk my own reputation (and perhaps my beloved family) even by telling such stories. But I risk it for a most cogently compelling reason. I know that there are many pastors and lay people in the body of Christ who have encountered similar experiences, who have not told anyone for fear of being labeled a "kook" or weird, or even being thrown out of their church as a spiritist or spiritualist!

Over forty years ago I renounced all mysticism and said to the Lord, "I want no experience of any kind unless it happens only by the Holy Spirit." How many Christians, especially the newly born, have had similar things happen to them, and who has known to listen to them without blame? Who has known how to minister to them or recognize the need?

Suppression and isolation are not good. *It is healing to share in the right places. Small groups in churches are right places.* Friends can discern and pray. We must take away the aura of judgment and condemnation and share properly, inside the Church, where our brothers and sisters can pray for us and protect us. Whether such happenings are recognizably good or bad, loneliness from fear of being shunned because of having a mystical experience can wound the spirit.

I have debated and prayed a long time before deciding to share these stories. I believe that there are burdens of confusion and wondering that need to be lifted from a great many of our brothers and sisters. The risk of our reputation is worth it for their healing. I do *not* expect or hope that the body of Christ can answer the questions of those who have had similar experiences. I certainly can't, not even of my own. To dwell too much on these matters would likely be a delusory distraction keeping us from concentration on more appropriate and fruitful pursuits. This side of heaven there will always be "...more things in heaven and earth...than are dreamt of in your philosophy."[1] But we can end the loneliness and the wondering whether those who have mystical experiences are crazy or weird by our acceptance of such people and our willingness to hear, support in prayer, and offer loving discernment (and in some cases, gentle correction). Having come out of an extremely mystical heritage, I know firsthand the ravages of loneliness that strange experiences can engender! I know the hunger for sharing in safe places within the body. I know the need for Christians in our midst who are sensitive to spiritual encounters of this kind not to feel isolated, but to feel themselves enfolded in the love and prayerful balancing concern of people who may never have had such experiences.

Christians in our midst who have had gray-area experiences need earthy people to stand by them and with them. Earthy people also need the challenge of hearing experiences outside their ken. Too long an atmosphere of fear and ridicule, scorn and judgment has prevailed, silencing and isolating those who have had these experiences. We tend to fear what we do not understand. So many times brothers and sisters have come to us greatly wounded because they did share a happening, only to find themselves under condemnation and greater isolation and loneliness than what impelled them to speak in the first place! We plead with the body not to be arrogant and insensitive, especially when called upon to warn a brother or sister.

I do not condone or whitewash such experiences or those who have them. I only plead for healing. Those in this pragmatic age who are sensitive to such things are left vulnerable to many things by isolation. The body needs to gather around and protect them in its midst, lest they be carried off into delusion or be shut down by the body's unwillingness to venture. They can become unfruitful even in the clearly valid gifts of the Holy Spirit. When isolated, they become too bruised and lonely to function even if they remain willing to do so. Let us be determined to be healing emissaries of Jesus first rather than swift swords of judgment—though if healing love is present, swift swords can also be healing instruments.

HEALING FOR THOSE INVOLVED WITH
SPIRITUALISM/SPIRITISM

Great healing is needed for those who have been involved in spiritualism and/or spiritism. All the effects and prescriptions for healing listed in the previous chapter pertain here as well, with several additions and emphases.

First, spiritualism, far more than most other occult things, exposes participants to the sights and inroads of the powers of darkness. Whether people actively participated or were somewhat innocently involved by others, they need to be more assiduously hidden from the eyes of devils and more rigorously shut off in all centers of their soul from access by the devil.

Defilement is more severe. Unclean spirits may have attached themselves to the person or may have entered them. Exorcism is most likely required in such cases.

Deposits—thoughts and emotions, recollections of seeming to have talked with a departed dear one—may have been left in the mind and may plague and clamor to be accepted and to be repeated. Sometimes people are convinced that departed ones have commissioned or commanded them to do something that would prove lack of loyalty or love if denied. The entire plot of *Hamlet* revolves around his belief that his dead father has appeared to him and commanded him to take vengeance on his brother for killing him and usurping his throne and his wife. Honor seems to be at stake. Misplaced zeal tears at them to act, usually in wrong ways for a wrong cause, as vengeance should not be Hamlet's but the Lord's.

Such deposits should be broken by the voice of authority, dispelling spirits' words by the Lord's name. Demons usually want to stir people to do some great wrong thing to right some supposed great wrong—or even to do some seemingly right thing to prevent or correct some wrong happening. Many times Christians have been convinced that if they could only convey a forgiveness seemingly from the other side, a person could come to rest about a guilt, or perhaps they hope to express for a departed person a love that person failed to express while on Earth so that someone's longing heart might be healed. But those longings are not to be fulfilled by spiritualism. The Holy Spirit has other and better ways to address those needs. When needs as these seem to have been fulfilled through spiritualism, a ministering one must even appear to wound the person being ministered to in order to heal them. "Mary, that message came from spiritualism. I know it has been a comfort to your heart, but it's a false comfort. Don't you see that you still question? Your spirit is not at rest, even though your mind has latched onto that message. Let's let go of that message. We don't have to know whether or not it could have been something your loved one would have wanted to say to you. Our Lord is our only true comfort. Let's listen only to Him and wash yourself of all defilement. OK? Will you pray with me about it?"

Remembrances of messages or experiences nag continually at the mind and heart for acceptance. A brother or sister may come from a séance and say to one who has never even thought of attending anything spiritu-alistic, "Dad came to us last night, and he wants all of us in the family to know he loves us. He wants you, George, as the eldest, to watch over the rest of the family, especially David, who he says is heading into trouble." That may seem innocuous, even helpful. But George probably would have taken responsibility anyway. The message confuses. If David does head into trouble, George's mind and all the rest of the family's thoughts may be plagued with thoughts that perhaps spiritualism is OK after all. If George does watch out especially for David, he is bothered by the apprehension that after all he may be doing the bidding of a spiritualist's counsel, so that even a right duty in the family is tainted by questions of uncleanness. If a prophet were to have given the same counsel to George, and David were kept from trouble, God would receive the glory. But who gets the glory if circumstances are otherwise?

Those who pray for deliverance and healing should petition for cleansing of the person's mind and heart from temptation. Prayer ministers should avail themselves to the cleansing power of God's Word.

> The law of the LORD is perfect, restoring the soul; the testimony of the LORD is sure, making wise the simple. The precepts of the LORD are right, rejoicing the heart; the commandment of the LORD is pure, enlightening the eyes. The fear of the LORD is clean, enduring forever; the judgments of the LORD are true; they are righteous altogether. They are more desirable than gold, yes, than much fine gold; sweeter also than honey and the drippings of the honeycomb. Moreover, by them Thy servant is warned; in keeping them there is great reward.
> —PSALM 19:7–11

A prayer minister would be well advised to read several passages like that to the person to whom he ministers and to assign daily reading of Scripture, like all of Psalm 119, John 12–20, or the letter to the Romans. Jesus was not speaking figuratively when He said, "You are already clean *because of the word which I have spoken to you*" (John 15:3, emphasis added). His Word is the power unto salvation (Rom. 1:16).

Demons love to incite family troubles by supposed messages in séances. One purporting to be a departed sister may say, "Watch out for Martha; she is telling tales about you where she should not." "Dan's wife is making eyes at your husband. Be aware." To mask the intents of creating suspi-cion and sowing seeds of unrest and division, the demon behind the scene may throw in some good advice, such as "Be compassionate" or "Try to forgive," knowing that the person will be more likely thereby to treasure the message without suspecting it. The demon knows those seeds of suspicion and division will do their dirty work in the heart anyway. The person may try to throw the message off, but in the back of his mind questions and resentment may continue to gnaw away.

Let us be clear about the difference between the Lord's words and those from flesh and demons. A prophet of the Lord may also give warnings, perhaps even with the same admonitions or counsels to be compassionate and to forgive. When the prophet speaks, it is the Holy Spirit speaking through him. His words carry the Lord's anointing. They affect the heart with His purposes. They bring forth good, "for it is God who is at work in you, both to will and to work for His good pleasure" (Phil. 2:13). When a gossiper spreads stories, flesh is at work.

> A worthless man digs up evil, while *his words are a scorching fire.*
> A perverse man spreads strife, and a slanderer separates intimate friends.
> —PROVERBS 16:27–28, EMPHASIS ADDED

Flesh may or may not be impelled or aided by devils; the slander may come only from flesh. But when it comes by the agency of spiritualism, it always has behind it and working through it demons and their defilements. It carries Satan's "anointing" and worms its way into people to pander to the basest motives of flesh. God's Word calls forth His righteousness within us. Satanic words seduce to the worst of the flesh within mankind.

It is important that we comprehend this distinction, for many have said, "I don't see what's so wrong about that word from the spiritualist. My pastor said the very same thing to me in the same words. I just took it as confirmation." Not so. Those words from the spiritualist are not identical to those from the pastor even if identical in word, expression, and tone. It is the distinctive power and source of each that is the deciding factor. God needs no confirmations from the devil. His Word is only sullied by the leaven of additions from evil sources. We are to keep our hearts and minds, souls and spirits *only* to Him who is the fountain, who has the words of life (John 6:68).

People who have been involved in any form of the occult should be urged to renounce it aloud before others in prayer. For those involved in spiritualism, it is not merely a wise urging but an imperative. The spoken word contains power, most especially in confession, as in James 5:13–19, which is the command to confess our sins before others.

It is important in all prayer concerning occult involvement to make use of the blood of Christ, especially for those tainted by spiritism and spiritualism. The blood, the Word, and the cross are the most powerful weapons of our warfare in healing those involved in occultism, especially spiritualism.

Since Leviticus 20:6 says, "As for the person who turns to mediums and to spiritists, to play the harlot after them, *I will also set My face against that person and will cut him off from among his people*" (emphasis added), there are therefore two prime effects of spiritualism that ought to be addressed by healing prayer:

1. The person needs to be restored to the favor of God. Reconciliation should be voiced in prayer until the person knows he is again within God's good graces. Moreover, blessing ought to be reestablished. A person may feel accepted again but perhaps only as a third-rate citizen who is again allowed access to God, but of course no good thing would ever come his way again. Therefore the person must have God's blessing pronounced over him until he again believes that God's angels and saints go before him to seek his good and he could again be entrusted with an important task. His confidence as a child of the King who provides for him needs to be reestablished.

2. Those involved and now repentant of spiritism and spiritualism must be restored to their families and to the family of God. From the moment of occult sin, the irresistible forces of the law of sowing and reaping act to cut a man off. That curse of the law has been stopped on the cross of Christ. God nailed all the demands of the law to the cross and canceled all those legal requirements. (See Colossians 2:14.)

As with all sin, spiritualism demands retribution. Forgiveness does not mean God overlooks sin but that He paid the price of our redemption from sin by taking it in pain upon Himself. Nevertheless, that awesome, complete, and glorious price He paid waits upon prayer to apply it. The prayer minister or healer must not fail to pray for full and complete termination of the effects of spiritualism! We say this because to our great chagrin and the continuing harm against the body of Christ, we have all too often heard of those who have spoken of their dereliction and consequent repentance, only to have their hearers fail to pray or do anything about it! That is almost as grievous as the sin of the involved one. Prayer is the first access of the grace of God to mankind. Understanding is not enough. Acceptance is not enough. Only prayer applies the blood and the cross and completes the work.

Any kind of occult involvement, including spiritualism, sends harm through family lines for generations to come. Those who pray are called also to stop the descent of harm through generational sin.

Demonic Oppression, Inhabitation, and Demonization

Though any kind of occult involvement may result in demonic oppression or inhabitation, demonization is almost certain in the case of spiritualism. Spiritualism, especially on the part of the medium, is not only an attempt to contact spirits. While in sorcery an attempt is made to work with and through demons, spiritualism gives direct invitation to enter and work *through* one's own body. Thus, more than in any other occult involvement, spiritualism results in demonic inhabitation.

There are those who believe that no Spirit-filled Christian can be inhabited by a demonic power. We have not found this to be historic fact, no matter how appealing the theology that the Holy Spirit and demons cannot inhabit the same area. The fact is, it happens. We have exorcised hundreds of Spirit-filled Christians, some of whom have been not only Spirit-filled for many years but well-recognized, powerful servants of the Lord! Thank God that once the Holy Spirit enters, all other spirits *inevitably must leave.*

Sometimes, in deference to the beliefs of some, we have simply said that a believer has become "demonized." That makes no distinction as to where the demon is, whether inside or outside the person. Perhaps those who believe a demon cannot inhabit a Christian are correct that in those deepest regions of Christ's indwelling through His Spirit, no demon can abide. It may be that the demon we exorcise merely inhabits some more exterior area of a person's character and personality. Therefore, we use several terms to distinguish degrees of being demonized.

Infestation

The first level we call "infestation." By that we do not mean that the person is inhabited but that satanic hosts swarm about him like a stirred-up hornet's nest. Through uncrucified areas of his flesh, they can occasionally activate and sometimes motivate him to wrong actions. They hook into him in unguarded areas from outside his person.

Inhabitation

The next degree is simple inhabitation. A demon has entered but is relatively ineffective. It is as though, to use an analogy, a virus has invaded the bloodstream but has no ill effect because the immune system is strong enough to keep it in check. Temporarily at least, the strength of the person's character has fought it down, unable to cast it out, but able to render it largely ineffective. After the person has received the Holy Spirit, the Lord's power forces the demon to surface, be revealed, and cast out.

Scripture presents numerous examples of Christians who were demonized to varying degrees. Unresolved anger can give demons a foothold (Eph. 4:26–27). In the last days, some Christians will become demonized through heresy (1 Tim. 4:1). Paul urged Timothy to gently instruct apostate Christians, so that "they may come to their senses and escape from the snare of the devil, having been held captive by him to do his will" (2 Tim. 2:26). Paul handed Hymenaeus and Alexander "over to Satan, so that they may be taught not to blaspheme" (1 Tim. 1:20). When a man cohabited with his father's wife, Paul said, "I have decided to deliver such a one to Satan for the destruction of his flesh, that his spirit may be saved in the day of the Lord Jesus" (1 Cor. 5:5). Nonresistance invites demons: "Resist the devil and he will flee from you" (James 4:7). When Ananias and Sapphira donated money, they lied about the amount they had gotten from the sale of their land. To this, Peter replied, "Ananias, why has Satan filled your heart to lie to the Holy Spirit...?" (Acts 5:3). The Greek for the word *filled* is "pleroo," the same word used in "filled with the Spirit" in Ephesians 5:18. Thus, those who are filled with the Spirit can be filled by a demon, if they grant him access.

That was true in my case (John's). Raised in an extremely liberal church, I was well instructed morally but not grounded in the Word or in a personal relationship with Jesus Christ. In my search for reality, I had dabbled in studies, some of which I did not even recognize as occult, in the years before the Lord found me. Along the way a demon had entered. I was not aware of any symptoms other than fatigue. Surely that demonic thing must have at least blunted sensitivity, warped my theology and my sermons, and postponed the Lord's capture of my heart. But the strength of God's hold upon my unregenerate old man was apparently enough to corral and render that devil mainly mute. I received the infilling of the Holy Spirit in October of 1958. Great glory and joy surrounded all that happened at first. But then in November that demonic thing could no longer maintain its place and surfaced.

I know by what I experienced how dreadful are the pain and terror demons feel under the application of the true light of God and His blood and cross. As that demon surfaced, I was no longer comfortable and capable of rejoicing in the presence of a powerful servant of God. It had been a joy to visit with Ed Bender, then pastor of the Open Bible Church of Streator, Illinois. But the demon within me became fraught with fear. Wilbur Fogg, my Episcopal rector friend, playfully tossed holy water at me one day while I was chatting with him in the sanctuary of the Episcopal church. To that demon whose emotions registered as mine, that was a moment of stark terror! Those globules of water sailing toward me appeared as mountains of smashing fire! In the exorcism, done by Wilbur and his wife, Alice, the mention of the blood of Jesus caused actual physical pain, and the cross engendered sheer terror. I felt it when that demon could stand it no longer and left me.

I have since ministered to many hundreds of people whose history was similar to mine. Perhaps those who maintain that Spirit-filled people cannot be inhabited by demons are correct in the sense that Spirit-baptized persons cannot *remain* inhabited, as the person comes more and more into the fullness of the Holy Spirit. But people certainly can still be inhabited for a while after receiving the Holy Spirit. I was, and so have many to whom I have ministered deliverance.

NEW WINE IN OLD WINESKINS

Many people have wondered how it can be that immediately after a highly anointed time—or sometimes during a greatly blessed service—unholy desires pester the emotions, or base thoughts course through the mind, or even curse words. Sometimes families and churches explode into rancor and divisiveness during or immediately after a tremendous revival movement in the church. Secular counselors have told Paula and me that after a great revival has come through an area, their offices, more than at any other time, are filled with desperate clients. This is because we neither understand our nature nor the function of the Holy Spirit.

Picture it like an old dry well. Sticks and leaves, spiders and insects litter the bottom. Now let a great rain fill that old well with water. All that trash, along with its living inhabitants, rises to the surface of the water. In the same way, the water of the Holy Spirit forces to the surface whatever rotten old things have been lying dormant in our character. Malachi prophesied that the Messiah would do this very thing: "He will sit as a refiner and purifier of silver; he will purify the Levites and refine them like gold and silver" (Mal. 3:3, NIV). Who are the "Levites" today? We are—the priesthood of believers (1 Pet. 2:5). We may have become freshly so refilled and anointed that we want to think we must really be holy, else the Holy Spirit couldn't be that much with us and in us. But that attitude is only delusion and false pride. The first function of the Spirit who is called holy is to convict of sin. He Himself dislodges and causes those old things to rise up within us. He is neither surprised nor offended. He knew all along. We are the only ones astonished at what is revealed. The following diagrams may help:

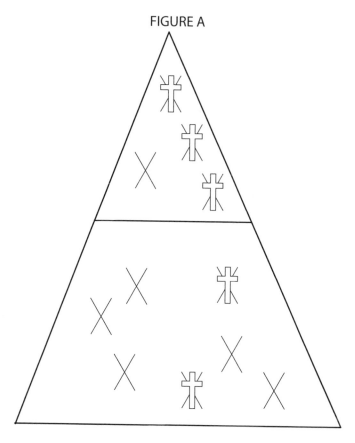

FIGURE A

The top portion of the triangle represents our conscious mind. Each *x* represents a wound or sinful aspect of our character. The superimposed crosses stand for problem areas we have already recognized and successfully reckoned as dead on the cross (Rom. 6:11). The bottom section pictures our hidden heart or subconscious areas. The line between the two signifies our common unwillingness to discover what is actually in our heart.

Our personal spirit, the breath of God in us, wants to reveal the remaining troubled areas to consciousness to be seen. "All things become visible when they are exposed by the light, for everything that becomes visible is light" (Eph. 5:13). But we are normally unwilling to admit or face the unknown in us, so we push those things down and build walls, as in Figure B.

FIGURE B

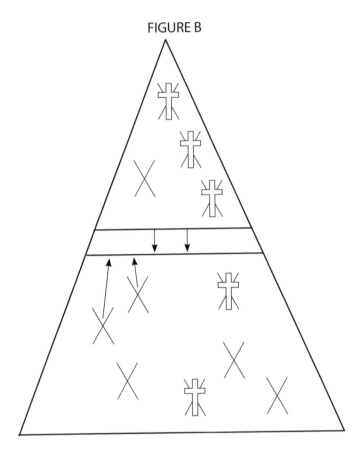

So long as our spirit does not obtain sufficient power, our conscious mind can win the battle. We gain a false peace, while the inner one smolders like a volcano. We shut off our inner voice and will not hear, though our spirit sends signals through dreams and insights, and perhaps by psychosomatic illnesses.

But let a person be filled by the Holy Spirit, and our own spirit gains the ability to act with undeniable power. Let a wife, husband, relatives, or friends touch the heart with real love, and power transfuses into the spirit of the person. The personal spirit now possesses sufficient power to demand a hearing. The Holy Spirit is wise and will not drive us into a mental breakdown. But our own spirit can act like a tempestuous child, demanding by a nightmare or by some kind of emotional outburst that we recognize that particular sin or admit that we do have some problem in our life. Thus the battle is on, as in Figure C.

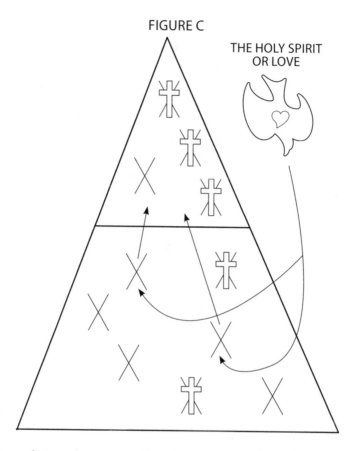

FIGURE C

This explains why, as so often happens, family and church battles occur immediately *after* great and anointed times. Our inmost being, as St. Paul said, delights in the law of God and has been blocked by the war in our members, but thanks be to God in Jesus Christ, we have been given power to break through. (See Romans 7:22–25.) When the church, spouses, friends, or we ourselves fail to understand the process, we may think Satan is attacking because he is angry at the recent victory. We may shout Satan away and wrestle ourselves under control again, only to miss the blessing that simple confession, forgiveness, and inner healing prayer could have wrought. Not Satan primarily, but flesh, was at work. At such times, we need to learn to hear one another compassionately, not frightened or disturbed as though something out of place were happening. In this instance, troubles do not mean that the anointing is leaving but rather the reverse, that the anointing is proceeding to the task for which it was sent.

Let the wisdom of the Lord forewarn and prepare. Let the body of Christ look not so much for times of great uninterrupted peace and blessing after the Lord has moved upon a congregation. That rarely happens. What usually occurs is that that new surge of power not only dislodges fortresses of flesh but also sometimes forces infesting and inhabiting demons to surface. Had the Church understood, it could have rejoiced and administered healing, thus prolonging and deepening the move of the Lord in its life. Unfortunately, His people are often destroyed for lack of knowledge, and since they do not understand the process, they also do not comprehend what is happening in their own characters. That means, then, that those sinful things that are surfacing find no proper access to the light of knowledge for what they are. Often, frightened Christians think, "Oh, no, how can I have such a thought—or this kind of feeling—when the anointing is on us all? I must be terrible!" So they repress that thing and rebuke the devil. Simple confession would have brought joyous healing: "Yes, Lord, I see I have that thing in me. Show me its root. Lead me to friends who can set me free." The rule is that when urges from within are denied access to proper action, they *will* come up, some way, somehow—perverted and destructive! In this way, movements of the Lord in congregations grind to a halt by rancor and disunity where counsel, confession, and prayer ought to have proceeded to sanctification and transformation.

Both the hidden perversions in our flesh and whatever demons may have been connected to them become dislodged by the power of the Holy Spirit. It will not do only to cast away the demonic and think of the problem as only exterior warfare with demons. Demons cannot inhabit a person without a house of character to hide in. It is that sinful area— an unforgiveness, some practice of "getting even," or an arrogant way of dominating or cowing others by fleshly strength, any kind of practice in as yet unredeemed aspects of our character—that is now being called to death on the cross by the present agency of the Holy Spirit. If we only cast away the demonic, seven worse demons are apt to return, and the person's last state will be worse than the first (Luke 11:24–26). What is important is to haul that house the demon has lived in to the cross where Jesus promised to destroy all the works of the devil (1 John 3:8). We short-change ourselves and fail the work of Christ when we think that because people have been born anew and filled with the Holy Spirit, the work is all done. It has only begun. Each visitation of God in the Church will plunge His people into dealing with whatever is caused to surface!

Deliverance and Exorcisms

Some time ago, early in the history of the Charismatic movement, the many newly Spirit-baptized, especially from mainline formerly liberal congregations, discovered that Satan is indeed real and that there are in fact real demons. Most of us who lived through that time (mostly in the 1960s) can remember how frantic some of us became with this new discovery. For a while, everything had demons in it! They were everywhere! Everyone who was anyone in the kingdom had to be into deliverance. Spit and vomit buckets appeared in prayer rooms, along with paper towels and napkins. As is usual with Homo sapiens, we rushed off balance into the weird and to the extreme. Fortunately, most of the body of Christ has matured through that time. But let us chronicle some of the lessons we learned—or should by now have learned:

1. Exorcisms do not have to involve shouting and screaming, rolling on the floor in convulsions, and vomiting.

Sometimes that happens, as in the case of the boy who lay in convulsions when exorcised by Jesus (Luke 9:37–43). However, some demonstrations happen only because some people are susceptible to suggestion and some are emotionally demonstrative. A lot of what went on early in the Charismatic movement happened because we expected it to. That gave Satan a playground. Exorcisms can be done by quiet authority and faith, without hyperemotion or physical demonstrations. The point is that mature exorcists need not send undercurrent messages to the exorcised to act out unnecessary emotional or physical demonstrations. Sometimes such reactions happen, but as healers we ought to mature in our task until we are neither needlessly allowing it nor unconsciously setting the other up to act in such ways.

In the early years of our ministry, exorcisms became prolonged struggles in which the exorcised acted out all manner of weird behaviors. Then the Lord taught us that all that strange activity could happen only because we believed Satan possessed that kind of power! Our belief structure presented him with a circus arena to put on a show. We learned that Satan could even delight in losing battle after battle to us. He knew he would lose anyway, but he could have a ball with us before exiting, so long as we were willing to let him have all that attention and let him glory in all that supposed power. When we learned that they really "overcame him because of the blood of the Lamb and because of the word of their testimony" (Rev. 12:11), and that Satan has no power any longer, having been totally defeated and stripped by our Lord Jesus Christ, our faith no longer gave the devil a theater to perform in. Now, exorcisms are usually short, simple, and easy.

Usually, this is the case, but not always. One night friends at a meeting in California were teaching about exorcism. They asked me to come up and offer some words of wisdom. I shared as we have here, that all such emotionalism and weird behavior is not necessary and that exorcisms can be conducted with dignity and authority. The Lord, in His humor, caused the first man, at the first word of authority, to slide out of his chair onto the floor in convulsions—and we were in a dramatic battle!

2. We do not need to command demons to name themselves, nor is it wise.

Whoever said that the devil would tell the truth? Jesus said that Satan was a liar from the beginning and the father of lies (John 8:44). We know of Christians who have spent all night in exorcism, casting out, by their own subsequent account, more than two hundred demons from one individual. Sometimes that may in fact have been the case. We are convinced that, unfortunately, most often what did transpire was that the expectancies and the methods of the exorcists invited the devil to play with them all night! If we need to know the name of a demon (and if it is truly wise and powerful to know a name), then let us ask the Holy Spirit! What have we to do listening to demons or giving them permission to speak and act through a person? Paula and I command the demon to be silent. We give him no permission to put on a show through the flesh of a person being delivered. Did we think the Holy Spirit less powerful or willing or truthful that we should turn to the devil for revelation?

Christians have derived this faulty practice from that one instance in which Jesus asked, "What is your name?" And the reply was, "Legion." But let us think about that. Can the reader for a moment suspect that the Lord of all the universe did not know the name? Of course He knew. He did not ask in order to find out, as many Christian exorcists do today, thinking they follow His precedent. Note the use of singular and plural in the text: "Then He [Jesus] asked *him*, 'What is your name?' And he answered, saying, 'My name is *Legion*; for *we* are many'" (Mark 5:9, NKJV). Jesus addressed the man, himself, not the demons. He asked "*him*," not "them." When a psychiatrist enters the room of a mentally ill patient (remember, this was an insane man living among the tombs), sometimes he asks him, "What is your name?" If the person can answer the question correctly, that tells the psychiatrist the patient is, for the moment, in control of himself. Answering sanely strengthens the resolve of the patient. Jesus, by asking, was giving to the patient the opportunity to stand in faith by trying to state his own true name, but it was the demons who answered, "...we are many." Since they spoke through the patient's vocal cords, the Scripture records that *he* replied, but the plural *we* informs us it was the demons who spoke through him.

Furthermore, although there are seven Greek words that can be translated "commanded," none of the writers of the Gospels used any of them to describe the way Jesus addressed the man with Legion. Instead, they say Jesus *asked* for his name. Such courtesy is appropriate only for humans, for to "ask" is to give your hearer the right to refuse to answer. Surely Jesus would never grant a demon such permission. In the Gospel accounts, the Greek word for "asked" is *eperotao*. It means to ask one whom you consider your equal. Surely Christ would not address a demon as His equal. But He could address a man this way. For Jesus was not only God; He was also a fellow human being. Can anyone in his right mind suppose that our Lord Jesus Christ required information from demons in order to have power over them? Jesus, as Lord of the universe, needed nothing from the devil! And neither do we! To ask demons to name themselves gives them permission to use patients' vocal cords, thus increasing rather than decreasing their hold.

In many cases, no name is needed. A deliverance minister simply commands a demon to leave, and he must. Such attitudes as lust, pride, fear, and so on are not demons, although we often use those names to identify demons that exacerbate those attitudes. They are aspects of our flesh, which demons sometimes wield. It is actually confession of that sinful attitude that prepares the way for us to cast them out. Since a demon requires a foothold in us, when that attitude is washed away in the blood of Jesus, the demon's hold in that area is broken and thus his energy or presence is made ineffective in that area. We need only, by the guidance of the Holy Spirit, to lead people to specific, detailed confession. When enough of a demon's lodging places are destroyed, we can easily exorcise him. That is why, after people have named a number of such attitudes as though they were demons, a person sometimes feels released. If he repented of the corresponding sin, then it was basically the power of confession and forgiveness that enabled whatever exorcisms may have happened.

3. Discernment of the presence of a demon is *not* a mandate to exorcise in *that moment*.

The body of Christ has done much harm by zeal without wisdom. If a person is not prepared to renounce his sinful ways, if he is not struggling to live Christ's way and is willfully choosing unrighteousness, then "it goes and takes along seven other spirits more evil than itself, and they go in and live there; and the last state of that man becomes worse than the first" (Luke 11:26).

At Elijah House, we seek to uncover root causes for the demonization, thereby to demolish the residence of the demon through forgiveness and the cross. We seek to discover whether there is sufficient resolve by which the Christian will discipline himself to try to walk in a new and holy way. We want also to ascertain whether his family and a church body will be there to support him. We want to see indications of repentance and of real hatred for the sins the demon has been perpetrating through the person. Only if such attitudes are present will we choose to exorcise, unless the Holy Spirit, for His own reasons, sovereignly initiates or orders us into the exorcism.

4. Exorcisms are best done by teams.

After the warfare of exorcism, exorcists and their team would be well advised to cleanse themselves by prayer, lest something latch onto them. Paula and I know of several who found themselves inhabited or demonized for quite a long while after becoming involved in doing exorcisms.

5. Women can do exorcisms.

Some have said that women ought not attempt to do exorcisms. We have not found that to be either scriptural advice or wise counsel. Women ought to follow the same counsel as any man, to do exorcisms only under proper authority, within the enfolding protection of a team whenever possible, and only when group wisdom says it is time. "Make war by wise guidance" (Prov. 20:18). But we see nothing in Scripture forbidding women to be exorcists. Many women are effective exorcists. It was Alice Fogg, the rector's wife, who took the lead in exorcising me when I needed it. Many pompous people make pronouncements when God has not told them to speak, and I greatly doubt any man's warranty in the Lord who protests that women are unfit for this ministry. Men more easily wield authority, but nothing prevents the Holy Spirit from expressing copious authority through a woman. I have seen strong men properly daunted when a saintly woman, under Christ's anointing, beetled her brows and spoke with sternness as His messenger.

Above all, we plead with the body of Christ not to rush around seeing demons behind every illness and each sinful propensity in people's lives! That is soulish and carnal nonsense. It gives glory to the devil. It turns eyes from the Lord toward fear and confusion. It edifies no one. It releases few, especially in any permanent way. Paula and I, in our more than fifty years of Spirit-filled ministering, have most likely done more valid exorcisms than almost any other servants alive and ministering in the body today! We do not speak from disbelief or unthinking disregard, but from years of learning by experience in our Lord Jesus Christ.

> Solid food is for the mature, who *because of practice have their senses trained to discern good and evil.*
> —HEBREWS 5:14, EMPHASIS ADDED

CONTINUED HEALING AFTER DELIVERANCE

It is, however, not mainly for correction that we write about demons and exorcism. It is for teaching concerning healing. Demonic presences sully and ravage the personal spirits of those they beleaguer. Exorcisms therefore should also contain prayers for cleansing and healing. Affection and much warm human contact should follow exorcism. Newly delivered people ought not to be left alone too soon afterward. Devils want to return, however wise and timely the exorcism. The protective presence of friends is needed. Wholesome earthy involvements will help, such as eating a good balanced meal, visiting about nonspiritual matters with family and friends, or working together with others doing simple chores that require some manual labor.

Most importantly, spouses need to be quietly held for relatively long periods of time in warm embrace. There is nothing wrong with a newly delivered wife curling up on her husband's lap and drinking from his presence. His balance and wholeness, his saneness and calmness settle and heal her spirit. Similarly, a husband may lie quietly chest to chest with his wife, enjoying her presence and her sweet nurture singing gently into his cells the song of wholesome earthy life.

Freshly delivered people may find it jangling to be plunged immediately into tension-filled situations or family hassles. An exorcism is somewhat like an engine overhaul. We do not want to run such a motor at full power until piston rings have had time to settle and seat themselves. Just so, we need time to accustom ourselves to the new us. Wise counselors will so advise.

Sleep is important. Many people succumb to demons in the first place because they have neglected good sleeping habits. Fatigue and nervous stress serve to weaken immunity not only to physical disease but also to sins that invite demonic inroads. After exorcism, nothing so invites reentrance of demons as a return to the same sins, but a close second is lack of sufficient sleep. Relatives and friends should not be reticent in insisting upon rest.

Simple cleanliness heals the person and thus helps to ward off the return of demons. Soaking in the tub is good for those newly reclaimed from Satan's empire. Being well groomed helps to restore a sense of well-being. Note that the Word of God records that after Jesus exorcised the Gadarene demoniac, the people "found the man...*clothed* and in his right mind" (Luke 8:35).

Relatives and friends would do well to protect newly exorcised people from the prying of nosey "well-meaning" friends and neighbors who ask questions like, "What's it like to have a demon?" and "How do you know they're all gone?" Sometimes Jesus told people, "Tell no one" (Luke 5:14; 8:56); other times, "Return to your house and describe what great things God has done for you" (Luke 8:39). Exorcised people can profit by the wise counsel of mature Christians about whether and when to share, how much and how often.

Finally, relatives and friends should persist in watching over an exorcised person for several weeks following the exorcism. Relapses are possible. Secondary exorcisms are often forthcoming, like aftershocks following a major earthquake, as other hidden sins may shake loose.

A blessedly healing conclusion to all exorcisms is frequent visits to the Lord's table in Communion.

> I am the bread of life. Your fathers ate the manna in the wilderness, and they died. This is the bread which comes down out of heaven,

so that one may eat of it and not die. I am the living bread that came down out of heaven; if anyone eats of this bread, he shall live forever; and the bread also which I shall give for the life of the world is My flesh....He who eats My flesh and drinks My blood has eternal life, and I will raise him up on the last day. For My flesh is true food, and My blood is true drink. He who eats My flesh and drinks My blood abides in Me, and I in him. As the living Father sent Me, and I live because of the Father; so he who eats Me, he also shall live because of Me. This is the bread which came down out of heaven; not as the fathers ate, and died, he who eats this bread shall live forever.

—JOHN 6:48–51, 54–58

CHAPTER 9

IDOLATRY AND SPIRITUAL ADULTERY

You shall not make for yourself an idol in the form of anything in heaven above or on the earth beneath or in the waters below. You shall not bow down to them or worship them; for I, the LORD your God, am a jealous God, punishing the children for the sin of the fathers to the third and fourth generation of those who hate me, but showing love to a thousand [generations] of those who love me and keep my commandments.

—DEUTERONOMY 5:8–10, NIV

O ur purpose in this chapter is to reveal how to heal the results of idolatry and spiritual adultery. We will first examine idolatry and later spiritual adultery.

Since in today's Western culture few people make figurines and set them in niches to worship, we need to see idolatry in a different sense. There is no sin that does not involve idolatry. If we steal, we have valued whatever we took more than we value God. If we commit adultery, we have elevated that woman or that man as more important to us than God. If we choose not to be in church on Sunday, we have made an idol of whatever we wanted more than obedience—pleasure, business, repairing the house, laziness, and so on. If we do not tithe, mammon is our god, no matter what we say. We may protest with our lips that we love God, that we are born anew, that we have all manner of wondrous experiences with God, but if we have not put our money where our mouth is, all our belief and experiences testify only to God's grace, not our faith. Apart from works, faith lies dead (James 2:17). Proof is written unequivocally in the history of our giving.

> No man can serve two masters; for either he will hate the one and love the other, or he will hold to one and despise the other. You cannot serve God and mammon.
>
> —Matthew 6:24

We are all inveterate idol makers. We do it by nature. For example, all we need is an anointed worship service, and the next time we get together we will try to copy what we did last time. We are no longer seeking the Lord Himself. We want that experience of power and the goose bumps. These things have for the moment become our God, the idol we worship.

We often idolize pastors and other spiritual leaders. That is why we often hate them so when they fall. They shattered our god.

If we check the many hundreds of little unconscious, unnoticed ways we break God's laws, we will see that even if we have tried, attended church and prayer meetings, and paid our tithes, we are still habitual idol-makers. How about when the wife is angry? We don't tell her the whole truth because we want to "keep the peace." Peace is now the idol we have served that justified lying. God said through St. Paul, "Do not provoke your children to anger" (Eph. 6:4). When we keep pushing the children away because they interrupt the ball game on TV, we have worshiped TV more than God. When the boss not only fails to compliment but also criticizes, and we blow up, it's a sure tip-off that we serve the idol of self. And so it goes, through every aspect of life. Idolatry is the first and greatest sin behind all we do.

Idolatry in Marriage

The most common form of idolatry that we have to deal with as prayer ministers is in relation to marriage. The command is: "Submit to one another out of reverence for Christ" (Eph. 5:21, niv). We have found that that command contains an unrelenting principle: in whatever degree we are not subject to Christ, we cannot be subject to one another! But more to the point, in whatever degree we are not in reverence for Christ, we idolize one another. There is a God-sized hole in us. Nature abhors a vacuum. If we do not fill it with Jesus, we *will* fill it with something—commerce, friends, sports, hobbies, and so on. Most often we ask more from our mates than they were intended to give.

Idolatrous requests wound the spirit because the mate feels the weight of demand. People placed in that position *know* they cannot supply what is wanted. No one can fulfill our need for God. Since both the asking and the attempt to respond are subconscious, both partners are filled with anxiety and frustration, and strain is added to the marriage.

Many husbands have spoken to us of their wounding and confusion. They say they love their wives. They always desired to be loving. They can't understand why they cannot simply rejoice and give the love they want to. "I just feel 'checked,' like something's wrong, and I don't know what." The truth was that their wives had put them into an idolatrous situation, and their spirit sensed it and recoiled. The great relief they express after we have explained how idolatry blocks tells us how much being put in that position wounds and confuses their spirit. The confusion and inability to express love for their wives had greatly undermined their confidence and their identity as husbands. Their spirits sensed and properly refused idolatry, but their minds had not understood.

If in their childhood either spouse had been neglected, rejected, or abused and now is insecure, prayer ministers should look immediately for signs that they are wounding their mate by idolizing them. Frequently, husbands whose mothers failed to affirm and give affection not only idolize their relationship to their wives, but they also relate to them as mothers, which wounds even more. Rejected and neglected girls also tend to relate to husbands as to fathers. In these instances, teaching is part of the healing.

Prayer ministers should instruct couples how to recognize when they are being projected wrongly into a parental position or being asked to fill God's shoes. The counsel of transactional analysis is quite correct, to teach them to say "I am not your mother" or "I am not your father." The same can be said in relation to God. "You're asking me to give you what only God can." This kind of counsel is predicated upon instruction and trust that the couple can hear one another and discuss their problems rather than blow up!

In the meantime, the prayer minister should be exploring roots of insecurity in each, applying healing, and attempting to evangelize the heart so as to fill that gap with God. Until that interior vacuum is filled, understanding the problem cannot be sufficient. No matter what our mind knows, our spirit searches for fulfillment. Not finding it, it nurses resentments. Unhealed roots send repeated shoots of trouble to the surface. It will not be enough to forgive resentments and bring self-defensive and aggressive practices to death on the cross. Only a full infilling of the love of Father God can take care of that vacuum and heal a wounded child's spirit. "Though my father and mother forsake me, the LORD will receive me" (Ps. 27:10, NIV) is true here for healing also. We must invite Father God to fill their hearts and then incubate them in His love, somewhat in and through us as prayer ministers, until they can believe and sense His fullness within their own hearts, apart from us.

IDOLIZING AUTHORITY FIGURES

The second kind of spiritual fornication commonly observed by prayer ministers is in relation to authority figures. We make gods of pastors, presidents, teachers, political leaders, parents, husbands, wives, our counselors, and prayer ministers. The tragedy is that we crucify our gods! We make scapegoats of authority figures, projecting our sins and all blame onto whoever is handy. Unconsciously we hate our sin in the other and crucify it. Any pastor worth his salt has suffered from being idolized and consequently persecuted. If he has not, I suggest he most likely was not preaching God's Word or being very effective!

The man who was most formative in my (John's) schooling was Dr. Ernst Jacob, a rabbi who had fled from persecution in Nazi Germany. At Drury University, Springfield, Missouri, he taught me European history, Old Testament history, prophets, and German. I shall never forget how one day, when he had taught us about all the miracles God wrought for Israel in the Exodus and during the forty years in the wilderness, we asked him, "Rabbi, when the Jews had seen God work all those miracles for all those years, and they knew God was real, how come they so quickly turned to worshiping idols? Why did they turn from the God they *knew* was absolutely real, to worship idols they made with their own hands?"

Rabbi Jacob leaned back, grinned a great, wide smile, and said, "Ven Gott ist Gott, Gott is Gott. Gott insists on being Gott. Gott ist in control. But ven mann hast ein idol, mann ist Gott. Mann ist in control!"

That lesson burned all the way through my heart and mind, and I thought of the Scripture, "But these enemies of mine, *who did not want me to reign over them...*" (Luke 19:27, emphasis added). The issue is always, "Who is in control?"

Whenever a pastor truly preaches God's Word, that Word is sweet to
the taste but bitter as gall in the stomach (Rev. 10:9). It enters the heart
and disturbs. Its truth exposes sin and forces decisions. People whose lips
honor God but whose hearts are far from Him (Matt. 15:8; Mark 7:6)
find themselves idolizing their pastor for the greatness of his ministry, but
then so often they choose to persecute him rather than face sin and die
on the cross! "He who separates himself seeks his own desire, he quarrels
against all sound wisdom" (Prov. 18:1). Any pretext will do.

Evangelist Earle Tyson was persecuted because he set up his tent in
the backyard for his children to play in. According to his accusers, he
was building additions without a permit! I was criticized because I went
to weed my garden barefoot—disgraceful! I was also criticized because
I wore colored socks in the pulpit rather than black. Of all things for a
pastor to do! The Word forces decisions; we must either change or find
something wrong with the messenger—anything—to justify our unwillingness to face sin.

There is in us that which hungers for the King of kings and Lord of lords.
That is why teenagers who do not truly worship God fasten such devotion
upon rock stars. We *must* worship something. Worship is built into us as
fundamentally as breathing. We can't live without it. That hunger rushes
to locate somewhere, fasten onto something, and express itself. There is
a cult whose members worship the memory of Elvis Presley! One young
man came to our door for counsel, convinced that Elvis was the reappear-
ance of Christ! And a more recent cult was sure that Michael Jackson was
the Messiah!

Look what has happened in the Charismatic movement. Every teacher
God has raised up we have idolized! What a dangerous pedestal we have
placed these men upon! God, who is rightly jealous because He loves us,
had to move to deliver both the teacher and His Church. He warns and
remonstrates, but if the teacher does not hear, or if he hears but his constit-
uency does not, God has to bring him down! God raised up five great
teachers—Bob Mumford, Charles Simpson, Derek Prince, Don Basham,
and Ern Baxter. Who among us in the early days of the Charismatic movement did not gratefully sit at their feet! But who heeded the warnings?
Shepherding and discipling went off balance and brought them crashing
down! They still taught, but their ministry to the whole body was at least
temporarily damaged.

I cut my eyeteeth on the teachings of Ken Hagin and quoted from him in *The Elijah Task*. He and Ken Copeland led into faith teaching, which for a season went off balance (no blame intended to them). God raised up our friend Father Francis MacNutt to minister across the world to Roman Catholics and Protestants alike. We were called to speak together in a Camp Farthest Out in Hawaii, he on healing, I as a prophet. I warned all there that whenever anything or anyone is elevated too far, God Himself must smash that idolatry. I received a tremendous outcry of angry protest. Then God took away their idol. Within a few months, Francis married Judith and was disfellowshiped, his books banned in many Catholic places! I grieved for my friend, that none could hear the warning. In the very moment of rejoicing for Francis and Judith in the happiness of their marriage, Paula and I grieved for the loss of his ministry to his own church.

I love and honor all these men. They are still, one and all, great teachers. We especially love Francis. The point is that by God's mercy, one way or another, He has smashed the pedestals on which all of them stood and graciously saved them for further service in the kingdom! God will not suffer idolatry to continue.

Nevertheless, healing is needed. Many throw away faith altogether when their idols fall. Disillusionment breaks the heart of many. Confusion and lack of understanding provide fertile ground for seeds of division in the body of Christ. There is no need to argue whether shepherding and discipling were all wrong or had valid points we all should hear. There is no need to discuss whether the faith teachings were right or wrong, or whether Roman priests should be allowed to marry. All that is beside the point. Once we established those men on pedestals, God was forced to do something about it. Had it not been the way history's leaves fell, some other thing—maybe less gracious—surely would have happened. The result is the same in every case. The idol worship is gone, forever smashed. Let the body draw a breath of thanks and repent, for we did it *to* them.

I have little hope we shall have learned our lesson. We'll do it again. But let every prayer minister and prophet become a watchman who warns as in Ezekiel 33. Paula and I are grateful that there are those on our Elijah House board who act regularly as faithful watchdogs to keep us humble. Most of the time, however, our clay feet leave such muddy tracks that we bring ourselves down all by ourselves with little need for help from anyone else!

Prayer ministers should look for more than those internationally known instances of idolatry. It happens all around us. Some sure indications are as follows (concerning the way we relate to our church, pastor, teacher, or political hero—whomever):

Inordinate defensiveness. "Don't you dare criticize that man!" Scripture tells us to be prepared always to make a defense for our faith (1 Pet. 3:15) and that there is a friend who sticks closer than a brother (Prov. 18:24), but idolatry is indicated when defense, usually with rancor, continually blocks out what should be heard and heeded.

Bias that blinds. True relationship is not naïve. It sees both the blessings and sins of friends, and loves anyway. But those in idolatry gloss over faults. Their eyes are full of stars of fancy. They make excuses for faults rather than confront in love.

Persecution complexes. This involves seeing reactions of people to our idols not as possible warnings of error but as persecution for righteousness. Since sometimes persecution is indeed because of righteousness, the distinctive factor is unwillingness to see both possibilities. It *has* to be persecution. That conclusion is seized without waiting for all the facts or for clarification or verification from the Holy Spirit. Error is ruled out, and with it repentance.

False martyrdom. True martyrdom ordinarily is not sought. It happens *to* the saint despite his attempts to live quietly. (See 1 Thessalonians 4:11.) True martyrdom gives glory to God. Somehow those who idolize only sniff the winds of possible martyrdom and trumpet the cause so that the hero receives the glory. "You're making a martyr of him!"

Sexual confusions and attachments. Both women and men are tempted to throw themselves at figures they idolize. How many hundreds of times have we heard of some saint whose ministry was ascending to the heights who came crashing down by falling into adultery? Sexual trouble is the natural end of idolatry, as surely as water flowing downhill must eventually find a body to rest in. Conversely, servants with purified hearts seldom find people attaching to them sexually or trying to seduce them. What emanates does not send such signals. Flesh attracts flesh. Spirit attracts spirit.

For the one who sows to his own flesh shall from the flesh reap corruption, but the one who sows to the Spirit shall from the Spirit reap eternal life.

—GALATIANS 6:8

Twisted teachings. Too much emphasis begins to be placed on a few scriptures, more and more understood out of context. This is so whether the teacher himself is out of balance, puffed up in his own arrogance, or defiled by the idolatry of others. What started out as truth goes too far, and the weak and immature suffer.

Anger. Somehow, everybody seems to become overinvested in the project and becomes quickly or inordinately angered. Just as fury overtook Nebuchadnezzar (in Daniel 3:19), anger, sometimes followed by violence, is a sure sign of the presence of idolatry.

Each man to his own tent. Armed camps. Division in the body. Isolation. When idolatry is *not* present, participants can hear the sound advice of Gamaliel to wait and see whether this thing is of God. If it's not of God, it will die of its own accord. If we oppose it right away, we may find ourselves opposing God (Acts 5:34–39). But when idolatry *is* present, there is no waiting. Participants must choose sides, right away.

Satan's work has always been to cut up and divide. Look at the residue from shepherding and discipling and the faith teachings. There are still far too many sitting in pockets of loneliness saying, "We were right after all, and why don't you see it and receive us?" Understand, we do not blame the teachers who began the movements. It was idolatry, far beyond their ken and control, that carried things to their natural end.

Paula and I, and every other teacher in the body, should pray fervently and regularly that we and our teachings may be delivered from the defilements of idolatry in the body, and that these movements of which we have spoken may yet be recovered from whatever effects still bedevil and sour what would otherwise produce good and wholesome fruits. Each leader must bear his own load, but the sin has been that of the entire body. Therefore, *the repentance and the cry for mercy should come from the body, too.*

HEALING FOR IDOLATERS

Individuals who have been involved at either end of idolatry, as leaders or as those who have idolized them, need to find healing in the church or in a counselor's or prayer minister's office. Law has been transgressed. Iniquity *will* be visited with judgment. The Lord will visit "the iniquity of the fathers on the children, and on the third and the fourth generations of those who hate Me" (Deut. 5:9). How often we have seen the children and grandchildren of spiritual leaders suffer all manner of tragedies! As prayer ministers used to hearing stories of tragedy, even we are amazed how often, when investigating family histories, we discover behind a singularly tragic family record an ancestor who was a pastor or spiritual leader of some sort. It seems their descendants ought to be most blessed, and indeed we are sure most often they are.

> A good man leaves an inheritance to his children's children.
> —PROVERBS 13:22

Without statistics, could we guess that 90 percent of the time such descendants are most blessed? But there is a risk in serving God. Servants can fall into snares and traps.

> Let not many of you become teachers, my brethren, knowing that *as such we shall incur a stricter judgment.*
> —JAMES 3:1, EMPHASIS ADDED

In Deuteronomy 5:9 we learn that it is primarily the sin of idolatry that causes judgment to be visited upon the descendants of the sinner, and idolatry is the most common error to which teachers and leaders fall prey!

When prayer ministers discover idolatry, they should pray to stop the descent of harm to *future* generations by the blood and cross of Jesus. It would be well to check the history of the ancestry as well, to determine whether patterns of idolatry have descended through *past* generations. Those who may think it harsh of God to visit the iniquity of parents through several generations would do well to read no further until having read chapters 8–10 of *The Elijah Task* and chapters 4–6 and chapter 8 of *Transforming the Inner Man.* God is neither unjust nor unkind, as those chapters explain.

The individual himself should be led through prayers of repentance and forgiveness. If he is one who has idolized a leader, it may be wise to counsel him to go to that leader and confess, asking forgiveness, if he had close enough contact to warrant such an approach. If he is the leader who in one way or another sought others to put him on a pedestal, or even if it only happened to him, the prayer minister should pronounce forgiveness for the sin of playing God. He should lead the leader through the Abraham-Isaac prayer, in which his ministry is treated as his Isaac and left as dead in Christ at the altar. God will restore his ministry, but no longer as his to be possessed and defended. It will belong to God alone.

It is "grass-eating time." When Nebuchadnezzar failed to heed the warnings of the Holy Spirit through his dreams and through Daniel's interpretations (see Daniel 1–4 and chapter 17, "Nebuchadnezzar's Image," in *Restoring the Christian Family*), the watchers proclaimed that he would be driven from his kingdom to eat grass until his mind should some day (after seven periods, Dan. 4:32) be restored to him (Dan. 4:34). If repentance and self-humbling do not soon enough allow the grace of God, the servant must learn the hard way. He goes off balance. He makes a fool of himself. He may even lose his sanity in megalomania. He must eat grass for a while. The simple meaning of this in our modern vernacular is that he is "grounded." For a while, God will allow him no more flights of fancy and imagination, no more mystical heights. God humbles, even humiliates His servant again and again until even onlookers want to cry out, "Enough is enough!" But enough isn't enough until the servant is so crushed he never again wants the taste of being idolized, nor does he want the taste of idolizing another. It must be written in indelible ink on his heart and in his mind.

The prayer minister's part in all this is to be a friend. Prayer ministers must not try to ameliorate the situation. We must only stand by. Our compassion and understanding will help the afflicted one comprehend what and why he is suffering, but no more than that. We must not blunt the sword of God's judgment. There will come a time when the servant ceases Job's lament and, like him, cries out, "I have declared that which I did not understand, things too wonderful for me, which I did not know....I have heard of Thee by the hearing of the ear; but now my eye sees Thee; therefore I retract, and I repent in dust and ashes" (Job 42:3–6). Until that time, what the one in God's grinding machine needs is a friend who has faith in God to know he will come all the way through, when it seems to him he'll never make it. Love *"believes* all things" (1 Cor. 13:7, emphasis added); love believes for us when we can't believe for ourselves anymore.

There may be others involved. A man may have dragged his family, against their better judgment, into following some would-be Christ.

> Many false prophets will arise, and will mislead many.
>
>   —MATTHEW 24:11

> For false Christs and false prophets will arise and will show great signs and wonders, so as to mislead, if possible, even the elect.
>
>   —MATTHEW 24:24

> Do not go after them.
>
>   —LUKE 21:8

That form of spiritual adultery requires several prayers:

1. That all the words and thoughts implanted during that sojourn be brought to nothing by the fire of the Holy Spirit, that every false teaching be rooted out, leaving only the deposits of wisdom and wariness.

2. That the servant's family be likewise delivered and cleansed.

3. That he be helped to eat humble pie by talking it out with whatever participating family members will sit down with him.

4. That forgiveness and reconciliation be voiced and acted out in and beyond the family.

5. That somehow the prayer minister works to restore respect for the person in the family. If the man is a husband and father, then headship and trust in his leadership need to be restored. This latter may require teaching the rest of the family that what we go through can make us wiser and prepare us rather than disqualify us to lead.

Good-natured joshing and teasing is a grand reentry tool—not ridicule, which demeans, but rather banter that asserts and teases in an attitude of respect. Those who have been "on a trip" into idolatry have taken themselves too seriously. They need to be helped to laugh heartily at their mistakes.

Experiences in the out-of-doors should be prescribed for those who have been delivered from idolatry. It was not accident that the prescription for Nebuchadnezzar's healing was that he should eat grass! We need to soak up good old earth for a while. The great poet Wordsworth used to become so caught up in mysticism that he would grab hold of a tree until balance returned. Lots of work in the yard and garden are a grand tonic for the self-important.

Spiritual Adultery

We have spoken so far of the many ways we can idolize and worship what we ought not to, but there are many ways to commit spiritual adultery without idolizing. Whenever we give to someone else what belongs only to our mate, we have committed *spiritual* adultery. Physical adultery occurs when we proceed beyond that to give our *body* to another. The Lord spoke of spiritual adultery when He said:

> You have heard that it was said, "You shall not commit adultery"; but I say to you, that every one who looks on a woman to lust for her has committed adultery with her already in his heart.
> —MATTHEW 5:27–28

Many Christians circumspectly keep their hearts from thinking lustfully and so congratulate themselves that they have never been involved in spiritual adultery. But the ways of our heart are more elusive than that.

By the grace of God, I have never been to bed with anyone other than my wife. And I have been careful never to allow myself to dwell on sexual thoughts concerning any other woman. I have been well aware of the scripture that says, "Do not desire her beauty *in your heart*" (Prov. 6:25) and of the wise old proverb which says, "Look not long upon beauty belonging to another." But that did not keep me from *spiritual* adultery.

In the early years of our marriage, Paula and I had not yet crossed the bridges of communication by the spans of wisdom and the cross. We were often at odds. Paula did not know how to reach past my bristles to comfort me, nor did I know even what I wanted, which was really only her whole being to hold and nurture mine as God intended.

That left a vacuum. I was vulnerable. I gravitated to whatever men or women in less-threatening secondary relationships could comfort, affirm, or flatter me. I could open up and share easily with them what should have been discussed only, or at least first, with Paula. Many times Paula was grievously wounded when at a social function she would overhear me easily telling someone else something I had not yet shared with her. That was spiritual adultery. I had given that communion of heart, that deep fellowship that belongs between a man and his wife, to someone else.

When Paula tried to talk with me about it, I would try to remember, attempting to decipher by logic what was hers alone and what could be shared with others. It was sweaty work, and unsuccessful, because the problem was in my heart. My heart had not yet learned to find its only source of manhood in relation to Paula. I was still set to find self-fulfill-ment and self-definition elsewhere. That is spiritual adultery at root level, looking for somewhere to happen. Naturally, it happened again and again.

When Paula would fuss and storm about it, my mind easily saw—at that moment—that she was right. But since my heart was still not right, my mind would lose it again and again. Remorse did not become repen-tance. But her fuming convinced my frightened heart not to open to her, the very one whom God had designed for its refreshment! That increased the vulnerability, for nature abhors a vacuum.

Even while becoming aware of the problem and determining to be faithful, I became worse. Men, but especially women who seemed to be wise and understanding, gentle and comforting, became so tonic to my lonely soul that I unconsciously sought more and more excuses to spend time with them. Both my grandmothers had been able to hear me, so I sought out the grandmothers and unburdened my heart to them, not realizing that was spiritually adulterous. Nor was I aware that undealt-with areas in my heart dulled and warped my judgment so that I often accepted as wise counsel and comfort only that which did not challenge or threaten, as Paula's counsel seemed to do. I was also naïve concerning the hidden needs and motives of others and unprepared to recognize the difference between clean affirmation and manipulative ego building. Some, who were equally lonely and spiritually adulterous, latched on to me in return. At last, though I never ever hugged another woman wrongly, kissed anyone, or even let myself think a sexual thought, Paula cried out, "We aren't even alone in bed anymore!" She could feel the pull of those other women who had latched onto me.

Fortunately, the Lord's grace had built me so morally, mainly through the strong morality of my ancestry, that the Lord could catch me before I went any further. At last He revealed to my *heart* what Paula was talking about, and I could come to repentance rather than to mere remorse. Together we prayed through everything we could think of, among them unfulfilled needs for mothering, desires to turn women on for ego's sake, fear of true vulnerability that left me vulnerable at lesser levels, unconscious hatred of women that wanted to draw women to me and then punish them by turning them away unfulfilled, ways of taking vengeance on Paula by giving what was hers to someone else, and so on. One large blockage that had to come to the cross was that I had, because of the tension in my childhood, learned to separate comfort, ease, refreshment, and gentle nurture from anything having to do with "home." Home had become identified in me as tension and responsibility, not rest and refreshment. I had to bring many judgments and fears to death in order to discover the truth that Paula had (not always graciously in her frustration) tried to communicate, "Someday you will learn that I'm the best friend you have and that your children can be refreshment, not always just a heavy responsibility!"

Most importantly, Paula and I learned not to identify one another as antagonists. We *joined together* to fight hand in hand against the blockages in each other's flesh that kept us apart. Even so, long after beautiful bridges had been built and we had crossed many times to find glorious picnics in each other's parks, I still had to fight tendencies to flee. I found I desperately feared total vulnerability. I could even warp Scripture to justify my flights: "Do not give your strength to women..." (Prov. 31:3). I told myself I could be swallowed up or lose my headship—anything would do to justify fleeing from vulnerability and commitment. I found it necessary to pray again and again, especially when the sweetness of marital sex had threatened to open all my gates, "Oh, Lord, I *choose* to be vulnerable. Open me to Paula. Don't let me flee out!" I could tell when my heart was beginning to close. God gave me a barometer—my tongue. When it wanted not to talk with Paula and found itself easily waggling with other people, I knew I had to battle again with my old self!

The Lord has won the battle with us. We may slip occasionally, but He has us, and we are "locked on target." Our oneness is now what validates our message to many. But our story is not unique. We have ministered to thousands more like us in the matter of spiritual adultery than concerning any other problem in human nature.

Though women also have ways of fleeing from full partnership, we find that men much more often than women resist true union. Most likely the greatest root derives from men having fought off, as boys, mother's tentacles of control. Few mothers have known how to give their boys nurture without smothering. We have learned early on not to tell women our secrets: they have elephantine memories and are determined to use them on us! Many women unconsciously castrate their husbands and sons. Little sisters find power over stronger brothers by tattling. Countless hurtful ways may have to be tracked down to set a man free to relate to his wife. Deeper than all these is the memory of every man all the way back to Adam. It is no joke that we remember what Eve got Adam into! The cross of Christ must find the reasons for the problems in all our relationships before we are fully free.

God said to Eve, "Your desire shall be for your husband" (Gen. 3:16). Women tend to press in, seeking to find their place with their man. At the deepest level, sin has forfeited woman's place as the full and equal partner of her husband. In Christ, woman's place is restored, but that, like other things, must also be worked out. Therefore, something in her deep mind remembers and presses to recover that position. That, so long as flesh governs it, comes across as demand to husbands, from which they flee. Osage Indians used to say, "When you see a white man coming to you with a gleam in his eye to help you, run like the wind the other way!" So do men from women, like Li'l Abner from Daisy Mae on Sadie Hawkins' Day!

Though sometimes women find shelter and strength in some other man and so commit spiritual adultery, the most common thing we deal with in prayer ministry is that kind of confusion that happens when wives unconsciously transfer to the Lord what belongs only to the husband. The fact that Christ is the groom to all the church (His bride) becomes a temptation rather than a blessing when a woman's heart is not right. Her husband senses the adultery and may react violently. How can he compete with such a rival? In retaliation some men have left the church in anger. We have encountered a number of women so vulnerable by not having connected emotionally with their husbands that seducing spirits have actually convinced them that the Lord is so much their husband they are entitled to enter into sexual union with Him. Spirits have so seduced some women that they have experienced the feelings of intercourse, including orgasm. That kind of spirit is called an "incubus." (The same kind of seduction can happen with men, in which the spirit is called a "succuba.")

Women may find in prayer groups the security they should have found in their husband's headship. Leaders who rightly attempt to be father figures for all in their group may find confusing kinds of relationships and feelings developing in the group, as women unconsciously—or consciously and sinfully—attach themselves. Because of so many unhealed wounds in so many hearts in so many prayer groups, spiritual adultery is perhaps the most common sin in the Charismatic movement.

Affairs usually do not commence as affairs, at least among Christians who intend to walk in His way. It is unconscious spiritual adultery that hooks both participants. When true union fails, particularly in the areas of communication and heartfelt sharing, husbands and wives are left open to another who may *seem* to be able to fill that gap. Many who have fallen to physical adultery have said to us in prayer ministry, "I don't understand it. I had good sex at home. My wife is great sexually—this other woman can't even hold a candle to her—so what am I doing wanting her? I don't get it!" Or women have ranted and raved and cried out, "He had all he wanted! Whatever can he see in her?" However, it was not sex that was wanted. It was that union of hearts and spirits of which sex is only the climax. Because sex is the climax, other kinds of adulterous union naturally gravitate there.

There are no heroes in this kind of warfare. There are only holy cowards. People must be taught to avoid encounters once entered. They cannot remain in relationships that have become spiritually adulterous and remain pure and safe. Sooner or later they will plunge over "Lover's Leap" unless grace intervenes to heal in full each heart and each marriage.

Sometimes continuing relationships cannot be avoided. A brother-in-law or sister-in-law is likely to remain in the family. We may not be able to withdraw graciously from a prayer group and join another. Besides, if the heart's condition is not healed at root level, we will find the same problem with someone in the next group, and sooner or later we are going to run out of groups! Certainly we don't want to be transferring from church to church, firing secretaries regularly, or dropping out of club after club.

The rule is that when relationships have been so deeply engaged that tracks of familiarity have been built and danger of further fulfillment lurks, whatever price must be paid must be paid, even if we have to indeed change churches or jobs or towns altogether. But if dabblings have been caught in time, we can remain where we are while ministry discovers and heals roots. The second rule is, however, that participants in spiritual adultery, at whatever stage, must not be allowed to be the ones to decide how safe or not safe they are. That decision must be entrusted to the wisdom of friends and prayer ministers. Fools think that they are still safe and that they can stop anytime they want to. Discerning friends are protection from folly.

HEALING FOR SPIRITUAL ADULTERY

Spiritual adultery requires healing on two levels. The presence of tendencies to spiritual adultery ought to be taken as a sure indication to prayer ministers that root troubles exist in relation to mothers and fathers. Deep inner healing should be engaged, particularly in search of roots of bitterness regarding lack of fulfillment, deprivation of affection, criticalness and wounding, inability of parents to appreciate and foster talents, and most specifically in relation to possible hearts of stone and inner vows not to be vulnerable. Once the inner one is healed of resentments, that vacuum must be filled with love. Then the prayer minister can deal with present frustrations and blockages and instruct the married couple in the art of true sharing and meeting.

One thing about spiritual adultery is more insidious than most other sins: it may not seem like sin at all. It appears to be good to be able to enter into seemingly deep relationships with people, especially if we are strongly moral people; we "know" we will never let things get out of hand. The fellowship appears to be tonic to our soul. The esteem of others inflates our ego. It may nag at the back of the mind as a curiosity, or even be a painful awareness, that we can share so easily with someone else but not with our own spouse. But if we have some training in psychology or sociology, we can easily chalk that off to the common knowledge that one can almost always be nicer to secondary people than to primary. It may be difficult to hate it enough to stop. Our advice: look at it from another angle. Stop justifying it out there. Start seeing it as harmful to your spouse. Put yourself in your mate's shoes and feel the loneliness, the desolation, and the betrayal. Learn to hate it for what it does to loved ones rather than measuring it by your own feelings.

Perhaps we should not leave the subject without mentioning that spiritual adultery is not confined to marital relationships. When we wander from pastor to pastor and church to church, that is spiritual adultery. If Paula and I serve under the anointing of an inviting pastor to teach and leave, that's fine. But if we pull his people after us, that's adultery. If in a church we minister to people the pastor appoints, that is good. If we let too many find help from us who should be obtaining if from their own group or from his counsel, that becomes adulterous. We could list a thousand ways, all assumable under the simple definition that whenever we drink from some other cistern than God has appointed, we engage in adultery.

Occasional listening to another teacher is not adultery (lest we lock ourselves into cultish rigidity through the above definition). "One sows, and another reaps" (John 4:37). No one husband, wife, pastor, teacher, or friend can be *all* to anyone. Trying to be everything to another can itself become idolatrous, and thus, adulterous. The mark of distinction is in the heart. If our heart is attached where it belongs, whatever other source of refreshment becomes ours will only heighten our basic attachment. But if we begin to disrespect where we belong and hunger for something else and more, then we are in danger, and any other source will become adultery. We need to be watchdogs of our hearts (Prov. 4:23). So long as we seek first and fully our own mate and church and friends, we are on track. But when hungers and lusts arise, we must take these as signals and flee to our own mate and whatever friend, counselor, or prayer minister can help us to discover what is the matter.

ADULTERY TOWARD THINGS

We can also be adulterous toward things. Many wives have had good cause to hate their husband's job, or the car, because he caresses it and not her. TV, football, golf, chores, hobbies—anything can become the object of our adultery. Women are not so likely to be adulterous in those areas, but how many mothers have given to their children what belonged to their husbands and then justified it because he "left them" first? We fall into adultery toward things for the same reasons as with people, and healing is accomplished in the same way. Adultery with things, however, may be more insidious since it is generally less recognizable as such, and ways to deal with it are more difficult to live through. A man cannot quit his job, and a woman may feel as though her husband is asking her to worship him more than God when he fusses about her giving so much attention to the church rather than to him. Nevertheless, the price must be paid. Half of the game is won when we truly see it, the other half when we determine to pray it all the way through.

Spiritual adultery and idolatry are similar. There is only one difference. In idolatry we put someone or something in God's place and worship it. In adultery we put God or some other person or thing in our mate's place and love it. Spiritual adultery and idolatry merge when we also idolize the person or thing we present ourselves to. It usually is not long before adultery also becomes idolatry. In one sense it is idolatry at inception, for whatever is more important than what God has given us is already our idol. Idolatry is unavoidable; we idolize because that is the basic sin of our flesh.

THE KINGDOM OF SELF

Behind every other idolatry is one worse than all. It lies at the core of all of us. It is the kingdom of self, where self rules all our hidden motives. The throne may be given to Jesus, but self still fancies itself the power behind His throne.

The core of us is so infected with evil it cannot be healed, only slain and resurrected. Ever since Adam, we have been determined to be like God. There is a ruling center so devious as to allow us to role-play all the actions of surrender to God or service and love to others, without ever allowing itself to be detected, much less brought to death. Prayer ministry and our progress in the Lord can be described as a gradual peeling of an onion, skin by skin, not to uncover sweetness but to find rottenness and roaring defiance within, unbowed and unsurrendered.

Countless times Paula and I have watched the "pilgrim's progress" of a brother as he became what seemed to him saintlier and saintlier. We knew, as we observed, that there would come a time, when he was ready, that Christ would uncover the last shrouds of deceit to discover sheer sin, untouched by goodness! There is great risk at that time. Even the Lord cannot force us to choose rightly. The way of life and death lies starkly before us at that moment. A choice must be made. It is predicated on bare and simple *trust*. At that moment the sinner must be willing to say, "Yes, Lord, I *will* see it. I *will* own it. I *am* totally corrupted and helpless." It does little good to confess the depths of our sinfulness theologically before that moment. We have seen many fundamentally sound brothers who have come to that moment of full experiential acknowledgment and have fled from it in sheer terror! It is amazing how, after years of being in Christ, we still want to hang on to some tiniest shred of righteousness or some merest inch of control, as though our salvation depended on that!

The brother pastor of whom we spoke in the chapter on defilement (chapter 5) and his wife were members with Paula and me and an elder and his wife in a small support group. One day we were all sitting in the warm sunlight on the elder's balcony. The Lord had been working in the pastor's heart for weeks, revealing, step-by-step, further and further interior caverns of his heart filled with filth and webs of deceit. Now, our gentle Lord was opening more to this pastor He loved. The brother's words still ring in my ears. "I don't believe I'm going to like what I see when I get in here." Sure enough, it was too much for him. He fled out—and shortly thereafter the defilement of delusion caught him. He has never returned to full and joyous faith.

On the other hand, we have seen many come to that point and laughingly enter rest. "Well, what do you know. I don't have anything to defend anymore. I'm shot through with sin, and I'm loved anyway. Jesus has me. His righteousness is mine. I don't have any. Hallelujah!" St. Paul came to that point and chose the righteousness of Jesus:

> For I *know* that *nothing good* dwells in me, that is, in my flesh.
> —ROMANS 7:18, EMPHASIS ADDED

> It is because of him that you are in Christ Jesus, who has become for us wisdom from God—that is, *our righteousness*, holiness and redemption.
> —1 CORINTHIANS 1:30, NIV, EMPHASIS ADDED

At the depths of all of us is a spirit that masks its basic idolatry all our life until that moment of revelation in Jesus. We want to be God! We are jealous of Jesus who was elevated to be Lord of all. We are full of striving, therefore, to establish the kingdom of self, none more so than those who have learned the secret of service to others. How better to play God? The sin of self-idolatry causes all our works for the Lord to be shot through with self-aggrandizement and self-glorification, no matter how many times we say we will give Him all the glory. The truth is, we have to say we will give Him the glory precisely because we are inclined not to. Self-idolizing means that while we smile and rejoice in our brother's success, inwardly we grind our teeth in jealousy and surreptitiously "rejoice in unrighteousness" (1 Cor. 13:6) when our brother stumbles. We are compelled to put everyone else down and elevate self, without ever realizing we do it!

We are all shrikes at heart, for self-vaunting is the ruling attitude in every person's hidden heart. The moment we see our basic sin of idolatry and how it is the spider at the center of all our webs of deceit, we enter rest—if we choose to let go and let Jesus. But not all choose rightly.

> And this is the judgment, that the light is come into the world, and men loved the darkness rather than the light; for their deeds were evil.
> —JOHN 3:19

What deeds? Listen to it the other way around.

> "What shall we do, that we may work the works [deeds] of God?" Jesus answered and said to them, "*This is the work of God, that you believe in Him* whom He has sent."
> —JOHN 6:28–29, EMPHASIS ADDED

The evil deed at the core is unbelief, distrust that Jesus actually is the risen and present Lord who can and will hold our life if we let go of it! How many times we have counseled brothers who lived in and for the Lord in the church, who celebrated the risen Lord every Sunday, who at this crucial depth did not know and could not believe that He is the risen Lord! The evil deed is to walk in oneself, to hang onto the center of control, to walk in one's flesh by unbelief, which is idolatry—the worship of self.

The choice is upon us.

> No one can serve two masters; for either he will hate the one and love the other, or he will hold to one and despise the other. You cannot serve God and mammon.
> —MATTHEW 6:24

Mammon is the god of this world's wealth, which is the meaning of the word in the context of Matthew 6. But that verse may as accurately be applied to pose the question, "Who is master of our spirit—self or Jesus

Christ?" I know by our years of prayer ministry that most who read this chapter will nod their heads knowingly, thinking they have been through this death and rebirth, but few have. There are many levels—practice runs, as it were—before the final revelation and death. It must be lived, all the way through.

One lady to whom I ministered over thirty years ago went to another prayer minister to receive further ministry. Having been through the process a few years ago himself, her prayer minister knew the path. He watched as week by week she came closer and closer. She made a covenant with him. "This time I will not flee out!" At last there came a day when the presence of the Lord came upon her and she broke through in a moment of full revelation to exclaim, "Oh, I see it! I have been like a black widow spider sucking the righteousness out of everyone around me—my husband, my children, everyone!" The prayer minister leaned forward and gently said, "Dolores,* at last you've become real!" She had indeed been a full-fledged shrike (see chapter 6); her diagnosis was true. God had shown her the core of self that subconsciously ruled all her doing.

The prayer minister left the session rejoicing in the Lord. "At last she has seen herself and faced her sin. She's come home, Lord. Thank You, Lord." He expected to see her at the next session at rest and radiant, but the kingdom of self was not that easily dethroned. She lit all over him with bitter railing and accused him of calling her a black widow spider! She was there to tell him she would have no more of that! It mattered not at all that the prayer minister's wife (who was working those days with her husband in team ministry) pointed out to her, "Dolores, my husband didn't say that to you. You said it to him!" She could not hear. Her heart's doors were closed. She *had* to have *some* righteousness. When her time came, she simply could not believe the grace of God. She fled to another prayer minister who, she hoped, would speak to her the easy things that her kingdom of self wanted to hear.

We write for warning, friends: "Humble yourselves, therefore, under the mighty hand of God, that He may exalt you at the proper time" (1 Pet. 5:6). Again, I say, *humble yourselves.* Don't flee out. Be determined to face it all the way through. You have nothing to lose but your wickedness. This is the core, the deepest thing, the center of all that keeps us from the fullness of the kingdom of God—self! Idol worship! Our spirit on God's throne

---

* Fictitious name

in us—years and years after our conversion experience! Let us press on for the prize of the upward call of God in Christ Jesus (Phil. 3:14).

Since we cannot die that death in reality until He brings us to it, "Choose you *this day* whom ye will serve.... As for me and my house, we will serve the LORD" (Josh. 24:15, KJV, emphasis added).

CHAPTER 10

GRIEF, FRUSTRATION, AND LOSS

A tranquil heart is *life to the body*, but passion is rottenness to the bones.

—PROVERBS 14:30, EMPHASIS ADDED

A joyful heart makes a cheerful face, but when the heart is sad, the spirit is broken.

—PROVERBS 15:13

A joyful heart is good medicine, but a broken spirit dries up the bones.

—PROVERBS 17:22

We have written somewhat about grief in chapter 4, "Depression," and in some aspects about frustration and loss in our upcoming book *Transforming Wounded Relationships* in the chapter on "Destiny Malaise." There are many excellent books on the subject, one of the best being *Healing Life's Hurts* by the Linn brothers. This chapter is not to repeat what has already been covered, but to address the subject from the more specific aspect of how grief, frustration, and loss affect our personal spirit, and thus our bodies, and how such effects can be healed.

Grief, frustration, and loss come in two kinds. There is that which befalls us from loss of aspirations, frustrations in vocation or job, or loss of income or cherished objects. These are all hurts in relation to things, a dream, or a hope being as much a thing to our heart as a cherished teapot handed down from Grandmother. But there is also that kind of grief, frustration, and loss that happens in relationships to God, others, or oneself. Of the two, the second is far more formidable. Lost things become only a memory. God and people continue to live, and their life calls to our life. Their continued existence alone summons us to redress and restoration.

When we come into the world, our spirit is not something apart from our body and our heritage. It is integrally involved with both. This means that our spirit instinctively looks to no one as primarily as to our own father and mother for definition and fulfillment. To lose a parent, especially in the formative years, is not like the loss of a limb. One can lose an arm and still adjust because the central core of the person remains intact, along with supportive systems of friends and relatives. But a parent has a far more foundational function in our life than even our own limbs. A child's spirit drinks definition and fulfillment daily from his parents, and their presence sings to the very DNA of his being.

There is a direct relation between the health of our spirit and body to how healthy our relationships are with the primary people in our lives:

> An excellent wife is the crown of her husband, but she who shames him is as rottenness in his bones.
>
> —PROVERBS 12:4

Grief also affects our physical health:

> My life is consumed by anguish and my years by groaning; my strength fails because of my affliction, and *my bones grow weak.*
>
> —PSALM 31:10, NIV, EMPHASIS ADDED

> Is it nothing to you, all you who pass by? Look around and see. Is any suffering like my suffering that was inflicted on me, that the LORD brought on me in the day of his fierce anger? From on high he sent fire, sent it down into my bones. He spread a net for my feet and turned me back. He made me desolate, faint all the day long.
>
> —LAMENTATIONS 1:12–13, NIV

Stress affects our spirit and thus our health, specifically our bones:

> A tranquil heart is life to the body, but passion is rottenness to the bones.
>
> —PROVERBS 14:30

It should be mentioned that the word *passion* here does not mean proper healthy sexual passion but fleshly aggravations.

> A joyful heart is good medicine, but a broken spirit dries up the bones.
>
> —PROVERBS 17:22

Anticipation of stress likewise affects our spirit, thus our health, and most specifically our bones. Habakkuk prophesied of approaching judgment for sin:

> I heard and my inward parts trembled, at the sound my lips quivered. Decay enters my bones, and in my place I tremble. Because I must wait quietly for the day of distress, for the people to arise who will invade us.
>
> —HABAKKUK 3:16

Job, under the stress of loss and sorrow, suffered in his spirit and in his bones, and his friends spoke of sin affecting the spirit and bones: trembling so that all his bones shake (Job 4:14); his bones cling to his skin (Job 19:20); the night pierces his bones (Job 30:17, NIV); there is "unceasing complaint in his bones" (Job 33:19). On the other hand, Job described those who are blessed by God, who enjoy health, by speaking of their "bones full of youthful vigor" (Job 20:11); "wholly at ease and satisfied; his sides are filled out with fat, and the marrow of his bones is moist" (Job 21:23–24).

We can experience spiritual grief and loss because of sin that separates us from God. This immediately affects the spirit and thus the bones.

> There is no soundness in my flesh because of Thine indignation; there is *no health in my bones because of my sin.*
>
> —PSALM 38:3, EMPHASIS ADDED

> He also loved cursing, so it came to him; and he did not delight in blessing, so it was far from him. But he clothed himself with cursing as with his garment, and it entered into his body like water, and like oil into his bones.
>
> —PSALM 109:17–18

The discipline of the Lord directly affects our bones.

Make me to hear joy and gladness, let the bones which Thou hast
broken rejoice.

—PSALM 51:8

Why are bones so important? How does what happens to our spirit so
quickly and directly affect our bones? Listen to these simple facts:

Bone marrow…found within the cavities of large bones…is a
"cellular factory" that *makes more than 20 billion new blood cells
every day* throughout each person's life. A specialized cell type—the
bone marrow stem cell—is fundamental to the process. Bone marrow
stem cells have the ability to mature into red blood cells (*cells that
carry oxygen to all parts of the body*), white blood cells (*cells that help
the body fight infections and diseases*), or platelets (*cells that help
blood clot and help control bleeding*). These functions are essential
for a healthy life.[1]

Now let us hold in mind, while we read the following scriptures, the
startling fact that *every day twenty billion new blood cells* are released into
our body and that the bone marrow produces white cells that protect us
from disease:

Trust in the LORD with all your heart, and do not lean on your own
understanding. In all your ways acknowledge Him, and He will make
your paths straight. Do not be wise in your own eyes; fear the LORD
and turn away from evil. *It will be healing to your body, and refreshment to your bones.*

—PROVERBS 3:5–8, EMPHASIS ADDED

Pleasant words are a honeycomb, sweet to the soul and *healing to
the bones.*

—PROVERBS 16:24, EMPHASIS ADDED

A cheerful look brings joy to the heart, and *good news gives health to
the bones.*

—PROVERBS 15:30, NIV, EMPHASIS ADDED

Then you shall see this, and your heart shall be glad, and *your bones
shall flourish like the new grass*; and the hand of the LORD shall be
made known to His servants, but He shall be indignant toward His
enemies.

—ISAIAH 66:14, EMPHASIS ADDED

In Isaiah 58 the Lord calls for men to serve Him as they ought, and says:

> Then your light will break out like the dawn, and your recovery will speedily spring forth; and your righteousness will go before you; the glory of the LORD will be your rear guard. Then you will call, and the LORD will answer; you will cry, and He will say, "Here I am." If you remove the yoke from your midst, the pointing of the finger, and speaking wickedness, and if you give yourself to the hungry, and satisfy the desire of the afflicted, then your light will rise in darkness, and your gloom will become like midday. And the LORD will continually guide you, and satisfy your desire in scorched places, and *give strength to your bones.*
>
> —ISAIAH 58:8–11, EMPHASIS ADDED

The psalmist spoke of his bones rejoicing in the Lord:

> And my soul shall rejoice in the LORD; it shall exult in His salvation. *All my bones* will say, "LORD, who is like Thee, who delivers the afflicted from him who is too strong for him, and the afflicted and the needy from him who robs him?"
>
> —PSALM 35:9–10, EMPHASIS ADDED

One of the promises of God concerning righteousness and bones was fulfilled by the fact that the soldiers did not break the legs of Jesus, as the custom was, but only pierced His side:

> Many are the afflictions of the righteous; but the LORD delivers him out of them all. *He keeps all his bones; not one of them is broken.*
>
> —PSALM 34:19–20, EMPHASIS ADDED

In reading the above scriptures we conclude the following:

1. Men's bones and spirits have a special direct relation to God.

2. There is something precious and important spiritually and physically about bones—more so perhaps than other parts of the body.

3. The health and wholeness, "dryness" and "moistness," of bones directly register sin and righteousness.

4. Sin sometimes results in broken bones.

5. Confession, repentance, and the favor of the Lord are refreshment to the bones, and thus in health to the whole body.

Amazingly, we see in 2 Kings 13:20–21 that bones become such a repository of spirit and light that even long after death they can contain healing power!

> And Elisha died, and they buried him. Now the bands of the Moabites would invade the land in the spring of the year. And as they were burying a man, behold, they saw a marauding band; and they cast the man into the grave of Elisha. And when the man touched the bones of Elisha he revived and stood up on his feet.

What can all this say about arthritis? Bursitis? Leukemia? Tendonitis? The ability to rebuild body strength through the blood? What can it reveal to us about all the blood and bone diseases to which we sometimes fall? What may it say about the effect of rejection in utero? About attempts at abortion? Quarrels between parents while a child is in utero? Violence to pregnant mothers? And so on?

On the other side, what does it say about the power of prayers that apply the blood of Christ? About the value of the sacrament of Communion? About the salutary effect of the indwelling of the Holy Spirit? No wonder the Word promises that "those who wait for the LORD will gain new strength; they will mount up with wings like eagles, they will run and not get tired, they will walk and not become weary" (Isa. 40:31).

It has long been noted that those who receive our Lord and walk in Him often look years younger. Their vitality mounts. I (John) can testify not only for myself but also for many acquaintances that athletic coordination increased dramatically. Let us cease to think of the spirit like water and of our bodies like glasses, as though our spirit only inhabited a body, unrelated to it, unaffected by it, or the body by the spirit. That is docetic heresy (the notion that Jesus only *appeared* to have a physical body). The Holy Spirit inhabits all of our spirit, like the fluid in a living sea sponge or the electricity in the filament of a light bulb. Something new and tremendous results. The Holy Spirit and our spirit infuse, flow through, live in, breathe through, saturate, activate, revive, refresh, and empower every cell of our bodies! The Holy Spirit works to make us new in every way.

The entire import of this chapter so far is to make us aware that when we speak of the baptism of the Holy Spirit, of prayer, of sin and stress, of redemption and the blood of Christ, we are addressing down-to-earth, tremendously practical realities! Let us banish from our minds that falsity of thought that long compartmentalized life as though what we did on Sunday took care of God, and the rest of the week we could spend on the real and the practical. Only the foolish would think that the Sermon on the Mount was ever intended to be lived by anyone but naïve idealists and cloistered saints! Faith, living with God, and communing with His Spirit are practical and life-giving. The Sermon on the Mount was not only intended for practical living, anything less is less than practical! God's Word is eminently practical. Man's ideas and customs produce death. God's Word is life:

> The law of the LORD is perfect, *restoring the soul*; the testimony of the LORD is sure, making wise the simple. The precepts of the LORD are right, *rejoicing the heart*; the commandment of the LORD is pure, *enlightening the eyes*. The fear of the LORD is clean, enduring forever; the judgments of the LORD are true; they are righteous altogether. They are more desirable than gold, yes, than much fine gold; sweeter also than honey and the drippings of the honeycomb. Moreover, by them Thy servant is warned; *in keeping them there is great reward*.
> —PSALM 19:7–11, EMPHASIS ADDED

St. Paul commanded his followers:

> Finally, brethren, whatever is true, whatever is honorable, whatever is right, whatever is pure, whatever is lovely, whatever is of good repute, if there is any excellence and if anything worthy of praise, *let your mind dwell on these things*.
> —PHILIPPIANS 4:8, EMPHASIS ADDED

Too many of us have thought, "That's nice," while also thinking, "But of course it's not really relevant. We have to live in the real world." Thus we fail to receive the benefit of the next verse.

The things you have learned and received and heard and seen in me,
practice these things; *and the God of peace shall be with you.*
—PHILIPPIANS 4:9, EMPHASIS ADDED

St. Paul went on to say in the next verses that he had learned the secret
of facing everything and that he could do all things through Him who
strengthens him.

Secular science has been learning—unaided by the safeguards of God's
Word—to apply positive words to illness, often with spectacular success.

In a study conducted at the Cancer Counseling and Research Center
in Fort Worth, Texas, it was found that cancer patients typically shared
similar experiences in their childhood—isolation, neglect, despair, and
difficulty with interpersonal relationships.[2] In early adulthood, patients
were commonly noted to have been able to establish a strong meaningful
relationship or found great satisfaction in his or her vocation. They poured
tremendous energy into the relationship or role. The relationship or role
was then removed. As a result, the "bruise" left over from the childhood
despair was painfully struck again. Because these individuals were so
accustomed to letting despair and hurt bottle up, they were unable to let
other people know when they felt rejected, angry, or hostile.

The cancer patients tended to be the kind of people who were tremendously concerned to minister to the needs of others, but they did not feel
free to share their own feelings or problems with others. They didn't want
to be a burden to anyone. In their innermost thoughts they saw the end as
a disaster they had always half expected. Superficially they continued to
function, but the zest went out of their lives. Seventy-six percent of five
hundred patients interviewed shared this kind of history.[3]

The Simontons also reported that the major differences between heavy
smokers who get lung cancer and heavy smokers who do not are "poor
outlets for emotional discharge" in the former.[4] In addition, the fast-
growing tumors are often related to an extreme desire to make a good
impression, to ego-defensiveness, and loyalty to one's own version of
reality.[5] Our own teachings on performance orientation, bitter roots, and
inner vows certainly confirm this information.

The Simontons explained in simple layman's terms that psychological
stress on the physical body results in an imbalance of adrenal hormones,
greater susceptibility to carcinogenic substances, suppression of immune
activity, and an increase of abnormal cells and cancerous growth. In their

treatment program the Simontons attempted to introduce elements of hope and anticipation to create changes in perceptions of self and problems. They insisted that it is not stress itself, but the way of reacting to stress, that makes a difference in susceptibility to disease. By psychological intervention to change the patient's ways of reacting to stress, the destructive process in the body can be reversed to result in cancer regression.

In his actual healing regimen, Simonton calls for healing through relaxation. We agree with that. But in the later stages, his plan also includes imagining oneself as going from sickness to health with the help of an "inner guide" (a personification of the wisdom of one's own heart). We believe it is not our wisdom we must rely on but God's. We also view visualizing healing into existence as a kind of magic and, as such, forbidden by Scripture. We would do better to picture our healing as a hopeful forecast of what God has promised, but not as a fleshly means to make it happen. Even if Simonton's cure is flawed, his understanding of the source is correct. If many have been cured through these man-made techniques, how much more if the cure were a biblical one!

We believe that some secular modes of the healing art can be vehicles or packages for healing, insofar as they are biblical; therefore, God Himself is the content of the package—the power that makes the vehicle move. Prayer fully applies that power.

> I pray that the eyes of your heart may be enlightened, so that you may know what is the hope of His calling, what are the riches of the glory of His inheritance in the saints, and *what is the surpassing greatness of His power toward us who believe.*
> —EPHESIANS 1:18–19, EMPHASIS ADDED

HEALING FOR THE GRIEVING, FRUSTRATED, AND HURT

All of this means that when we hear of a great loss, we have power to heal and be healed by asking Jesus to identify with hurt and grief and take it into Himself.

> He was despised and forsaken of men, a man of sorrows, and acquainted with grief; and like one from whom men hide their face, He was despised, and we did not esteem Him. Surely our griefs He Himself bore, and our sorrows He carried; yet we ourselves esteemed Him stricken, smitten of God, and afflicted. But He was pierced

through for our transgressions, He was crushed for our iniquities; the chastening for our well-being fell upon Him, and by His scourging we are healed.

—ISAIAH 53:3–5

Whatever the hurt, whatever the loss, however great the tragedy, every Christian counselor and prayer minister needs to hold in mind Romans 8:28.

And we know that God causes *all things* to work together for good to those who love God, to those who are called according to His purpose.

—EMPHASIS ADDED

If we only comfort and heal, our patient may find himself also confirmed in his self-pity. He may remain unwilling to let go of his dour feelings because that stance of self-pity seems to purchase rewards from important people around him. Prayers for healing should contain assurances that God will make that pile of bitter ashes into a fountain of glory for ministry to others. Subsequent ministry needs to call for a discipline of prayer and faith that looks *through* problems and determines not to hug pain to oneself, for whatever reason.

It may be well worth it to repeat (from the chapter on depression) that grief may be worked through, healed, and resolved by faith, whereas sorrow may return many times. Sorrow and tears are not marks of lack of faith. Sorrow is a healthy release of loss and hurt. For many months after grief is assuaged, tears may well up, especially at holidays or when some incident triggers a cherished memory. *Such sorrow is not something to be done away with or banished, as one would cast away a demon, nor is it something to be healed too quickly.* It is not something bad or evil. It is something to be endured and sweetened by. It is a mark of love's knowing the pain of loss. It will pass away naturally in time, when its work is done in the heart.

Sorrow does evil work only when we fear it or otherwise handle it badly. Repressed sorrow eats into the marrow of the bones and destroys vitality. It can result in many psychosomatically caused diseases. Sorrow can be used as a tool wielded to control others. If we fear the need to express sorrow, we can see an increase of emotional tantrums.

The trouble is that we may have pockets of sorrow never yet released to tears. We did not let ourselves grieve at the proper time and have persistently repressed the sorrow, which then becomes something else more akin to anxiety. It rumbles around like a freighter in a fog-bound ocean looking for somewhere to head in. If no lighthouse of revelation pierces the darkness to let it unload its freight wholesomely in the proper dock of awareness and expression, it may flounder and strew its contents in many inappropriate places. The hurt of loss is often behind psychosomatic illnesses, depressions, and mental conditions.

One teenager in a congregation I served had had many conflicts with his father. He never felt he had come into easy acceptance and approval. Before he had an opportunity to talk things out so they could work through their problems, his father suddenly and tragically died. Now everyone eulogized the father. It seemed the height of disloyalty to say or even let himself think anything negative of this man whom the community honored as a servant to all. This son's sorrow was locked up along with all his other undealt-with emotions. He reached out to the Lord in an increasingly frantic attempt to find someone big enough to lift the weight off of him and hold his world together. One day he invited us to his home to see a picture of Christ that he had purchased for the dining room. It covered an entire wall! For him the largeness of the painting was an expression of his wanting Jesus to take over his entire life; he needed to rest in the enveloping presence of the Lord. But the exaggerated size of the painting was also to him a symbol of the enormity of the father image, impossible to live up to and beyond his reach.

At this point the young man's prayers, Bible reading, and the attempts of his pastor and friends to counsel him in order to bring him relief and rest were interpreted by him to be more that he had to live up to. The result was depression that became so unremitting and severe that he had to be committed to a mental hospital. This became the only recourse. Many people in the community did not understand what he was going through at all and blamed his breakdown on "religious fanaticism." When he had fully recovered, his psychiatrist said that the very fact that he had reached out to God was his way back to sanity and health. Meanwhile, not sorrow but inability to express it had become his prison until the Lord finally reached his heart.

When we do not deal with grief and sorrow at the right time and in the right way, it becomes repressed but in no way silenced. At some time it *will* have its day in court. We are thrown into painful mental and psychosomatic "prisons," and we do not get out until we have paid the last emotional penny! This echoes a principle in one of Jesus's parables.

> Make friends quickly with your opponent at law while you are with him on the way, in order that your opponent may not deliver you to the judge, and the judge to the officer, and you be thrown into prison. Truly I say to you, you shall not come out of there, until you have paid up the last cent.
> —MATTHEW 5:25–26

In our modern court system, lawyers often attempt to bargain before an issue comes before a judge, sometimes settling out of court, usually at lower cost than had the case proceeded to trial. In biblical days much the same happened. Both the plaintiff and defendant and their counselors were forced to travel together, sometimes long distances, to wherever a judge resided who could settle the issue. It was common practice to hash things out on the way, and everyone knew that it always cost far more if the judge did have to make a judgment. Although Jesus was speaking of reconciling with a brother, the same principle can be applied to grief: face griefs (or anger, hatred, fear, whatever) while it is rising to consciousness ("on the way with you"). Hardening the heart rather than expressing sorrow, hurt, or forgiveness is likely to result in painful cost, as our young friend suffered when pressures blocked his ability to handle grief.

Simple things such as having to move away from friends, the loss of a beloved piano teacher, or the death of a pet may lie behind a closed heart. Whether loss was early or late, mild or severe, a person may unconsciously or consciously decide that love costs too much. He may shut up his heart, making an inner vow never again to love or to be vulnerable. Hardened hearts are the most common result of undealt-with, buried sorrow. As we have seen earlier, such withdrawal often results in disease.

Shock after a loss is not faith

Unfortunately, Christians sometimes mistake the effects of shock for faith. When loss traumatizes the inner being, the homeostatic or balance principle within us may shut off all feeling for a while as protection from what threatens to become too much emotional stress. The resultant false peace may be taken by the Christian as victory due to faith. I think of one friend whose husband died. She sailed smilingly through the funeral and its aftermath, certain that her faith had given her victory over sorrow and tears. She was fond of quoting, "He shall wipe away every tear from their eyes; and there shall no longer be any death; there shall no longer be any mourning, or crying, or pain; the first things have passed away" (Rev. 21:4). But we could sense in our spirits the gusher of grief she was suppressing. Fear of letting down, of displaying emotions in public, of not demonstrating what she thought was faith, caused her to disregard the simple fact that those first things have not yet all passed away and the time for that prophecy to be fulfilled in total has not yet come. About three years later, physical problems signaled inner trouble, and after much counsel she broke down and cried the tears she should have allowed to flow much earlier.

Anger at God after a loss

Loss often results in anger. Inevitably the heart's cry is, "Where were You, Lord? Why did You let this happen?" It is not lack of faith to think such thoughts. It is not always sin to be angry with God. (See chapter 5 for a fuller discussion about anger at God.) Many Christians have been burdened with guilt because they thought anger itself is a sin. Jesus never sinned, yet Mark 3:5 says, "And after looking around at them with anger, grieved at their hardness of heart, He said to the man, 'Stretch out your hand.'" In Ephesians, St. Paul commanded, "Be angry, and yet do not sin; do not let the sun go down on your anger" (Eph. 4:26). What we do with anger makes it either righteousness or sin. Even those who know that with their mind often seem not to know it in their heart. All too many suppress anger, failing to locate it properly and deal with it specifically through forgiveness. Even though we may know it's OK to become angry, nevertheless it does not seem right to be angry with God. The mind says He is perfect, and how could He be at fault? But the heart could not care one whit for such logic. Anger can be healthy—initially. It says we believe in God and therefore expect that He ought to be there for us. Later we may come to some wisdom about how our sin or circumstances blocked Him from acting. For the moment our anger can say we love. St. Paul knew this, and so wrote to the Corinthians:

> Now all these things are from God, who reconciled us to Himself through Christ, and gave us the ministry of reconciliation, namely, that God was in Christ reconciling the world to Himself, not counting their trespasses against them, and He has committed to us the word

of reconciliation. Therefore we are ambassadors for Christ, as though God were entreating through us; we beg you on behalf of Christ, *be reconciled to God.*
—2 CORINTHIANS 5:18–21, EMPHASIS ADDED

We have grieved to hear people report that they finally worked up enough courage to admit to someone their anger at God, only to hear, "Oh, now, let's not be foolish. You have no right to be angry with God. Let's come off that." Worse yet someone might have said, "That's blasphemy. You know better than that." Please hear this, prayer ministers—God can take it. He doesn't need you to defend Him! Let people express their angers. What such people may be doing is simply cathartic. Catharsis is outpouring of pent-up emotions. Never interrupt a catharsis. Let people spend themselves. There will be time enough later to talk rationally. Further talk may not even be needed, for in the outpouring of emotion a person may see and repent. When prayer ministers jump in to shut off catharsis, the truth is they are afraid of such emotional outbursts, most likely because they are afraid of their own pent-up feelings. God is not an immature earthly parent who cannot allow His child to express anger at Him. Not only does He allow us to share our angers, but He also helps us to do so, as He did in some of the psalms, such as Psalm 88.

Some people express anger at God and actually mean it. They do really blame God for their troubles. It is not that they, like all of us, have normal present angers at parents, or at the Parent. Unconsciously, they project their unrecognized (or unknown) stored-up angers and judgments at their parents onto God. They feel that God (actually their parents) has let them down. They want to know why a good God can allow such things as tragedies to happen. "Either He doesn't care or He is impotent," is their cry of outrage. They may launch into complicated philosophical delvings of the entire question of the existence of good and evil, trying actually to justify God to themselves because they lack sufficient blind trust to rest in Him.

We have taught much about this biblically and theologically in chapters 8 and 9 of *The Elijah Task.* It is not our purpose here to explain the workings of God relative to His dealings with evil; rather, our purpose here is healing. Therefore our counsel is not to defend God at all. He is not the problem. We simply say, "What was your father like?" We want to know what kind of judgments have been formed against fathers and mothers who were unaffectionate, not present, violent, could not listen compassionately, or leapt to conclusions and judged unfairly. This also is developed further in chapter 2 of *Transforming the Inner Man*, "Seeing God With an Unbelieving Heart." What is important here is to realize that expressions of hurt and anger are not so important in themselves as they are clues to areas needing healing in the early life.

Having healed the inner man of ancient hurts and transformed resultant structures, we may not yet have sufficiently dealt with the hurt itself. Our personal spirit is different from our memory stream and our soul's structure. Our personal spirit may yet need to be comforted and soothed. We accomplish that by continuing to pray, after we have prayed for transformation of memories and structures, that the personal spirit be comforted by God. We may quote Psalm 27:10, "For my father and my mother have forsaken me, but the LORD will take me up," and we ask God to make up to them the years "that the swarming locust has eaten, the creeping locust, the stripping locust, and the gnawing locust" (Joel 2:25). We declare that they "shall have plenty to eat and be satisfied, and praise the name of the LORD your God" (v. 26). We ask God the Father to gather the person into His arms again and again, until the child within *knows* in every particle of his being that he is loved and chosen, that he belongs and is cherished.

It is not enough merely to take the negative to the cross. The child within needs to feed on that time of cherishing until he is whole and free. That means he needs to be encouraged to participate in small-group and church worship and in small fellowships and primary relationships until his inner spirit no longer is starved but entirely fed and made whole. Hugs and laughter, friendship and fun are in order to put into the person the wholesomeness of childhood he never before possessed.

The value of emotional release

There are those who overexpress sorrow and anger for many reasons. Most commonly, however, what we as prayer ministers must do is release to the surface what has long been suppressed or forgotten. Sometimes people are wounded without knowing it.

> Even in laughter the heart may be in pain, and the end of joy may be grief.
>
> —PROVERBS 14:13

I (John) am one of those who may be terribly hurt without realizing it at the moment. As a child in a sometimes tempestuous home, I built in a capacity to shut off present feelings so that their only function would be to inform my mind, which became steeled to analyze and handle calmly whatever threatened to become chaotic. That discipline has served me well through the years. However, along with that has come a tendency to become lost from my own true feelings, and years later I suffer increased pain from what could have been lightly experienced nearer to the moment.

Many men have built in such disciplines. I have had to learn to say to the Lord, as did St. Paul, "I am conscious of nothing against myself, yet I am not by this acquitted; but the one who examines me is the Lord" (1 Cor. 4:4). "Against myself" can be changed to, "I am conscious of no feelings of sorrow or anger or resentment, Lord, but they may be there. You search me out, Lord, and either cause me to feel them or deal with them by faith."

> Create in me a *clean heart*, O God, and *renew a steadfast spirit* within me.
> —PSALM 51:10, EMPHASIS ADDED

People who have learned to wall off feelings in order to remain calm and efficient under stress should be counseled not always to handle things alone in private prayers. Just as a man who is his own lawyer may have a fool for a client, so whoever always counsels and heals himself has a fool, and someday a collapsing Christian, for a counselee. As we learned earlier, 76 percent of those who contract cancer are those who would not let others minister to them. Friends see our hurt when we don't. Friends feel our sorrows when we have covered them even from ourselves.

> The way of a fool is right in his own eyes, but a wise man is he who listens to counsel.
> —PROVERBS 12:15

> The tongue of the wise brings healing.
> —PROVERBS 12:18

> He who neglects discipline despises himself, but he who listens to reproof acquires understanding.
> —PROVERBS 15:32

Anxiety in the heart of a man weighs it down, but a good word makes it glad.

—PROVERBS 12:25

The teaching of the wise is a fountain of life, to turn aside from the snares of death.

—PROVERBS 13:14

Often, in counsel or prayer, both prayer minister and the one to whom he ministers may inadvertently tap into an underground river of tears. Many times in discussion or prayer, or by a single question, people have suddenly broken into crying so heavily it seemed they could barely catch their next breath. Neither that person nor his prayer minister should fear such occasions, nor try to top off the geyser. Such crying releases pent-up energy. Tears are a gift of heaven. Such sudden outbursts of tears are nearly incontrovertible evidence that the quest has neared the mark of truth. Prayer ministers have only to wait out the sobs, perhaps kneeling beside the person and placing an arm of comfort over the shoulders, as if to say, "Have at it; I'm here to stand beside you. It's OK." Usually the aftermath of such outbursts is a time of quiet revelation. The force of the crying tells the person beyond argument how great his hurt was. The emotional release usually opens doors to insight. He may then begin to remember long-forgotten or repressed details. Precious ground may be covered in the afterglow of tears.

A prayer minister wins trust by letting the person sob it out, without scolding or trying to shut it down. Once he has shared his greatest depths of sorrow and let go of his self-control in emotional outbursts, and his prayer minister has not said, as perhaps his parents did, "Oh, dry up!" or "Crybaby! Get yourself under control!" or "Shut up that bawling, or I'll give you something worth crying about!" his heart knows it can take refuge in the prayer minister. He knows then that he will not be rejected. That acceptance grants his spirit courage to face truth and share it. The prayer minister need only be patient and quietly insistent, encouraging him to continue to share. Several times in one session a person may suddenly be overcome, once the floodgates have been opened. That in itself may frighten him. The prayer minister should assure him that he is quite normal and that such feelings and expressions are OK and healthy. By the prayer minister's quiet strength and calmness, it is expressed that it is all right and the person being ministered to feels that he can continue and live it all the way through. It is a matter of rejoicing when people break through into great gushers of sobbing and tears. Let us never be afraid of it.

There are some people, of course, who fake tearful uprisings and outbursts. The Lord can provide the prayer minister with discernment to know the difference. I have never known real tears to be anything other than a sign of deep healing.

Often, if a person has been starved for affection or for understanding, when someone bids to supply that long, pent-up need, great tears are the result. By that fruit, we may discern the depth of deprivation.

Allowing such outbursts may not seem very real, important, or necessary for people to embarrass themselves by talking about old things. They may want to escape, to seek some pretext to avoid more pain, but I have never known anyone who has experienced a sobbing catharsis of sorrow who has not immediately seen its reality and value.

Such persons know they cannot have faked that kind of outburst. They feel peace following the release. They know what it means then to cleanse their inner house. We insist to prayer ministers that they never say, "Oh there now, don't cry." So many times we have heard of "Job's comforters," who missed the entire import of what was happening! "Rejoice in the Lord always; again I will say, rejoice" (Phil. 4:4), the person is becoming real. He is getting at where it really is. "Let your forbearing spirit be known to all men [including those to whom you minister]" (v. 5). "The LORD is near to the brokenhearted, and…crushed in spirit" (Ps. 34:18). "Be anxious for nothing, but in everything by prayer and supplication with thanksgiving let your requests be made known to God. And the peace of God, which surpasses all comprehension, shall guard your hearts and your minds in Christ Jesus" (Phil. 4:6–7).

Prayer ministers, knowing the value of cathartic release, may be tempted to try to force it to happen. Please don't! The Holy Spirit is the great physician. He knows when boils are ready to be lanced. He knows when wells of stored sorrow are ready to be drained. He knows when the grapes of the heart are ready to be squeezed for the best wine for the feast. Be at rest. Our Lord will minister. Sometimes I have thought, "Surely now that this person sees it, he will feel something. Surely he will express it." Nothing seemed to happen. Six months later, even three years later, hearts have suddenly (it seems) broken into tears or anger, fear or hate. It took that long for the heart and mind to ripen to the moment of expression.

Prayer ministers should not be dismayed or frustrated with people who can't seem to feel anything. Feelings may be unnecessary altogether, or perhaps the Lord will release a geyser later.

Some people feel that what is bottled in their heart can never be dealt with because, "After all, he's dead and gone. I can't go back and ask his forgiveness or tell him how he hurt me." Many times they don't really believe that. They know in part of their mind that such thoughts are only a dodge. They know they can settle it by confession. They only want a convenient excuse not to have to go through the process. We seldom tackle that delusion head on. Earlier we said that anger is inevitable. All of us have had anger at God and anger at parents whether we were ever aware of it or not. We normally want to congratulate ourselves that we don't have resentment and bitterness. We want to assure ourselves that we are in control of our life. To be made aware that we have hidden emotions and drives is, therefore, to be told that we are not as much in control of ourselves as we had thought. That may be more threatening than the possible existence of anger.

Loyalty can block expression of negative feelings

Many people labor under the delusion that if we love someone, we of course can have no negative feelings toward them. It seems disloyal to admit resentment for lack of affection from a father who knocked himself out in every other way to provide for us. We don't want to admit we were hurt and cherished resentment at the critical tongue of a mother when our mind tells us she was overworked and under great stress. Loyalty locks frustration and sorrow into silence.

Grieving people need to be told that thoughts like these are only the admirable way the mind tried to handle their hurt, but that it did not suffice to clear the heart of wounding. There is no shame in admitting the other side of our feelings. No dishonor is intended toward a parent we mean to honor when we cry out the hurts we have long repressed.

It is as simple as when our child comes running to leap into our lap and we can readily see that he is hurting and angry with us. We say, "Come on, honey, tell me. What is it?" Our child's blurting out what he is hurting about, even if it involves talking about things we did wrong, does not dishonor us. It tells us our child loves us enough to suffer real hurts. It honors us that his trust of us is strong enough that he can be honest with us and know we will accept and love him anyway.

Just so, sharing with a prayer minister does not dishonor our parents.
It heals. If the parents, or whoever else involved, have gone on beyond
the portal of death, the wounds of the one who has been left behind can
still be healed merely by the prayers of the prayer minister. Who is to say
that our loved ones are not aware and blessed on the other side as they
dwell with the Lord? Jesus's story of Lazarus and the rich man seems to
indicate that the departed do see what happens here (Luke 16:19–31).
Whether they see or not is inconsequential to a person's healing. Prayer
reaches beyond inner portals of the heart to heal. We must never allow
fear of embarrassment, hesitancy to dishonor, or any other thing to block
us from becoming whole.

To accomplish healing in all aspects of sorrow, frustration, and loss, it
is not enough to discuss hurtful incidents. It is not enough to haul to the
cross resultant structures such as hearts of stone and inner vows we have
made not to be vulnerable. To pray about those things is necessary and
good, but incomplete. Our personal spirit still hungers for supply of what
was lost. When loved ones are gone, only our Lord can fully meet that
need Spirit to spirit. We, as prayer ministers and Christian brothers and
sisters, are called to be present as His instruments for touch, assurance,
acceptance, and affection, but only His fullness of spirit can bathe that
wounded spirit and breathe vitality into him again. We pray simply for the
Lord to accomplish that, loving the person into wholeness and fullness,
remembering as prayer ministers that:

> The Spirit of the Lord GOD is upon me,
> Because the LORD has anointed me....
> He has sent me to bind up the brokenhearted,
> To proclaim liberty to captives,
> And freedom to prisioners;
> To proclaim the favorable year of the LORD,
> And the day of vengeance of our God;
> To comfort all who mourn,
> To grant those who mourn in Zion,
> Giving them a garland instead of ashes,
> The oil of gladness instead of mourning,
> The mantle of praise instead of a spirit of fainting.
>
> —ISAIAH 61:1–3

NOTES

CHAPTER 1
THE FORGOTTEN FUNCTIONS OF OUR SPIRITS

1. African-American spiritual, "There Is a Balm in Gilead." Public domain.

2. Michael D. Marlowe, "Ancient Heretical Literature," http://www.bible-researcher.com/canon7.html; and "Orthodoxy vs. Heresy—Story and Theory," http://www4.wittenberg.edu/academics/phil/Reed'sCourses/Anc&Med/Anc&MedHeresy.html (accessed June 19, 2007).

CHAPTER 2
THE SLUMBERING SPIRIT

1. We strongly recommend that the reader study the introduction to *Crisis in Masculinity* by Leanne Payne for corroboration of these statements.

2. Marshall L. Hamilton, *Father's Influence on Children* (Chicago: Nelson-Hall, 1977), 51, 141, 166–167.

3. Tess Forrest, PhD, "Paternal Roots of Female Character Development," *Contemporary Psychoanalysis*, (1966), 3:21–37, http://www.pep-web.org/document.php?id=cps.003.0021a (accessed June 19, 2007).

CHAPTER 4
DEPRESSION

1. "Into the Woods My Master Went" by Peter Christian Lutkin and Sidney Clapton Lanier. Public domain.

CHAPTER 6
IDENTIFICATIONS AND SHRIKISM

1. William Shakespeare, *Hamlet*, 3.1. Reference is to act and scene.

CHAPTER 7
OCCULT INVOLVEMENT

1. *Oxford Universal Dictionary* (Clarendon Press, 1933).

2. Ibid.

3. M.A. Atwood, *Hermetic Philosophy and Alchemy* (New York: Julian Press, 1960), 7, emphasis added.

4. Ibid., 26, emphasis added.

5. Ibid., 42, emphasis added.

6. From notes from class on the Old Testament taught by Rabbi Ernest Jacob, Drury University, 1949.

7. William Shakespeare, *Macbeth*, 1.5, emphasis added. Reference is to act and scene.

8. *Macbeth*, 2.2, emphasis added. Reference is to act and scene.

9. Agnes Sanford has become the favorite whipping girl of shoddy scholarship by many apologists today. She made some statements that appeared to be occultic. For instance, she said that Moses had more occult power than the magicians of Egypt. A student of astronomy, Agnes was only using a term that meant "hidden." Later, that word became associated with occultism. Agnes hated the occult. I was with her when she spoke in many places to drive occultism out of the Church. None of the apologists checked with Francis MacNutt, Leanne Payne, or me. They thought they knew, yet they accused her falsely.

CHAPTER 8
SPIRITUALISM AND DELIVERANCE

1. *Hamlet*, 1.5. Reference is to act and scene.

CHAPTER 10
GRIEF, FRUSTRATION, AND LOSS

1. Oncologist-approved cancer information from the American Society of Clinical Oncology and the ASCO Foundation quoted in "Donating Bone Marrow," People Living With Cancer, http://www.plwc .org/portal/site/PLWC/menuitem.169f5d85214941ccfd748f68ee37a01d/ ?vgnextoid=ac9b04a3c5982110VgnVCM100000ed730ad1RCRD& vgnextchannel=95d5bf8f21e3a010VgnVCM100000f2730ad1RCRD (accessed June 20, 2007), emphasis added.

2. Carl Simonton, MD, Stephanie Matthews-Simonton, and James Creighton, *Getting Well Again* (New York: Bantam, 1992).

3. Lawrence Leshan, *You Can Fight for Your Life: Emotional Factors in the Causation of Cancer* (N.p.: M. Evans and Company, Inc., 1980) as quoted in Simonton, *Getting Well Again.*

4. D. M. Kissen and H. J. Eysenck, "Personality in Male Lung Cancer Patients," *Journal of Psychosomatic Research* 6 (1962): 123–127, as quoted in Simonton, *Getting Well Again.*

5. E. M. Blumberg, P. M. West, and F. W. Ellis, "A Possible Relationship Between Psychological Factors and Human Cancer," *Psychosomatic Medicine* 16 (1954): 227–286, and B. Klopfer, "Psychological Variables in Human Cancer," *J Proj Tech* 21 (1957): 331–340, as quoted in Simonton, *Getting Well Again.*

OTHER BOOKS BY JOHN AND PAULA SANDFORD

Transforming the Inner Man
Transforming the Child Within
Transforming Wounded Relationships
The Elijah Task
Healing for a Woman's Emotions
Healing Victims of Sexual Abuse
Why Good People Mess Up
Renewal of the Mind
Choosing Forgiveness
Awakening the Slumbering Spirit
Restoring the Christian Family

For further information, contact:

Elijah House Ministries
317 N. Pines Road
Spokane Valley, WA 99206
Web site: www.elijahhouse.org